The Novel and
the American Left

The Novel and the American Left
Critical Essays on Depression-Era Fiction

edited *by* JANET GALLIGANI CASEY

University of Iowa Press ⊔⊓ Iowa City

University of Iowa Press, Iowa City 52242
Copyright © 2004 by the University of Iowa Press
All rights reserved
Printed in the United States of America

Design by Kaelin Chappell

http://www.uiowa.edu/uiowapress

Printed on acid-free paper

Library of Congress Cataloging-in-Publication Data
The novel and the American left: critical essays on depression-era fiction /
edited by Janet Galligani Casey.
p.   cm.
Includes bibliographical references and index.
Contents: Introduction / Janet Galligani Casey—Taking tips and losing class /
Donna M. Campbell—"My little illegality" / Joy Castro—"Shriveled breasts
and dollar signs" / Angela Marie Smith—Monstrous modernism / Joseph
Entin—The objectivity of nature in Josephine Herbst's Rope of gold / Caren
Irr—Agrarian landscapes, the depression, and women's progressive fiction /
Janet Galligani Casey—The avengers of Christie Street / Lee Bernstein—
"Smashing cantatas" and "Looking glass pitchers" / Lawrence Hanley—
Marching! marching! and the idea of the proletarian novel / Jon-Christian
Suggs—Time, transmission, autonomy / David Jenemann and Andrew
Knighton.
ISBN 0-87745-880-4 (cloth)
1. American fiction—20th century—History and criticism.   2. Communism
and literature—United States—History—20th century.   3. Socialism and
literature—United States—History—20th century.   4. Politics and
literature—United States—History—20th century.   5. Right and left (Political
science)—History—20th century.   6. Right and left (Political science) in
literature.   7. Progressivism (United States politics).   8. Depressions—
1929—United States.   9. Working class in literature.   10. Progressivism in
literature.   11. Depressions in literature.   I. Casey, Janet Galligani.
PS228.C6N68 2004
813'.5209358—dc22   2003066271

04 05 06 07 08 C 5 4 3 2 1

Contents

Acknowledgments

The editor and contributors wish to thank the anonymous readers for the University of Iowa Press, who offered useful suggestions for improving individual essays and the collection as a whole. We would also like to acknowledge Prasenjit Gupta and Holly Carver of the Press for their prompt and careful consideration of the manuscript, and for vetting it through the final stages of production.

The following institutions have granted permission to quote from archival materials: Special Collections Research Center, Morris Library, Southern Illinois University at Carbondale (Papers of Edith Summers Kelley); Special Collections, Washington University, St. Louis, Missouri and the Estate of Josephine Johnson Cannon (Papers of Josephine Johnson); and the Newberry Library, Chicago, Illinois (Jack Conroy Collection).

Introduction

(Left) Contexts and Considerations

JANET GALLIGANI CASEY

How to narrate stasis? The question cuts to the core of fictional expression during the Great Depression, acknowledging the special artistic concerns of an America in crisis. Aesthetically speaking, one unique element of the cultural moment lay in its resistance to linear notions of progress, of movement, of hope—precisely those notions that had driven the most powerful American narratives to date. The story of the crash, of social and economic impasse, was not easily accommodated within a national imagination propelled by the great forward-looking mythos of manifest destiny or the boy-makes-good, rags-to-riches paradigm of Horatio Alger's dime novels. As Tillie Olsen was to write of this period some twenty years later, the 1930s were more aptly represented by the monotonous actions and circuitous thoughts of a dispossessed middle-aged woman, in the throes of unending housework, reflecting on her young mother-hood "during the years of depression, of war, of fear" ("I Stand Here Ironing" 12).

In 1934 James Agee, writing for *Fortune* magazine about the American roadside industry, asserted that the American spirit is inherently "restive," and that the "hunger for movement" is "very probably the profoundest and most compelling of American racial hungers." What's more, he added, we move not for any substantive reasons, but "for the plain unvarnished hell of it." If we are to believe Agee, and many observers since, then the paralysis engendered by the Depression in the United States posed not just physical hardships, but metaphysical ones, necessitating cultural maneuvers that would relieve the fear associated with stagnation. Morris Dickstein, for instance, has suggested that the popularity of 1930s movies featuring Ginger Rogers and Fred Astaire is related to the sheer attraction of fluidity, of *motion*, for a culture that had been forcibly immobilized. Michael Denning advances a similar argument concerning the enormous symbolic resonance, in song, narrative, and film, of the Okie migration, a *movement* of epic proportions that held out the tantalizing promise of narrative resolution. And as one historian of the '30s remarked, the popular dance marathon, in which a cessation of movement meant the loss of a cash prize, was a quintessential Depression concept, encapsulating the dilemma of an exhausted populace running on empty, imitating "the aimless, endless movement of superfluous people around and around the country in rickety cars or on freight trains."[1]

For some artists of the decade, the "new" stasis became a kind of dark national joke, given our longstanding association of America with literal and figurative mobility. It seems somehow fitting, for instance, that October 1930 saw the publication of William Faulkner's *As I Lay Dying*, in which the ironic journey of a fetid corpse exposes the noble quest motif as a preposterous cultural-narrative framework for those in the lowest social classes. And at the other end of the decade, filmmaker Preston Sturges exploited the genre of the road movie to highlight, like Faulkner, submerged assumptions about class, movement, and representation: *Sullivan's Travels* (1941) features a socially-minded Hollywood director who hits the road in search of the downtrodden, but winds up, propitiously, on a chain gang. It appears that, in the context of the Great Depression, the classic American belief in movement as progress, in the journey as a means to an appropriate and desirable social or economic end, is not just invalid; it's hilarious.

Indeed, the tension in the culture between involuntary stasis and the desire for mobility offers a rich organizing framework within which to consider some of the most compelling artistic statements of the period, ranging from the black humor of Faulkner and Sturges, to the iconic potency of Dorothea Lange's photographic portrait, *Migrant Mother* (1936), to the distinctive image-*cum*-narrative genre of the "documentary book," including Erskine Caldwell's and Margaret Bourke-White's *You Have Seen Their Faces* (1937) and James Agee's and Walker Evans's *Let Us Now Praise Famous Men* (1941). Moreover, such artistic exploitations of the dichotomy between aimlessness and direction, fixity and locomotion, only extended the tensions implicit in a vocabulary that had grown up with nineteenth-century working-class culture but that achieved new currency with the large-scale labor disputes of the early twentieth century. Terms such as *speed-up*, *work stoppage*, *walkout*, and *strike* collectively demonstrate how assertions of movement or nonmovement, action or inaction, became counteractive strategies in a socioeconomic war.

Not coincidentally, the stasis/motion framework also elucidates the precarious aesthetic placement of the fiction that deliberately intervened in this war by narrating the stories of the workers. In short, the economic crisis also precipitated a narrative crisis—not only throughout the 1930s, but in the years preceding and proceeding that decade, years in which the plight of the laboring classes achieved unprecedented prominence in the cultural consciousness. For socially engaged writers eager to use fiction as a reformative tool, the development of appropriate narrative styles that could reach a large and varied audience was a constant challenge, especially given that the most obvious choice, conventional realism, was better suited to the traditional stories of bourgeois advancement than to the static reality of the workers. (It is surely an irony that realism, with its insistent telos, is so strongly identified with a cultural moment, and a class, characterized by stasis.) Various novelistic solutions were tendered, some more successful than others. The organized Left, for instance, eschewing the blatant narrative experimentation of high modernism because of its inaccessibility and perceived irrelevance to working-class concerns, produced many social-realist "conversion narratives," derided by literary historians as formulaic but nonetheless noteworthy for their effort to infuse stories of working-class inertia with (Marxist) momentum. In a different vein, more centrist social novelists, such as John Dos Passos in his *U.S.A.* trilogy, experimented with unique combinations of conventional narration and modernist stylistics, creating a sense of dynamism through dialogic structures. And certain left-leaning women novelists, concerned with the vicissitudes of gender as well as class, used a variety of figurative means to critique the female's gendered stasis and to interpolate her, too, into the arguments for progress, revolution, change. One of the purposes of this volume is to showcase some of the maneuvers—structural, theoretical, metaphorical—by which novels accommodated the culture's momentary resistance to linearity, propelling themselves in ways that urged, and continue to urge, new considerations of the relationship between fictional expression and social commentary.

A premise of this collection, then, is that the broadly leftist social-realist fiction of the 1920s, 1930s, and 1940s, which found symbolic cohesion with the Depression, constitutes not only a fascinating cultural enterprise but also an intriguing moment in the history of the American novel.[2] Despite assertions that the novel has been less efficacious in addressing working-class culture and concerns than such genres as autobiography or reportage,[3] the art of fiction in this period was at the forefront of left-intellectual inquiry in that numerous socially conscious novels were indeed written and the role(s) and theory of fiction were widely debated. Moreover, one novel—Steinbeck's *The Grapes of Wrath*—was arguably the century's most influential arbiter of Depression iconography and broadly leftist sentiment. The contentions, on one hand, that politics and aesthetics are not profitably mixed and, on the other hand, that all art is essentially political, have worked to minimize the specific achievements of a large group of Depression-era novels that can be construed as leftist in a rich variety of ways, and whose serious investigation has been even further, if unintentionally, constrained by the perceived necessity of pooling texts that share the same foundational forms of leftism. It is not the intent of this collection to downplay the importance of distinguishing among left-leaning stances and manifestations, nor is it to argue that the novel was the primary form of leftist expression; rather, it is to approach this large group of texts, most of which have remained historically marginalized, from an alternative perspective—as novels—in an effort to illuminate, among other things, the range of possibilities in the period concerning the successful marriage of fiction and social commentary. That such a perspective is not only possible but also appropriate at this critical-cultural moment is the direct result of the spate of scholarship on the Old Left that has lately emerged.

Recent studies of the 1930s have successfully reshaped the contours of a field that had been unhappily delimited by certain prevalent assumptions: that the decade was about economics rather than aesthetics; that its attempts at "serious" artistic expression resulted in simplistic and embarrassingly tendentious works; that the Left could or should be equated specifically with the Communist Party, whose programs were proven misguided at best and un-American at worst; that the practical and theoretical concerns of the 1930s constituted an anomaly, a brief and odd cultural moment with some internal coherence but with little connection to intellectual movements that came before or after. Such assumptions, of course, have been thoroughly reexamined by scholars such as Cary Nelson, Barbara Foley, James F. Murphy, and Paula Rabinowitz,[4] and the period has been critically reinvigorated as a host of theoretical approaches have been profitably turned toward reconceptualizing it. In particular, the 1990s emphases on identity politics and the multiplicities of representation have lent new legitimacy to the intricate social and political allegiances of the various intellectual figures of the time, as well as opening the door for the reconsideration of the roles of minorities and women, whose concerns had been preempted in histories of American radicalism that emphasized Left sociopolitical movements as both white and male.

This book inserts itself into the dialogue on these issues by broadening what has necessarily, to this point, been a somewhat narrow focus. While many of the scholars treating the period have lent sustained attention to the novel as a genre in the 1920s, 1930s, and 1940s, their revisionist efforts, while tremendously significant, have generally been undertaken within the context of specialized discussions of left-wing cultural politics. The present volume, in contrast to and in light of this crucial body of scholarship, offers discrete readings of specific leftist novels *as novels*, considering the ways that such texts not only iterated radical ideals, but also participated in the period's conversations about the ways and means of American fiction. The contributors herein "name names" (to appropriate a phrase with painful connotations in the history of the American Left) in a constructive sense, identifying specific authors, titles, and approaches by which to engage expansive theoretical questions concerning the role of the novel in the United States. In doing so they collectively bear witness to the vitality and cultural interest of these largely noncanonical works, and suggest new points of contact among literary schools that have traditionally been viewed separately. This more capacious context will, we hope, help to introduce these works to a wider academic readership—that is, to generalists of American literature and, by extension, to their students.

Moreover, in taking up a varied range of writers deploying a spectrum of progressive attitudes (Margery Latimer, Tess Slesinger, Meridel Le Sueur, Tillie Olsen, Pietro di Donato, James M. Cain, Myra Page, Mike Gold, Josephine Herbst, Edith Summers Kelley, Josephine Johnson, Albert Halper, Thomas Bell, Clara Weatherwax, Kenneth Fearing), this collection deliberately leaves open the notion of what can or should constitute "Left," allowing the contributors and their subjects mutually to demonstrate the many (contradictory) strands of left-liberal reformism in the period, and individually to consider the resulting tensions manifested in particular texts. As the reader will note, these essays assume no unified stance on the relationship between literature and perceived reality, including the possibility that art may effect social reform. Nor do they suggest a firm hierarchy of novels based either on political or literary standards. Rather, these pieces are united solely in their efforts to recoup certain works of fiction in terms of their engagement with ideologies of class, thereby pushing some of the more literarily sophisticated *or* culturally resonant *or* politically interesting left-oriented novels to the forefront of a serious critical inquiry that provides them with, as Cary Nelson has put it, "fresh opportunities for an influential life."[5] The moment for such (re)readings is especially auspicious because many of the novels discussed here are now available to a new generation of readers through reprint editions. Such editions, together with the kind of sustained critical attention that this volume represents, lend visibility and renewed validity to Depression-era fiction, contributing to a reassessment of not only the 1930s, but also the larger rubric of American modernism.

Thus the newly influential life that may be imagined for these works has much to do with their role(s) in reshaping the already fluid borders of a vast literary landscape that continually eludes critical efforts to contain it. The sheer variety of novels discussed here—popular and populist texts, narrowly proletarian texts, working-class texts lacking expressed partisan content, texts with high modernist or structurally experimental aspects, texts associated with differently inflected social movements such as eco-criticism—forces further reconsiderations of not only the Left, but also a host of categories by which critics and historians attempt to regularize a complexly variegated terrain of political-aesthetic expression. That these organizational categories have shifted substantially in recent years is reflected by the arrangement of this volume, which indicates some of the more compelling connections among the essays and also evidences the collection's participation in what Alan Wald calls "a qualitatively new and improved study of the epoch" that owes its genesis to 1980s-era developments in cultural criticism.[6]

For instance, as Wald points out, feminist scholarship has had a great deal of influence on studies of the Old Left, providing the impetus for the recovery of a number of texts from the Depression era that deal with working-class issues while also addressing the gender concerns that were frequently suppressed by class-based social analyses. It is fitting, then, that half of the essays included here employ feminist perspectives and/or read leftist texts by women as heavily gendered. Indeed, in the first three essays, Donna Campbell, Joy Castro, and Angela Smith concern themselves with literary articulations of the (female) body as a locus for bourgeois *and* leftist anxieties about class identity and sexuality. Campbell focuses on a specific gendered figure and its material manifestations—the waitress, signified by her uniform—in her consideration of James M. Cain's 1941 novel, *Mildred Pierce* ("Taking Tips and Losing Class: Challenging the Service Economy in James M. Cain's *Mildred Pierce*"). She perceives Cain as exploiting both the waitress and the social space of the restaurant to interrogate relations between the capitalist marketplace and the domestic sphere, as well as imbricated notions of service and production in regard to both food and sex. The mainstream popularity of Cain's novel (made into a classic and quite popular *film noir* in 1945) is understandable, Campbell asserts, in light of the middle-class anxieties about class, gender, money, and race that its all-white cast of characters delineates. Mildred's efforts to transcend her social sphere clearly point to the inapplicability of the Horatio Alger paradigm to Depression-era culture.

In "'My Little Illegality': Abortion, Resistance, and Women Writers on the Left," Joy Castro argues that the abortion plot in fiction by Josephine Herbst, Margery Latimer, Tess Slesinger, and Meridel Le Sueur functions, paradoxically, as a productive narrative moment that underscores the incompatibility of women's experience with both the bourgeois idealization of maternity and the Left's exclusively classist orientation. When female protagonists succumb to the pressure of their leftist partners to terminate pregnancies, argues Castro, their nonresistance is ironically framed as the resistance of the narrative itself, which indicts masculinist ideologies that bracket the needs and desires of women. The physical loss of the fetus becomes, then, a trope for other kinds of loss, both material and ideological.

In yet another reading grounded in ideas about corporeality, Angela Smith locates images of bodies, including mechanized bodies, within both materialist and modernist theoretical perspectives. Smith's essay, "'Shriveled Breasts and

Dollar Signs': The Gendered Rhetoric of Myra Page's *Moscow Yankee*," reads Page's novel as articulating radical new spaces for female bodies, in particular, while also leaning on chauvinistic rhetorics of modernism that link women to capitalist decadence. Ultimately, Smith suggests that even a proletarian conception of embodied subjectivity cannot escape the gendered dynamics structuring more conventional literary forms. Yet Page manages, in Smith's view, to create a vision of men and women reshaping their lives even as they bear the traces of bodies, and literatures, shaped by gendered tropes.

It is not only appropriations of the gendered body, however, that are of concern in this collection; on the contrary, Joseph Entin broadens the focus somewhat to consider "wounded proletarian bodies," specifically those represented by Tillie Olsen and Pietro di Donato. Entin's "Monstrous Modernism: Disfigured Bodies and Literary Experimentalism in *Yonnondio* and *Christ in Concrete*" considers the hybrid narrative forms resulting from a combination of rhetorical and materialist concerns. In both of these texts, Entin asserts, deformed bodies call attention to a mediation of the aesthetic realm of literary representation and the social realm of lived experience. Thus these novels play out simultaneously the self-reflexivity of "high" art and the political critique intrinsic to narratives of social justice, producing a version of modernism that is "monstrous" indeed.

Two essays address the relations between gender and the semiotics of landscape for women writers on the Left, echoing the interdisciplinary strain in contemporary criticism even as they continue to mine the rich possibilities opened up by feminist approaches. Caren Irr's "The Objectivity of Nature in Josephine Herbst's *Rope of Gold*" establishes Herbst as a point of reference for late twentieth-century movements such as deep ecology and eco-feminism. For Irr, Herbst's landscapes are overcoded with political and sexual significance, embodying a critique of unjust property relations that damage the natural world as well as underscoring women's deep connection to nature as removed from such corruption. Irr sees a latent utopian element in Herbst's representations of nature that differentiate her from male contemporaries such as Steinbeck, and that may have negatively affected her reputation. Gendered landscapes are also considered in my "Agrarian Landscapes, the Depression, and Women's Progressive Fiction," which takes up two novels—Edith Summers Kelley's *Weeds* and Josephine Johnson's *Now in November*—and their challenges to dominant clichés of American agrarian iconography such as, for instance, the sentimental parallel frequently drawn between the maternal body and the fulsomeness of the natural world. In contrast, these novels disrupt the period's investment in farm culture as the American way and, more specifically, in the female body as a "natural" means of propagating it. I argue that, by confronting both the spatial metaphors of a masculinist aesthetic *and* the gendering ideologies of constructed space informing the material lives of women, these farm novels reshape the contours of both the American literary landscape and the social landscape of the Depression.

If women and their concerns were underrepresented in previous assessments of the Old Left, then race issues were nearly absent; Lee Bernstein's essay, however, exposes the relevance of ideologies of race to class-oriented critique in this period. In "The Avengers of Christie Street: Racism and Jewish Working-Class Rebellion in Mike Gold's *Jews without Money*," Bernstein asserts that Gold's fictionalized autobiography articulates the author's development of working-class resistance through processes of racial projection and masquerade. The young Mike and his gang, including a Jewish boy nicknamed "Nigger," play alternately the roles of Native Americans and their mythologized killers, working out the gang's social relations through complicated alliances and breakups that mimic colonial power dynamics and call into question the construction of such terms as "Black," "Jew," and "Indian." Ultimately, the boys' exploitation of oppositional social-cultural positions enables an imaginative avenging of the real wounds inflicted by anti-Semitism and class prejudice; however, Bernstein also sees this play as prefiguring Gold's adult difficulties in transcending the particularities of ethnicity in the interest of a socialist future.

Both Lawrence Hanley and Jon-Christian Suggs consider the actual programs set forth for proletarian literature in the 1930s and the ways that specific novels succeeded (or failed) to conform to such ideals. In "'Smashing Cantatas' and 'Looking Glass Pitchers': the Impossible Location of Proletarian Literature," Hanley uses novels by Albert Halper and Thomas Bell to underscore the ways in which the presumed optimism of the proletarian literature project was disrupted by tensions between "bourgeois cultural authority and working-class cultural production." Proletarian narratives written by working-class writers, Hanley contends, are persistently weighed down by their own self-consciousness about their cultural positioning; working-class artists, both within fiction and as the creators of fiction, are caught in dilemmas of identity premised upon the "conversion of subaltern experience into cultural authority." According to Hanley, this "impossible location" manifests itself not only within these texts, as an "incoherence" that is too often deemed defective, but also through the academy's failure to consider the social implications of producing, reading, and interpreting "literature."

In 1935, Clara Weatherwax's first novel won the prize in a proletarian novel contest announced by the magazine *New Masses*; Jon-Christian Suggs discusses this text and its relation to ideals of proletarian fiction in "*Marching! Marching!* and the Idea of the Proletarian Novel." Suggs surveys not only prevalent attitudes toward proletarian novels, but also, notably, attitudes about proletarian short fiction published in American magazines; these contexts set the stage for a specific discussion of Weatherwax's attempts to respond to debates about the

appropriate form and content of radical fiction. In bringing this text to our attention despite its continuing neglect by the academy, Suggs attempts not only to
reconsider its innovative qualities, but also to show how difficult it was to grapple with "the problem of the proletarian novel as it was understood in the 1930s."

It seems fitting that the collection should close with an essay that pointedly
addresses the novel's radical, and radicalizing, potential. David Jenemann and
Andrew Knighton review the theoretical perspectives by which the novel has
been revealed, in its reification of subjectivity, as bourgeois; they then argue that
Kenneth Fearing's novels attempt to create an alternative structural paradigm
that inhibits, rather than advances, reader identification. In "Time, Transmission, Autonomy: What Praxis Means in the Novels of Kenneth Fearing," Jenemann and Knighton position Fearing as a writer intrigued by the novel's
subversive possibilities, and show how Fearing's fiction successfully undermines
the sense of totality (and totalitarianism) offered by the novel in its traditional
realist forms. Ultimately, their essay questions whether subjectivity in the novel
may exist outside of the dialectic between self and society.

This final piece by Jenemann and Knighton is perhaps the most direct in
suggesting that Depression-era leftist fiction successfully and unequivocally
advanced a cause, in this case an aesthetic as well as a social one: in decon-
structing the novel as he did, they argue, Fearing truly accomplished something
revolutionary. There is a genuine sense, however, in which *all* of the essays here
establish their subjects' progressivism in novelistic—rather than merely political—terms, so as to counter the notion that the fiction surrounding the Great
Depression was flat and uninteresting, rife with outmoded structures and formulaic ideas that were not especially well executed. Instead, these essays
uncover texts that are nuanced and provocative, and that yield richly to contemporary analysis, demonstrating that, even if the times in which they were
written seemed static, Depression-era novels managed nonetheless to embody
lively dynamisms. That these texts invigorate discussions about American modernisms seems clear. And if, as one critic has recently lamented, the "'theorisa-
tion' of resistance" has too often been substituted of late for the discussion of
actual political texts,[7] then this collection also points toward an alternative
direction for the interrogation of literature and the Left in the United States.

NOTES

    1. Dickstein, "Depression Culture: The Dream of Mobility"; Denning, *The Cul-
tural Front: The Laboring of American Culture in the Twentieth Century*, chapter 7; Caroline Bird, *The Invisible Scar*, 66.
    2. This volume is deliberately subtitled to invite a more capacious definition of "the
1930s." As Alan Wald has pointed out, some of the most important texts associated with

this decade were conceived, written, or published outside of it (see "The 1930s Left in U.S. Literature Reconsidered"). My use of the term "Depression-era" is intended as an inclusive gesture.

3. Denning, 241. Denning quotes Raymond Williams as having made the same point about the representation of working-class culture in the nineteenth century. And William Stott has argued that "the primary expression of thirties America was not fiction but fiction's opposite [i.e., documentary]" (*Documentary Expression and Thirties America*, xi).

4. Nelson, *Repression and Recovery: Modern American Poetry and the Politics of Cultural Memory, 1910–1945*; Foley, *Radical Representations: Politics and Form in U.S. Proletarian Fiction, 1929–1941*; Murphy, *The Proletarian Moment: The Controversy over Leftism in Literature*; Rabinowitz, *Labor and Desire: Women's Revolutionary Fiction in Depression America*.

5. Nelson, *Repression and Recovery*, 14.

6. Wald, "The 1930s Left," 20–22.

7. John Whalen-Bridge, *Political Fiction and the American Self*, 7.

The Novel and
the American Left

Taking Tips and Losing Class

Challenging the Service Economy in James M. Cain's *Mildred Pierce*

DONNA M. CAMPBELL

When James M. Cain's novel *Mildred Pierce* appeared in the fall of 1941, the reviewers seemed unprepared for this domestic drama from the man who had written *The Postman Always Rings Twice* (1934), *Double Indemnity* (1936), and *Serenade* (1937). In addition to the familiar complaints about Cain's amoral characters — "Southern California abominations" who wallow in "the deep, slow pull of the ancient ooze where worms and serpents crawled" according to Robert Van Gelder in the *New York Times Book Review* — contemporary reviews somewhat inconsistently faulted Cain for deviating from the fast-paced, violent world of his trademark "hardboiled" fiction (7). After trying to fit *Mildred Pierce* into the formula by claiming that Cain had "wrapped his iron fist in a silk stocking to knock together the sexy, highly sensational, and sometimes outright sentimental odyssey of a grass widow," or woman whose husband has deserted her, the reviewer for the *Nation* asked, "Who's been softening up Mr. Cain?" (409). What the reviewers expected was something more like the "fusillade of five shots in deliberate tempo" that marked the dramatic opening sequence from the successful 1945 film adaptation of the work (MacDougall et al. 71). The adaptation establishes a classic film noir ambience that promises — and delivers — all the elements of that genre: suspense, murder, and a "woman who uses men for her own ends, whose desires, ambitions and machinations match — or surpass — those of the male" (Fine 28).

Such a treatment, however, roundly belies the origins of the film in Cain's novel, which contains no flashbacks, no mystery — and no murder. As Linda Williams, Pam Cook, Janet Walker, and other feminist film critics have demonstrated, the film's "noir male discourse of a dangerous, nocturnal underworld" was in successive rewrites superimposed over the original screenplay written by

Catherine Turney, some of which remains in the "day-time woman's filmic discourse of Mildred's own story."[1] In other words, the film obscures its waitress-heroine's success narrative by substituting *noir* style for working-class substance. Further, it displaces Cain's true subject, which he described as "one woman's struggle against a great social injustice— . . . the mother's necessity to support her children even though husband and community give her not the slightest assistance" (Hoopes 349). Questioning the gratuitous insertion of a murder into this plot, Cain asked, "Why not tell that story, which at least has its own quality, rather than a murder story not very different from every 'B' picture that has been made for the last forty years?" (Hoopes 350). Cain's protest went unheeded, and the eclipse of the "woman's story" by an overpowering "noir male discourse" in the film has led to a similar critical eclipse of the novel's explorations of gender and class.[2] Written near the end of the Depression, *Mildred Pierce* probes middle-class anxiety about the already destabilized boundaries between worker and aristocrat, undercutting Mildred's Horatio Alger-like rise through a consistent devaluation of traditional markers of class and culture.

Like Cain's more familiar hardboiled novels, the book uses the conventions of popular fiction to explore issues of power, sexuality, and class, particularly of working-class characters' struggle for autonomy. As Edmund Wilson noted in his seminal essay on the hardboiled school, "The Boys in the Back Room," "the hero of the typical Cain novel is a good-looking down-and-outer, who leads the life of a vagrant and a rogue," but the position of antihero is not in itself proof against being assimilated into the dominant culture (E. Wilson 665). For Cain's characters, the quest for self-definition results less from a shift in class than a shift in self-perception: in key scenes in several of his novels, down-but-not-really-out characters confront, recognize, and thereafter reject what Cain calls a "varlet" mentality, which they implicitly define as the willingness to work for wages and tips instead of holding out for the big payoff from their carefully planned if improbable schemes. Like her male counterparts in Cain's earlier novels *The Postman Always Rings Twice* and *Serenade*, Mildred is inscribed in a cultural framework that defines both identity and sexuality in terms of class; like them, she struggles to retain her autonomy in a service-oriented, consumption-driven culture. In *Mildred Pierce*, Cain uses the figure of the waitress and the restaurant to examine both the marketplace's reproduction and exploitation of the domestic sphere and also the ways in which home and marketplace are constituted by the opposing ethics of service and production that govern the exchange of food and sex.[3] Paradoxically, the despised natural talents of cooking, service to others, and natural sexuality that define her as "waitress" and earn her the label of "varlet" become her means of resisting several forms of class-based cultural dominance: the failed middle-class dreams of her first husband, Bert; the decaying Pasadena aristocracy of her second husband,

Monty; and the social license of artistic superiority practiced by her monstrous daughter Veda.

In effect, Mildred's story is a three-act drama structured simultaneously by her successive occupations as "grass widow," waitress, and entrepreneur, and by the sexualized relationships that inform each of these periods of her life. Possessed of a face that would "pass in a crowd" (Cain 20), "an A-1 shape" including voluptuous legs (47), and "a gift [for cooking such] as few ever have" (87), Mildred is Cain's Everywoman, albeit an Everywoman raised above the rest by a squint that, when she is provoked, "hint[s] at something more than complete vacuity inside" (20).[4] Her first career is established in a scene that frames the book's principal issues of production and sexuality. In a prosaically described but idealized domestic picture, her husband Bert braces his avocado trees and waters his lawn outside the Pierces' Glendale home while Mildred frosts a cake indoors. The picture is perfect, from the "utile jewel" (5) of the green and white bathroom where Bert showers after his labors to the living room with its mass-produced "Spanish-style" furnishings, here as in *Double Indemnity* Cain's favorite metaphor for banal and imitative American culture. The image of a domestic idyll breaks down, however, when the reality behind it is revealed. As Bert and Mildred quarrel over his failure to find work and his relationship with the "grass widow" Mrs. Biederhof, it becomes evident that yard work is the only work that the unemployed Bert can get, whereas the lavishly described "beautiful" cake that testifies to Mildred's considerable gifts as a cook functions not as an icon of family togetherness but as a marketable commodity. The scene ends with his departure, ironically making Mildred herself the "grass widow" with two children to support. This section also introduces Mildred's daughters Veda and Ray, who comprise the first of Mildred's triangulated relationships with paired characters in the book. Veda and Ray represent contrasting aspects of Mildred herself, and her neglect of the warmhearted, impulsively affectionate Ray, "the picture of Mildred" (16), in favor of affected, ambitious Veda foreshadows Mildred's later single-minded quest for "the restaurant, which to her was a sort of Holy Grail" (152). At this point still a "grass widow," Mildred possesses as assets only voluptuous legs and a gift for cooking, parts of herself that she views dispassionately when taking stock of her situation after Bert leaves. Throughout the novel, Mildred tries to maintain a sense of self that controls these components of serving up sex and food while still using them to produce something of worth—a home, a restaurant, or a relationship. Her struggle results from her attempts to integrate these assets with her sense of self even as her culture tries to reduce her to simply performing these service functions.

Mildred's first attempt to preserve her status occurs when she risks this small capital—sex and a home-cooked chicken dinner—in a desperate gamble to land unattached family friend Wally Burgan as a new husband. His response causes Mildred to fear that she has entered a different sort of service economy, as she describes the encounter to her neighbor Lucy Gessler:

> "Lucy."
> "Yes?"
> "I'm on the town."
> "Well—you don't mean he actually left the money on the bureau, do you?"
> "All but." (37)

In Lucy Gessler's pragmatic moral code, grass widows are "fast" unless they adopt the protective coloration of a traditional wife, donning aprons and returning "right back to the kitchen, where all women belong" (30). But the apron provides no protection; indeed, Wally seduces Mildred when he enters her room to "pull those apron strings . . . as a gag" (35). Like Bert, Wally violates the supposed security of apron strings and kitchen by abandoning his responsibilities, leaving Mildred vulnerable once again since she has been denied the only profession she understands and is willing to accept, being "at home," as the census records put it. Wearing an apron in the home in service to her family is acceptable, but wearing it as an apron-for-hire as a housekeeper or waitress is, as the novel makes clear, metaphorically indistinguishable from selling one's body into prostitution. Significantly, when Lucy and Mildred fear that Mildred is now "on the town," Lucy identifies the key signifier of prostitution as leaving the money on the bureau, the traditional spot for leaving a prostitute's fee, another kind of tip for services rendered. Later, the prosaic Lucy reinforces the connection when she misunderstands Mildred's reticence about taking a job as a waitress, believing that she has taken a job in a bordello:

> "What kind of job?"
> "Oh—just a job."
> "I'm sorry . . . but if it's that kind of a job, I hope you picked a five-dollar house. You're too young for the two-dollar trade, and personally I wouldn't like sailors."
> "I'm a waitress. In a hash house."
> "It rhymes up the same way."
> "Just about." (60)

By casually equating the two professions ("hash house"/ "gash house"), Lucy confirms the significance of the social line that Mildred has crossed and also her fears about the loss of status she has suffered.

Mildred's transition from a production-based to a service economy thus introduces one of Cain's most problematic concepts: the psychological Rubicon between production and service, autonomy and dependence, that results from wearing a uniform and taking tips. Significantly, as Christopher Wilson notes in *White Collar Fictions,* the use of "service" to denote "the section of the economy that supplies needs of the consumer but produces no tangible goods" dates only from 1936, a fact that lends weight and timeliness to Cain's use of the concept if not the term itself (C. P. Wilson 274 n. 4). In *Tipping, an American Social History of Gratuities,* Kerry Segrave demonstrates that tipping had long been a contested issue in American culture. Some protests came from unions, which favored equitable wages and railed against the practice because it allowed employers to pay less than a living wage. A more universal dissatisfaction arose from a deep conviction that tipping was undemocratic and hence un-American. Its very origins were foreign, and the "plague of tipping," as William Dean Howells reported in a 1913 "Editor's Easy Chair" column for *Harper's Magazine,* spread like a disease from continental hotels and steamships where honest Americans encountered an incurable "national observance of the Open Hand" (313). As a speaker for the Society for the Prevention of Useless Giving put it in that same year, " We are growing to tolerate a kind of petty grafting that is not right, that is un-American. . . . It is this giving of gratuities that is unlike us; it is a custom copied from a foreign country where conditions are different from ours" (Qtd. in Segrave 30). In addition to contaminating Americans with corrupt practices from Europe, tipping reinforced class distinctions and as such was profoundly undemocratic. As one account from 1916 protested, "The tip goes always from a superior to an inferior; never from servant to master. It is not a recognition of service, for the inferior never tips the superior for the service rendered. That would be an insult" (Qtd. in Segrave 31). Racism was a significant component of this superior-to-inferior transaction, with the Pullman company encouraging tipping of its porters, all of whom were black, as a means of overcoming resistance to "insulting" white workers with tips; as the St. Louis *Republic* put it, "It was the Pullman company which fastened the tipping habit on the American People and they used the Negro as the instrument to do it with" (Qtd. in Segrave 18).

Yet anti-tipping associations like the Anti-Tipping Society of America, founded in 1904, polemics such as William Scott's *The Itching Palm* (1916) and the *Commercial Bribery and Tipping Review,* experimental "no tipping" hotels like the Grace Dodge Hotel in Washington, D. C., and even anti-tipping laws enacted by several states failed to stop the practice. By 1935, a study by Rae Needleman in the *Monthly Labor Review* estimated that there were "800,000 employees in tipped occupations," including 333,000 restaurant employees (Needleman 1314). An important step in the changing of public attitudes toward tipping occurred in 1937 when the Bureau of Internal Revenue and the National Recovery Act addressed the debate over whether tips should be considered wages in establishing a minimum wage. But in 1931 when Cain's Mildred applied for her first job as a waitress, tipping was still a legal battleground for the IRS, for the unemployment insurance commissions of most states, for employers, and for the public, and its social implications reflected the uncertainties of its economic status.

Cain first introduces the issue of tipping in *The Postman Always Rings Twice* (1934) when Cora balks at having her lover Frank Chambers "wear a smock, with Service Auto Parks printed on the back."[5] She explains to him why she married Nick Papadakis:

> "I got off the Chief with fifteen guys taking my picture, and two weeks later I was in the hash house."
> "And then?" . . .
> "Then two years of guys pinching your leg and leaving nickel tips and asking how about a little party tonight. I went on some of them parties, Frank." (11–12)

In Cain's novels, leg-pinching and sexual exploitation come with the territory for a waitress. Earlier, Frank socks Cora in the leg "so hard it nearly knocked her over" (10), an attack that, as Joyce Carol Oates points out, is "without provocation . . . a kind of act of love in itself" (120). Yet by this gesture Frank distinguishes himself from her other patrons and lovers, for his blow mimics and intensifies the customers' pinches and leg-groping, exposing the violence and sexual exploitation inherent in Cora's position. Similarly, John Howard Sharp, the washed-up opera singer of *Serenade* (1937), steals food and signs on as bouncer for a brothel without compunction, but he worries before a singing job:

> I had never taken a tip, and I wondered how I was going to feel about it. . . . They borrowed a tray from a waiter and passed it around and when it came back it was full of silver. He handed it to me, and I thanked him, and dumped it in my pocket. I had taken a tip, but I didn't feel anything.[6]

For Cain's characters, taking a tip functions metonymically for the model of the service economy that they will do anything to avoid—in the case of Frank Chambers and Cora Papadakis, even commit murder. In addition to the denial of individuality that attends the wearing of uniforms and smocks, accepting tips transforms the individual into a depersonalized commodity, a "varlet" whose identity is merely the sum of easily sheared-away and interchangeable service functions. As used by characters in *Mildred Pierce*, Cain's incongruous archaism "varlet" allows Monty and Veda to ally themselves with Cain's satirically depicted Pasadena *ancien régime*, but it also functions more generally as Cain's ironic shorthand for the pretensions of those who employ the term. Those who take tips become "varlets" because of their double servitude, an acknowledgment of "dependence on the customer as well as the boss"(C. P. Wilson 60). Susan Porter Benson's observation about the additional social burden on saleswomen is instructive here: "the addition of the client to the usual worker-employer dyad was always implicit in service work, but [now] the client was directly and emphatically present on the selling floor"—and, one might add, in the restaurant booth as well (125).

In *Mildred Pierce*, several of these features converge in the figure of the waitress, a symbol that gains additional significance from its association with feminine markers of food and sex. For Mildred, waitressing recontextualizes and consequently devalues her talents in both areas. Bereft of a larger purpose, her domestic skills lose value as she simply serves food instead of preparing it, and she resents the depersonalization that the profession demands. Cain plays on this signification in *Mildred Pierce* during several extended scenes in which Mildred looks for work but resists this occupation. Offered a job as a waitress, she tells Miss Turner at the employment agency, "I can't go home and face my children if they know I've been working all day at taking tips, and wearing a uniform, and mopping up crumbs" (49). Since "mopping up crumbs" arguably constitutes a great proportion of her day's labor as a mother in any case, the two other conditions that Mildred mentions—uniforms and tips—stand out in high relief. After witnessing a squabble over tip-stealing at a restaurant, however, Mildred, instead of leaving, "as though walking to the electric chair . . . head[s] to the kitchen" (53) and takes a job as a waitress. Later, when she recognizes that the entire world thinks she is good only for "putting on a uniform and waiting on other people," the blow to her pride makes her physically ill and hysterical. She later sobs to Lucy Gessler, "I—just—can't—do—it. . . .Wear a uniform. And take their tips. And face those awful people. . . . And one of them grabbed my leg. Ooh—I can feel it yet. He put his hand clear up to—" (61). The legs that she fetishizes as her sole beauty, narcissistically admiring their perfection in mirrors or when in bed with various lovers, devolve into a doubly debased tool of her trade: like Cora, she must "trot" all day as a waitress and also allow sexual handling of them for the sake of a tip. During this period of her life, her on-again, off-again relationship with Wally Burgan is similarly service-oriented. Their infrequent sexual encounters when Mildred's financial affairs are desperate or when she wants help in opening the restaurant lend credence to David Madden's observation that for Mildred, "sexual giving is basically barter" (Madden 80).

Although Lucy Gessler comforts her by saying, "Nobody pays any attention to that uniform stuff any more" (61), waitressing for Mildred clearly represents a Depression-era loss of status that operates on a societal as well as an individual level. Given the climate of the times and the culture's relegation of lower-status jobs to minorities, part of the stigma resulted from racism and xenophobia. In both *Postman* and *Mildred Pierce*, the restaurants where Cora and Mildred work are owned by Greeks, Nick Papadakis and Chris Makadoulis, whose claims to American identity are undercut and mocked by the novels' ethnic stereotyping, including a comic representation of dialect. In Cain's novels, the position of waitress exposes the "white" all-American woman to contamination by placing her in a subordinate position to those defined as ethnically other. For example, *Postman*'s Cora Smith feels tainted by her marriage to Nick Papadakis, whom she and Frank call "the Greek," and she bridles at Frank's praise for her enchiladas: "You think I'm Mex. . . . Well, get this. I'm just as white as you are" (5). Frank, who shares her prejudices, understands then that his presence restores her sense of ethnic superiority: "I knew for certain, then, what I had just taken a chance on when I went in there. It wasn't those enchiladas that she had to cook, and it wasn't having black hair. It was being married to that Greek that made her feel she wasn't white, and she was even afraid I would begin calling her Mrs. Papadakis" (6). William Marling suggests that "'Nick the Greek' is a seme for blacks, for Mexicans, for Italians, for eastern Europeans, for all immigrants," and that in marrying him, Cora has broken the laws of the tribe (Marling 173). In *Gumshoe America: Hard-Boiled Crime Fiction and the Rise and Fall of New Deal Liberalism*, Sean McCann suggests a more benign interpretation of the issue, seeing Nick's ethnicity as an economic rather than racial signifier, one distinct from the overt and dichotomous white/not white racist judgments of the KKK: "Rather than foreign corruption [. . .] 'the Greek' stands in *Postman* for a type of triviality that Cain describes as typical of *American* culture. Nick epitomizes 'a whole goddam country that lives selling hot dogs to each other.' That he is Greek simply marks the fact that he is somewhere near the bottom rung of a ladder whose acme is thought of as 'white'" (McCann 75). The opposition between ethnic and "American" identity, however, one that Cora and Frank articulate with their discussion of "white," "not white," and "as white as you are," suggests that more than economic pressures are at stake: the precipitating factor in their second, and successful, attempt to kill Nick is Cora's offensive determination not to "have [a] greasy Greek child" (30), a decision that predates her decision to better herself economically by fixing up the restaurant that she and Nick had owned.

In addition to the xenophobic threat of serving under foreigners, the profession of waitressing itself was a primary determinant of lowered status, in part because of its association with minorities. Peter Fearon notes in *The Origins and Nature of the Great Slump, 1929–1932* that "[d]omestic service and waiting-on-table[s], which previously had been monopolized by blacks, now attracted white competition" (137). Without race and ethnicity to delimit social status, only occupation and its easily shed badges such as smocks and uniforms can distinguish working-class Glendale from aristocratic Pasadena. Since the concept of class depends upon a clearly identifiable set of social markers, part of the class-based tension in *Mildred Pierce* resides in the attempts of its largely white cast of characters to establish their relative status absent the usual signals of ethnicity and wealth. For example, at the funeral of Ray, Mildred's younger daughter, Mildred's family mistakes Letty, the hired girl, for a family friend rather than a servant, a social gaffe that Veda capitalizes upon as a chance to snub her cousins. The film lessens this tension, since William Faulkner, one of its screenwriters, changed Letty's character from white to black (LaValley 35). By the time the film was released, the novel's parallels between Letty and Mildred had dissolved entirely, for Letty, played by Butterfly McQueen, had become a stereotypically scatterbrained maid whose malapropisms and non sequiturs provide a clear contrast to Mildred's single-minded and articulate pursuit of success. In the novel, by contrast, issues of occupation and identity complicate those of class: as a waitress, Mildred serves others, but she hires Letty to serve her family and to replace her as caregiver and housekeeper, an identity that Letty embraces until she is as much a worshipper of Veda as Mildred is. The exchange of identity between mistress and servant multiplies in other ways as well. In both novel and movie versions, Veda orders Letty to dress in Mildred's uniform, which Mildred has hidden from her daughters, as a means of humiliating her mother by exposing her secret and then taunting her with the knowledge: "Aren't the pies bad enough? Did you have to degrade us by—" (77). The only way in which Mildred can distinguish herself from Letty and reestablish authority over Veda is by leaving the service economy and abandoning the profession of waitress to open her own restaurant.

Mildred's second transformation, from waitress to entrepreneur, originates with her procuring pie contracts and ends with her ownership of a bakery and three restaurants. In addition, this period marks the convergence of several events that signify Mildred's new status. The compressed time frame is itself suggestive. During the course of one week, Mildred meets and spends the night with Monty Beragon, a man who picks her up at the restaurant; experiences the death of her daughter Ray, repository of Mildred's humanity as Veda is of her ambition; rededicates herself to Veda; and opens her restaurant. The restaurant is a stage set for Mildred's representation of her successful marriage of domesticity and the marketplace, and she is its star. No longer a nameless plate-carrier, Mildred, as Cain observes, "looked like the cook in a musical comedy" (139). Liberated by her status as owner from the necessity of *being* the waitress, Mildred is now free to enact, and subtly to transform, the *role* of waitress. Thus the anonymous $3.95 "uniform" of Mr. Chris Makadoulis's restaurant is transformed into a Mildred-designed "costume" that features her legs, which have returned to their status as private aesthetic objects.

The restaurant further presents a synchronic convergence of Mildred's present and past that is obscured in the movie version. The film has Mildred meeting Monty when she buys one of his properties from him as a site for her restaurant, a convergence of new commerce and decayed gentility that has Snopes and Sartoris overtones.[7] In the novel, she takes over the old Pierce model home built by her husband Bert as a sales office for his real-estate development, a family business that, like the house itself, he has lost to economic pressures. As Bert had prospered in the twenties by building houses, replicating the present-tense suburban American dream for middle- and working-class families, so the Depression-based Mildred now trades on past-tense nostalgia. Establishing her restaurant in the Pierce model home with "the old colonial architecture that Bert spent all that dough on" (92), using a gas waffle maker "because that's the old-fashioned kind of round waffle that people really like" (140), she constructs a factitious past, serving up memories of a vanished and mythical New England to the rootless denizens of southern California. Moreover, her own history is inextricably bound up in that place, for it was during her visit to the model home that Bert originally seduced her. Food, sex, and marketplace intersect as Mildred converts the location of her own sexual initiation and of Veda's conception, the bedroom of the model home, into a gleaming commercial kitchen that is the site of her birth as a businesswoman.

Mildred's relationship with Monty Beragon seems at first the fitting complement to her commercial success and a suitable conclusion to her rags-to-riches tale. Indeed, the plot of the humble heroine and the upper-class male has been a staple not only of classic literature like *Tess of the D'Urbervilles*, turn-of-the-century shopgirl romances like those of Bertha M. Clay, and contemporary middlebrow novels like Christopher Morley's *Kitty Foyle* (1939), but, as Janice Radway demonstrates in *Reading the Romance*, of genre literature as well. But sexual interest and class antagonism in *Mildred Pierce* fail to follow Radway's pattern of mutual love and the eventual restoration of the heroine's identity (134). Monty and Mildred meet prosaically, but at a significant point in her life: he is her last customer at the restaurant where she works as a waitress and the first to see the restaurant she is about to open as an owner. Wondering idly about his ethnicity—"whether his bald spot was brown by nature, or from sunburn" (104)—Mildred soon learns that Monty, a Pasadena man-about-town and polo player, has all the aristocracy that the rest of her acquaintances lack. Unlike the phony Spanish-style furnishings of Mildred's Glendale tract house, which he despises, Monty is the real thing.[8] His mother is from an old Eastern family, he tells her, but his father's family is Spanish, "one of the gay caballeros that gypped the Indians out of their land, the king out of his taxes, and then sold out to the Americans when Polk started annexing" (107). At once authentically upper-class and exotic, with his "slightly Latin" look and "decidedly Continental" clipped moustache (104), Monty defends class distinctions based not on achievement, like Mildred, or on dreams of achievement, like Bert, but on the

possession of inherited and inimitable class distinctions. Over the course of their
relationship, Mildred sees that to Monty she remains "a pretty varlet," "an amus-
ing servant girl, one with pretty legs and a flattering response in bed" (153), and
the gingham apron that connotes motherhood and candied crabapple pie for
middle-class Americans such as Bert and Wally is for an upper-class "Latin" like
Monty a garment that flaunts sexuality, "the greatest provocation ever invented
by woman for the torture of man" (183). In a reversal of the book's early chapters, Mildred's domestic relationships now threaten the reintegration of self that
she has achieved through her success in the business world, for Monty verbally
dismembers and depersonalizes Mildred much as the business world had done
previously, calling her "the best piece of tail I ever had" (168). Despite her status as the owner-manager of several restaurants, Mildred is forever a waitress in
Monty's eyes because in his rigid view of class, taking a tip is an irrevocable act
in defining status.

Much of his posturing may be defensive, however, for Mildred now dis-
penses tips instead of receiving them, supporting Monty with small "loans" until
he attacks not the money but the manner in which she requires work for it:

> "A lady doesn't care [about Monty's lack of work]. A varlet does. . . .
> Why, you scum, you—waitress. I guess that's one reason I love Veda.
> She wouldn't pick up a tip. That's one thing she wouldn't do—and nei-
> ther would I."
> "Except from me." (197)

Just as he has steadfastly refused to work for a living, Monty rejects the payment
for service model, hypothesizing instead, like Veda, a gift economy that figures
exchange without reciprocity. But as the narrative voice points out, Monty never
realizes the central paradox of class: that "a jaunty aloofness from money, as
though it were beneath a gentleman's notice . . . rested squarely on money: it
was the possession of money that enabled him to be aloof from it" (168). As befits
his status as the novel's representative from European culture, Monty accepts
the world of tipping and the class distinctions it represents, but the rigid rules
that govern the practice and the flow of money from superior to inferior, never
the other way around, force him into some linguistic gymnastics to square his
practice with the ideal. Thus Monty believes that a tip is not a tip if it is given
with humor and not in expectation of services rendered: "I once thought maybe
I'd been mistaken, that you were a lady, and not a varlet. That was when you
handed me the $20 bill that night, and I took it. . . . I even gave you credit for . . .
some sense of humor that only an aristocrat has, and *asked* you for money" (196).
By definition a tip is also not a tip, he implies, if it travels from an inferior such
as Mildred to her superior in the class system. Mildred, he points out, has the
varlet's unreasonable expectation of receiving goods or services if money

changes hands, whether that involves driving Veda to piano lessons or functioning as Mildred's "paid gigolo," as he calls himself (168). Like Bert, whose
failed entrepreneurial efforts encompass a range of southern California boom-
and-bust schemes such as growing grapes, growing walnuts, and finally carving
his ranchland into subdivisions, Monty believes that a gentleman lives only on
the unearned increment gained from the labor of others, and his accepting tips
from Mildred meets this criterion. Also like Bert, he has defined leisure as the
status marker of the gentleman. But in the novel's Depression-era setting of
1928–1937, the disappearing boundary between those who *need not* work and
those who *cannot* work quickly erases the distinction between gentleman and
discarded worker. In the economy of the era, an excess of enforced leisure
drives down the value of the rare and precious commodity of leisure that signifies class.

The conclusion of Mildred's entrepreneurial stage finds her neglecting, and
finally losing, her empire in order to serve the musical career of her daughter
Veda, an improbable plot point that is justifiably the source of much criticism of
the book.[9] Veda, described accurately by reviewer Clifton Fadiman as "as nasty
a bitchling as has ever been committed to paper" (63), exists as Cain's attempt to
account for what the book considers a genetic freak of nature, the coloratura
soprano. Snobbish, selfish, and vicious, with an inborn talent for music, Veda
ridicules Mildred and the "Pie Wagon" even as, like Monty, she spends Mildred's
money lavishly. Through sycophancy, extortion, and fraud, Veda finally triumphs as an opera singer, accumulating along the way Mildred's fur coat, her
wealth, and her second husband, Monty, whose attitudes toward "varlets" she
shares. Briefly put, Mildred's story is equally Veda's story, for Veda functions
throughout as Mildred's double as well as antagonist. Much film criticism has
centered on the mother-daughter relationship, particularly since the film
emphasizes the similarities between the two women through a variety of methods: two-shots framing the visually similar actresses Joan Crawford and Ann
Blyth, shots repeated with both actresses, and so forth. Even in the book, however, Veda is a dark funhouse mirror, a distorted medium through which Mildred's own actions appear exaggerated and refracted into more sordid versions of
themselves. For example, Mildred's seduction by Bert and their subsequent marriage due to her pregnancy resurfaces as Veda's blackmail of her lover Sam For-
rester over a sham pregnancy. Mildred's collusion with Bert's best friend, Wally,
to buy her restaurant suggests Veda's later shady pretense of injury to gain a fraud-
ulent release from a radio contract. Most significantly, Mildred's affair with and
later marriage to Monty predates Veda's affair with him. Given the sexual into-
nations of the "heat lightnings" (132) that Mildred feels for Veda at several points,
Mildred's jealousy about the affair and her anger at Monty for stealing Veda come
across as perverse in the incestuous possessiveness they reveal.

Juxtaposed with her mother's story, Veda's narrative exists in part to parallel and in part to deflate the waitress's popular rags-to-riches tale. Veda's medium of exchange and artistic expression is music, as Mildred's is food. She exists as Cain's version of his familiar fairy-tale theme "the curse of an answered prayer": as Cain himself suggested, Mildred wanted a talented child and God gave her Veda (Hoopes 348). As Mr. Treviso, Veda's singing teacher, puts it, "Da girl is lousy . . . Da singer—is not" (252). In Veda's counter-narrative, Mildred remains figuratively the fairy-tale peasant, the "varlet," guarding the foundling princess whose musical abilities constitute the novel's conception of natural aristocracy. Stuck in this fairy-tale plot, Mildred can never become a princess herself, but she can do what she does at the end of the book, what "varlets" in the historical sense have always done: rebel. Divorced from Monty and remarried to Bert, Mildred finally frees herself by cutting the cord that binds her to Veda, and since this is after all a Cain novel, hauls out a bottle of rye to "get stinko" (298). If the rest of the book is a paean to what the characters call "gump" or gumption and to middle-class aspirations, if it exposes the illogical strictures against tipping and other markers of class, the ending ironically instead confirms the fairy tale. The natural aristocrats, Veda and Monty, leave for points unknown and new hosts for their parasitical ways, whereas Mildred, now "thirty-seven years old, fat, and getting a little shapeless" (297) is back where she started, married to Bert and baking pies for a living. She has escaped the service economy, but only at the cost of destroying all she has worked for and of losing her two daughters in the process.

Attempting to classify *Mildred Pierce*, contemporary reviewers such as James T. Farrell, himself a Cain competitor, solemnly condemned the novel's "movietone realism" and emphasis on "things and money, commodities" (83). Part of Cain's point, however, is that Mildred's complex negotiation of class involves commodifying herself. As reviews indicated, Cain's novel is a confusion of genres, much as the film is a conflation of them. It cannot be called simply a success story for its waitress-heroine, nor purely a melodrama, a "hard-boiled" tale of sex and violence, a "suffering mother" tale, a novel of domestic realism, nor even a proletarian bildungsroman as described by Barbara Foley. Cain's creation of Mildred, too, is problematic, for his customary satire of her and all his working-class characters, more apparent here because of the uncharacteristic third-person narration, is tinged with more than a little of the Veda-Monty contempt toward "varlets." One way to look at the novel is to see it, as does Joyce Carol Oates, as a tale of thwarted wish-fulfillment:

> *Mildred Pierce* has at its center a forbidden wish made articulate: that a
> mother may possess her daughter completely as if the daughter were a
> lover, that she may control not only this daughter, but all people, all

men within her orbit, and even achieve a kind of apocalyptic economic
success out of the ruins of the Depression—exactly the formula for a
popular audience, though all these wishes are ultimately thwarted. (116)

In another sense, however, Mildred's true forbidden wish is to own not only her
daughter but also Farrell's "commodities" and the social class that they signify.
Paradoxically, the accumulation of markers of her status as waitress—an apron,
a tip—negates any further acquisition of higher-status goods or class on her part.
As a member of the newly devalued service economy in prewar America, Mildred Pierce prefigures both postwar entrepreneurship—her analysis of the marketplace is eerily prescient—and the cultural anomie that results when service
substitutes for the production of commodities. Seen as a commentary on class,
Mildred Pierce becomes not so much a departure from Cain's hard-boiled fiction as a far more extensive exploration of, and trenchant commentary upon,
the social forces of the service economy that drive his drifters and ne'er-do-wells
in Depression-era America.

NOTES

1. Linda Williams, "Feminist Film Theory: Mildred Pierce and the Second World
War," in *Female Spectators: Looking at Film and Television*, 13. See also Pam Cook,
"Duplicity in *Mildred Pierce*," in *Women in Film Noir*, ed. E. Ann Kaplan, 58–82; and
Janet Walker, "Feminist Critical Practice: Female Discourse in *Mildred Pierce*."

2. Although it was not one of Cain's best-selling books and would later be outshone
by the movie adaptation, *Mildred Pierce* still sold an astonishing 733,000 copies within
six years of its original publication (Hoopes 426).

3. David Madden comments perceptively on the general linkage between food and
sex in *James M. Cain*. See especially chapter 3, "The Love-Rack and the Wish-Come-
True," 61–91. A more recent essay on Cain's use of food is Robert Dingley's "Eating America: The Consuming Passion of James M. Cain." Dingley suggests that the diners and
barbeque restaurants in Cain's works are part of a broader cultural preoccupation with
fast food in a mobile society.

4. James M. Cain, *Mildred Pierce* (New York: Vintage Books, 1989). Subsequent references are cited in the text.

5. James M. Cain, *The Postman Always Rings Twice*, in *Three Novels by James M.
Cain*, 13. Subsequent references are cited in the text.

6. James M. Cain, *Serenade*, in *Three Novels by James M. Cain*, 87.

7. According to LaValley, "In MacDougall's version, which Faulkner follows, she
gets the old, run-down house from Monte Beragon" (34). (The name is spelled "Monty"
in the novel and "Monte" in the script.) The suggestions of Sartoris and Snopes are strong
here, although the book suggests instead the overtaking of upstart Snopes (Mildred) by
older Snopes (Bert, the false aristocrat).

8. Catherine Jurca's *White Diaspora : The Suburb and the Twentieth-Century American Novel* discusses Cain's extensive use of interiors as a means of establishing class. Jurca suggests that Cain sees standardization and mass production as the ally rather than the enemy of homemaking; the emergence of interior design as a means of middle-class self-expression during the 1930s appears in the work as Monty, functioning as a tastemaker or ideal designer, articulates its principles for Mildred.

9. For example, in his 4 October 1941 review for the *Saturday Review*, Phil Stong comments, "Mr. Cain writes, as usual, with great vigor and economy, but this book is neither so tight nor so dramatic as the frugal 'Postman.' The story wabbles [sic] seriously at the end where Veda, hopeless as a pianist, turns out incredibly to be a coloratura. Mr. Cain's observations on the low natures of coloratura sopranos—they should all be married to left-handed pitchers and the happy couple shot immediately—as expressed by Mr. Treviso, the music teacher, are very funny" (13).

"My Little Illegality"

Abortion, Resistance, and Women Writers on the Left

JOY CASTRO

"The real class struggle," contends a character in Tess Slesinger's 1934 novel *The Unpossessed*, "is the struggle between the sexes; and rebellion begins at home" (23). It may seem counterintuitive that within a movement predicated upon the notion of human equality women would be viewed as inferior citizens. Yet work by Paula Rabinowitz, Laura Hapke, Constance Coiner, and others has illuminated the many obstacles facing leftist women writers of the '20s and '30s: the refusal of leftist party politics to address women's issues, the resistance to women in positions of leadership, and the ideology that discouraged women's literary production. Mike Gold's famous description of the ideal proletarian writer—"a wild youth of about twenty-two, the son of working-class parents, who himself works in the lumber camps, coal mines, and steel mills"—excludes women and domestic experience by definition (Qtd. in Nekola and Rabinowitz 3). Moreover, during a period when literary references to nonreproductive sexuality were allied with pornography in the public imagination, as Adam Parkes points out in his study of the Nausicaa trial, for a writer to focus on not only female experience but also pregnancy termination was transgressive in the extreme.

Yet the abortion story can function, as Judith Wilt has argued, as a potentially rich and productive narrative moment, since it is always a site of profound anxiety both for the storyteller, who stands revealed as a potential locus of moral culpability, and for the reader, who must contend with a morally contested, emotionally explosive issue (5). In three novels by leftist American women writers of the Depression era, the abortion plot refuses to perform according to reader expectations in three ways.

First, abortion itself, which would seem to function as a guarantor of women's reproductive freedom, is figured negatively in these texts by feminist writers. Though the increased availability of abortion and contraception during the '20s and '30s would seem to serve as a liberating force for women, the ramifications of such technologies must be understood differently within the context of a male-dominated social movement that saw children largely as impediments to class struggle and as fodder for the factory and battlefield. Women who found themselves pregnant could be compelled, in the interests of political ideology, to forego childbirth regardless of their own desires. Its meaning contingent on larger social circumstances, reproductive technology can function as a method of control rather than as a means of freedom. Leftist women's writing that reveals this conflict demonstrates the way in which women's freedoms are differently inflected within different cultural contexts and exposes the link between masculinist privilege within the bourgeoisie and on the Left. In choosing abortion, women realized the degree to which they, like the working class, had been commodified—a lesson lost on their male counterparts in the movement. These texts usefully remind us that resistance to the dominant ideology within a resistant movement can appear superficially similar to the ideology of the larger dominant sphere.

Second, the structures of these novels do not conform to current theoretical analyses of the abortion story. Interpreting the work of more recent authors (Didion, Barth, and others), Wilt argues in her 1990 study, *Abortion, Choice, and Contemporary Fiction*, that abortion functions to resist control. Thus, briefly, if a man tries to control a woman with pregnancy, the plot resists with abortion. Conversely, if a man tries to control a woman by coercing or forcing her to have an abortion (as is the case in all three of the novels)—or if a woman tries to control "nature" by having an abortion—then the plot resists with continued pregnancy (4). Either way, Wilt argues, the possibility of abortion provokes resistance. Such resistance, however, is not operative in Josephine Herbst's *Money for Love* (1929), Margery Latimer's *This Is My Body* (1932), or Tess Slesinger's *The Unpossessed* (1934). Rather, when male characters—whether bourgeois or leftist—attempt to control women in these texts, the women acquiesce, only to suffer physical pain and emotional devastation. Nothing is gained; abortion functions exclusively as a trope for loss and failed promise. Rather than serving as a moment of resistance, abortion instead functions as a moment of submission—the moment in which women, submitting to the demands of their lovers, their class, their politics, realize the extent to which their bodies are commodities and to which ultimately dehumanizing technologies have supplanted nature in capitalist society.

Last, the texts subtly valorize "nature," which is controlled, in each case, just as the women are controlled, as against technology, depicted as invasive and dehumanizing. In taking psychological refuge in images of nature—fruit, trees—the women recognize or resist their own victimization. Yet this woman-nature alliance does not function retrogressively; in contrast to what Stacy Alaimo has observed in her analysis of leftist women's texts of the period, nature does not operate in these narratives as "feminism's foe," "essentialist with a vengeance as it reduces the protagonists to breeding bodies" (109). Rather, nature functions as a refuge, a metaphor for what the women are relinquishing or, in Meridel Le Sueur's short story "Annunciation" (1935), choosing to keep. Nature operates as an ally in resistance, a source of strength that reinforces women's desire. In this valorization of nature, these writers respond also to the futurist argument. Published in 1909, the first manifesto of F. T. Marinetti, the founder of Italian futurism, argued in favor of ridding art and literature of all sentiment and humanitarianism in order to valorize the speed, technology, and inhumanity of the machine age (Nicholls 85). While the apparent misogyny of futurism, long accepted, is now being complicated by accounts of those few women who adopted modified versions of its tenets, Marinetti's own creative vision included the novel *Mafarka* (1910), in which women's bodies become utterly irrelevant: human reproduction is performed solo by a machine-man. The futurist vision of a future that edits out connection, relationship, and the female sex itself in the embrace of efficiency is resisted and rejected by these leftist women's texts, which critique such an enthusiastic, unquestioning celebration of technology, presenting abortion as the invasion of technology into the warm human world of intimate relationships and embodied pleasure.

While abortion functions in these texts as a moment of submission, of acquiescence, tremendous resistance does inhere in the production of narratives that expose this ideological inconsistency, braving as they do the personal and cultural anxieties of both writer and audience. In writing narratives that feature abortion, Herbst, Latimer, Slesinger, and Le Sueur confound expectations to vet the connections and tensions between sexual and economic politics for women on the Left.

Money for Love

She wished she had old clothes on and was going to work in a factory. She felt as if she wanted to do some hard work and really see life.

Socialist journalist Josephine Herbst based her 1929 novel, *Money for Love*, on an earlier, unpublished work that fictionalizes her 1920 relationship with dramatist Maxwell Anderson. Anderson, who was married, pressured her to terminate an unplanned pregnancy, and Herbst unwillingly agreed. Complicating Herbst's views of abortion was the tragic death of her sister.

Recovering from her own abortion, Herbst advised her sister to go through with an abortion that would keep her from being tied to a life of rural struggle. Her sister, following Herbst's advice, died during the procedure; Herbst's grief and guilt were tremendous.

Money for Love, Herbst's last novel before her Rope of Gold trilogy established her as a socialist novelist, does not explore leftist politics explicitly. Instead, it investigates the impact of male economic privilege on sexual dynamics, demonstrating the connections between bourgeois society's sexual commodification of women and its comparable commodification of the labor of the working class. It offers its female protagonist a glimpse of solidarity with the working class, yet she rejects such an identification, instead reinserting herself into a bitter, ironic version of the bourgeois marriage plot.

A few years before the action of the novel begins, protagonist Harriet Everist has acquiesced to the demand of her married lover, Bruce Jones, that she end a pregnancy, only to have him then end the relationship. While the experience has permanently altered her personality, leaving her cynical and emotionally numb, Bruce, a successful playwright, has gone on with his life, his marriage, and subsequent affairs. Jobless and desperate as the narrative opens, Harriet appeals to Bruce for money, finally resorting to blackmail.

Unlike the abortions in both Latimer's and Slesinger's novels, which function as the structural climaxes of the narratives, the abortion experience of Money for Love's protagonist is long since past, and the novel does not revisit it in any detail. Rather, abortion is presented as the impetus for all of Harriet's behavior during the action of the novel. Harriet, rightly holding Bruce accountable as the cause of the abortion (for which she cannot forgive herself), also views him as the responsible party for all of her subsequent suffering; the action of the novel is propelled by her attempts to exact compensation from him. Yet the reader comes to see just how profoundly Harriet causes her own suffering, and it is the sordidness of her response to Bruce, not of Bruce's initiating behavior, that comes to dominate the narrative. Within the present action of the narrative, Harriet, not Bruce, is depicted as culpable—and strikingly unsympathetic. Bruce, in contrast, is portrayed as compassionate and humane, a fundamentally fair fellow left to deal with a desperate woman. Moreover, he does so in a generous manner, giving her more money than she demands even after the letters in her possession no longer hold the power to threaten him. His wife, the mother of their four legitimate children, magnanimously forgives his affairs while expressing only pity for Harriet.

However, readers quick to condemn Harriet's behavior fail to perceive the social structures also critiqued by Herbst, the fundamental systems of privilege that underlie and motivate all of Harriet's actions. As Michael Roemer comments in *Telling Stories: Postmodernism and the Invalidation of Traditional Narrative*, "The wrong that sets off a story is often a vengeful deed by one who has himself been gravely wounded. We call him a villain because his wound was struck in the past and his hurt has turned into malice, whereas the injuries he inflicts on others are done before our eyes and so arouse our consternation" (7–8). Such a dynamic controls *Money for Love*. While Harriet is the novel's most unsavory character, the Joneses reproduce the period's status quo: the bourgeois family structure, the double standard of male sexuality, and the behavior appropriate to a good wife. Herbst indicts the structure of marriage itself as fundamentally predicated upon male privilege, both sexual and economic. What the novel reveals is that, without substantial capital of their own, women — both kinds of women: the long-suffering, middle-class wives who functioned as angels in the bourgeois house, and their disposable working-class counterparts — are at the economic mercy of the men with whom they are intimately engaged. The gendered economic system, then — with its limited access to education and professional success for women — is responsible for the financial dependency of women upon men that turns women into sexual and/or reproductive commodities.

Harriet's failure is the failure of a naïve woman to perceive her status as commodity in an economic world. She is sexually innocent when she falls in love with Bruce Jones, and he is reluctant to make love to her until she makes up tales of past experience. Assured falsely that she is used goods — that he will not despoil her market value — he has an affair with her. She fails to secure any guarantor of economic support from Bruce, viewing sexuality not within an economy of exchange but within an economy of gift and desire. Just so, her later attempt to blackmail Bruce fails for she has forgotten to get a receipt from the post office, and the packet of Bruce's letters to her is lost during delivery. Although the packet of letters is finally returned, "torn open" and looking "as if it had fallen on a wet street," as tattered as Harriet herself (252), she stands publicly revealed as a blackmailer, for some anonymous person has read the letters before returning them to the post office — someone who knows the title of Bruce Jones's only novel, *The Man Who Loved Women*, and someone with a keen sense of irony: "Someone had written something in pencil in a fine even hand. She held it up and read slowly, 'The Man Who Loved Women,' and underneath on another line, 'At Eight Hundred Dollars Per'" (252). She has been revealed to a community of strangers as a commodity who puts herself up for sale.

It is after this final devastation, the novel's climax, that Harriet experiences the fleeting possibility of class solidarity: "At a corner Coffee Pot she had a grape fruit and a cup of coffee. A working man stared at her perched on a stool. She looked back at him in a friendly way. She wished she had old clothes on and was going to work in a factory. She felt as if she wanted to do some hard work and really see life" (273). Here she identifies with the working class, and her expression toward the male is simply "friendly," not sexually inviting or rejecting. Herbst subtly ironizes Harriet's sudden interest, however, by syntactically placing it at one remove: Harriet feels "*as if* she wanted to do some hard work"; she doesn't simply want to work. Harriet's notion of factory labor as a way to "really see life," too, is ironized here. She flirts briefly with the opportunity for class consciousness but draws away from the possibilities, giving Bruce's money to her current boyfriend, who plans to use it for medical school—and who still mourns his first wife, dead as the result of an abortion. The novel ends with Harriet's reinsertion into the bourgeois marriage plot as she weds. She will be, not a worker in a factory, but a doctor's wife.

Herbst's novel functions as a passionate, disturbing critique of the function of sexuality within the complex formed by gender and class. If Harriet is indeed immoral in her attempts to blackmail Bruce, or if she is amoral in her lack of remorse for doing so, it is abortion, the text contends, and the whole system for which abortion synecdochically stands, that is responsible for so demoralizing her. Abortion has been the great teacher, the initiator into a world of economics where women's bodies, emotions, and desires are commodities and the purse-strings are held by men. Her trajectory after abortion functions for Harriet, then, as a possible transition into the working class, the fall from the Edenic illusions of the bourgeoisie—with its ideal of the self as a special, precious individual—into the reality of a classed society and her own relatively powerless position within it. Realizing that the most intimate aspects of her body and emotions are seen as products for which there may or may not be a market, Harriet recognizes the fundamentally economic nature of her society and her own place in it. Learning the lesson all too well—but rejecting the possibility of struggle for social change—Harriet trades on herself to the bitter end.

The fact that Herbst presents this moment of identification with the working class as a failed possibility demonstrates a measure of hope that, if women make the connection between their own commodification and that of workers, a beneficial alliance could be forged. Latimer's and Slesinger's novels, which take leftist male privilege to task, proffer no such hope.

In *Money for Love*, Herbst diverges from the direct, plain prose style and traditional narrative structures advocated for their simplicity and realism by many leftist critics and writers, producing instead a narrative that mimics its protagonist's emotional state. Harriet is easy to dislike not only because of her behavior but also due to her lack of warmth, spontaneity, and passion; she is depicted as calculating and manipulative but in a lackluster, melancholic sort of way, without even the energy for true villainy. Harriet exhibits a reduced ability to respond to her life and interact with the world—an "inability," according to Winifred Bevilacqua, "to cope with guilt and loss that impel Harriet to suppress any meaningful emotional life she might have had and to resign herself to operating unhappily within very limited horizons" (28). Such emotional withdrawal corresponds to the "reduced responsiveness" caused by "unsuccessful attempts to avoid or deny painful abortion recollections" identified as one of the symptoms of postabortion syndrome (PAS), a type of post-traumatic stress disorder, in 1992 (Speckhard and Rue 95). The very structure and prose style of Herbst's entire novel are remarkable for their extraordinarily flat affect; Herbst articulates the action with "a minimum of suspense and surprise and no emotional peaks or minor climaxes" (Bevilacqua 28). A public debate about the prose style, in fact, unfolded in terms suggestive of abortion itself. Katherine Anne Porter raises but does not pursue the issue of a link between style and content in her review of the novel for the socialist journal *New Masses*: "In her second novel, Josephine Herbst strips her vocabulary to fighting trim and goes for poor lost middle western human nature with a kind of cold detached ferocity that makes my hair rise. . . . [H]er lack of human pity is her own business. She has made a fine job of destruction. What, precisely, is she trying to kill?" (17–18). Published subsequently in the *Nation*, Herbst's response to her reviewers refutes the critical contention that, with her deliberately bare, flat prose, she was attempting to imitate what was then considered Hemingway's simplicity or naturalness of style. Of *Money for Love*, Herbst writes that "the people were pared to the bone, not to be realistic or natural, as you claim, but to suggest an even completer bareness of life than the actuality of the characters could portray. I believe you assume too much when you conclude that the end and aim of *my* writing, at least, is to be natural." She concludes: "I succeeded so well that I never want to do this sort of thing again. But in adhering to this method I was under no compulsion to exalt 'simplicity' but to attain a certain end. The machinery dominated the content in this case, and not by chance. I believe such a procedure always fails" (275–76).

With her use of stylistic and structural innovations, Herbst deliberately produced a novel that, in its very textuality, embodies the "reduced responsiveness" of postabortion syndrome. In so doing, she partook of the contemporary high modernist concern for exploring and depicting subjective states of consciousness. She describes her strategy in terms suggestive of medical, technological intervention ("machinery," "procedure"), perhaps in response to Porter's and others' unsubtle baiting. While assessing her narrative strategy as successful, Herbst views it ambivalently, describing it as one that "always fails," a "sort of thing" she wants never to repeat.

This Is My Body

"If I had a baby I'd knock down these buildings to get money for it. I'd kill all these people out airing themselves."
   "Gee, what's the matter now?" he cried in irritation.

So closely based upon her tumultuous Greenwich Village relationship with noted leftist poet Kenneth Fearing that critics refer to it unproblematically as a roman à clef, Margery Latimer's 1930 *This Is My Body* offers an incisive critique of the intersections of class difference and sexual politics at the locus of pregnancy (Ryley *ix*). The narrative hinges upon protagonist Megan Foster's reluctant agreement to abort the pregnancy her lover does not want. A subplot focuses on Megan's friend, a university student who, impregnated by the married dean of her college—a representative of bourgeois respectability—is tricked by him into visiting a doctor who performs a forced abortion while she struggles and screams.

In each narrative thread, a young woman wishes to keep her pregnancy. Each presents verbal arguments in favor of continued pregnancy and exhibits emotional distress at the prospect of termination. In each case, the male partner pushes her to abort by using social, political, and economic arguments, which—the narratives make clear—function to conceal his own personal reluctance to make public an illicit relationship, to reconceive the relationship as other than a sexual playground, or to cede primary importance in the eyes of the female. The Kenneth Fearing figure, Ronald Chadron, is a bohemian poet who derides bourgeois morality and espouses socialist ideals, yet he listens to his partner no more than does the dean. Although he does not, like the dean, employ physical restraint, the narrative carefully delineates his emotional violence: after using economic and political arguments to coerce Megan into terminating her wanted pregnancy, he leaves her to go for the abortion alone and to pay for the procedure herself. Only after Megan submits, moreover, does Ronald at last consent to touch her again, "press[ing] her arm warmly like a comrade or a husband"; Latimer's use of "comrade" here suggests her equation of party power structures and the male-dominant structure of the bourgeois household (325). After Megan's sacrifice, the relationship ends when she finds a paid prostitute replacing her in Ronald's bed.

Latimer's focus on the body as a site for cultural critique is highly self-aware. Early in the novel, Megan goes to the dean of the college—the same dean who later tricks his young lover into a forced abortion—and, claiming that her prescribed courses do not interest her, requests a special seminar on Descartes and Spinoza (35). The dean refuses. Latimer thus anticipates the work of contemporary feminist theorists such as Elizabeth Grosz, who sees the philosophical differences between Descartes and Spinoza as so fundamental to our contemporary understanding of the body that she opens her 1994 *Volatile Bodies: Toward a Corporeal Feminism* with a discussion of their work, arguing that Descartes accomplished not merely the bifurcation of body and mind,

> but the separation of soul from nature. Descartes distinguished two kinds of substances: a thinking substance (*res cogitans*, mind) from an extended substance (*res extensa*, body); only the latter, he believed, could be considered part of nature, governed by its physical laws and ontological exigencies. . . . The mind, the thinking substance, the soul, or consciousness, has no place in the natural world. (6)

While the Cartesian attitude toward the body—that it is "a self-moving machine, a mechanical device"—lends support to the arguments of characters like Ronald, Latimer's work functions to resist this "exclusion of the soul from nature, this evacuation of consciousness from the world" (Grosz 6, 10). In rejecting definitions of body-as-machine, Latimer simultaneously traces the sexual politics of her time to their root in Enlightenment philosophy and refutes the mechanistic ideology of the futurist argument.

Technology and machines are allied in the text with the degradation of female subjectivity. After hearing her friend's experience of being strapped down for an abortion, Megan responds by craving vegetation, water, and soil as sources of comfort, reading nature as stable and reassuring:

> She could feel nothing but fear and nausea, a great panic as if she must catch hold of wood, earth, anything solid and clean. . . . She thought in a flash of a tree that she could bind her arms around and clench herself close to so that when lightning came she would be holding a part of the tree even if it split apart and went rolling down the cliff. Then when the great tremendous floods of water came she would be holding part of the sweet firm wood. She would be borne out into the dark sea clinging to part of it, her arms wrapped around it.

The passage combines the imagery of a fundamental split with biblical flood imagery of retribution. As long as she can hold on to part of nature before it is bifurcated, Megan believes, she will be saved. But modernity offers no such refuge. When the two women leave the restaurant in a taxi, "Megan pressed against the glass. She tried to find something hard to grip hold of but there was nothing but the steel bar on the driver's seat. She crouched closer and smaller, one shoulder drawn up as if she thought someone was going to strike her, the other down against the glass" (311–12). Technology, machinery, offers no comfort; Latimer repeatedly uses the word "against" to describe its relationship to Megan's body.

The abortion scene itself emphasizes technology and Megan's lack of agency, since the literal tools of the procedure command center stage. In her study of abortion and class in Australian women's socialist novels of the period, Nicole Moore focuses on

> the moment at which an abortion episode stops, or draws the curtains — whether the reader's gaze is blocked at the moment the client enters the clinic, or when the client is offered anaesthetic (or not), whether the intrusion of speculum or knitting needle is mentioned, whether the presence of the foetus is allowed, or even the methods of its disposal — this moment is the mark of the degree of the revelatory impact of an abortion in narrative. (9)

In Latimer's text, the abortion occurs entirely offstage. The doctor announces, "It will take one hour to sterilize the instruments. You can wait in there" (327); an abrupt section break follows. The opening line of the section that follows finds Megan entering her apartment. "It's over," she tells Ronald; readers must infer the entire procedure (328). The focus thus falls on the technology, the instruments, and upon Megan's own lack of agency in the face of technology's power.

Afterward, she expresses her grief in terms of the material detail of abortion: "I ache. That iron scrapes all the time in my head" (330). Associating the technology of abortion with the changes of modernity and urbanization, the novel's final line depicts Megan's resignation to a bifurcated identity: "And now it seemed as if she walked on her knees behind herself, pushing her body forward through the waves of mindless faces, her stockings, her skin scraped off her moving knees, the raw flesh at last on the dull cement" (351). Like *Money for Love*, *This Is My Body* functions as a bitter novel of education for its commodified protagonist. But in Latimer's work, bourgeois men and men on the Left are revealed as equally responsible.

While the narrative is beautifully attentive to material detail and economic conditions, Latimer blends this focus with the use of archetypal symbolism, a strategy typical of high modernism. The abortion itself, as described by a waitress Megan knows, is figured as an everyday economic transaction, requiring the performance of class position: "He'll do it for thirty dollars," she tells Megan. "[W]ear old clothes or he'll charge a hundred" (326). Later we learn that Megan has in fact dressed the part, performed her class position, for when Ronald asks the cost, she replies, "Thirty." Latimer twice strikes the note of the price, drawing our attention to the figure. When considered in context, its resonance with the thirty pieces of silver for which Judas betrays Christ becomes clear, for Megan's lament is infused with the language of betrayal: "Oh, you've let me betray myself. . . . I've betrayed myself. I've punished and violated and betrayed my own self" (329–30). We remember the novel's title, *This Is My Body*, and realize that Latimer has audaciously couched the abortion narrative in Christological imagery. Latimer's biblical allusions, however, go entirely unremarked in reviews of the novel, suggesting the lack of comprehension with which most women's explorations of such structures met during the period. As Elaine Showalter argues,

> Even when women produced feminine versions of modernism, reimagining myths, for example, from female perspectives (such as Bogan's "Cassandra" and "Medusa," Millay's "An Ancient Gesture," describing Penelope, and H. D.'s "Eurydice"), as James Joyce and T. S. Eliot had modernized the myths of Ulysses and the Grail, [the women's] experiments were ignored and misunderstood. (109)

No reviewer considers the possibility that Latimer would dare to compare a young woman's story of embodied self-sacrifice to Christ's. Critics of *This Is My Body* fell so wide of the mark in interpreting Latimer's allusions, in fact, that the *New York Times Book Review* attributes the title and epigraph ("This is my body, friends, world—Oh, take my body and eat—") to Walt Whitman: "Miss Latimer has taken for her text a paraphrase of Whitman's introduction to 'Leaves of Grass'—'who touches this book touches a man.' Only her version of it is somewhat more diffuse" ("Hungry" 9). Unrecognized in her contemporary reception, Latimer's narrative strategy resembles that of the high modernists, which many leftist critics rejected as effete and politically disengaged. Yet Latimer uses the biblical structure to assert the primacy, the centrality to Western culture of her protagonist's social, sexual, and economic plight.

This aggressive blend of modernist technique and material detail grew out of Latimer's situation as a leftist intellectual who rode the crests of multiple movements. While her ambitious experimentalism drew her toward the modernist project, the material circumstances of her life kept her close to class struggle. In 1922, for example, Latimer's father supported a family of four with an income of only a little over $1,000, the rough equivalent of $10,000 in today's terms (Loughridge 218). In 1983, poet Carl Rakosi recalled with chagrin his youthful misperception of Latimer's financial condition: "In those days young women were not expected to support themselves, and I assumed therefore that when she lived away from home, she was on an allowance the way Kenneth [Fearing] and I were. I was shocked to learn from her biographer that there was no money for this at home . . ." (95).

Latimer won scholarships to finance her college education, worked at the Henry Street Settlement House with young immigrant women, and supported herself in New York with clerical jobs while struggling to write. Her work

appeared in *New Masses* and *American Mercury* as well as in experimental little reviews such as *transition* and *Pagany*—though even *Pagany*, as Cary Nelson notes, while "hardly a politically oriented magazine, nonetheless published
poetry and prose in sympathy with the impoverished and unemployed" (102).
Melding high modernist symbolism and archetypes with socialist attention to
material contingency, *This Is My Body* complicates traditional boundaries
between leftist and modernist canons while offering a simultaneous critique of
bourgeois morality, leftist sexual politics, and futurist ideology, indicting the
mind-body bifurcation that underpinned all three.

The Unpossessed

"The fruit, Miles!" she said; "you've forgotten the fruit."
"The fruit can wait," he said bitterly.

Slesinger's scathing and witty 1934 novel *The Unpossessed* uses
the free indirect narrative point of view of Katherine Mansfield's "Prelude" and
Virginia Woolf's novels to indict the sexual politics of the leftist intellectual
movement from the inside. Slesinger's husband, Herbert Solow, was an assistant editor at the *Menorah Journal*, which had begun as a vehicle of Jewish
humanism but had shifted toward Marxist ideology by the beginning of the
Depression. The young writers associated with the journal would eventually
form the foundation of what became New York's influential literary Left.
Divorced by 1932, Slesinger mined her experiences with Solow and the journal
to explore the link between political ideology and sexual politics.

   The Unpossessed chronicles two simultaneous trajectories, those of a socialist magazine planned by three long-time male friends in New York and of the
pregnancy of the wife of one of the friends. Each trajectory is characterized by
a troubled, effort-filled rise and a premature fall. The married protagonist Margaret Flinders, who has a highly developed class consciousness and is deeply
committed to left-wing politics, agrees to the abortion her husband wants; her
subsequent emotional devastation functions as the structural culmination of a
sharply satirical look at the inner workings of a leftist magazine. In her 1991
study, *Labor and Desire: Women's Revolutionary Fiction in Depression America*,
Paula Rabinowitz notes that in *The Unpossessed*, "Slesinger exposes the essentialist and bourgeois aspects of the metaphors of proletarian masculinity even
as she reanimates them" (150). Abortion represents not the failure of the bourgeois family romance but rather the failure of left-wing politics itself to address
the issue of justice between men and women in their private lives and to address
the term of the body within social revolution. The narrative, while structurally
privileging the Flinders's relationship—it begins and ends with Margaret and

Miles—also follows the story of another couple involved, Jeffrey and Norah, revealing that both male characters use socialist rhetoric as a cover for their emotional problems and sexual desires.

Miles employs political arguments as a cover for his own deep repudiation of the feminine. Raised in a punitive, violent New England family whose unquestioned patriarchal authority he incorporates even as it wounds him, Miles later comes to embrace socialism as the explanation for the harsh economic realities that confirm his most deeply held beliefs about life. He remembers his mother as "the Limb of Satan" for "her sin of being pretty," and fears the vulnerability entailed by physical and emotional intimacy with his wife (45). Unfortunately for Margaret, his antipathy toward the feminine is only reinforced by the rhetoric of their leftist intellectual friends, who describe bad politics as "pink," "soft," and "emasculated" (185). For Miles, "who sat and explained the nature of economics and forgot to consider his pulse-beats," political debate provides a safely abstract refuge from the threatening realms of embodied and emotional experience (59).

Jeffrey uses leftist rhetoric differently to rationalize away objections against maintaining the world as a male-dominated sexual playground. Monogamy is "so utterly bourgeois," he exclaims (56). His self-serving use of socialist ideology allows him to seduce without guilt the wealthy Merle Middleton for her money—in order to support the magazine—and Comrade Fisher for her party connections. All the while, he comfortably relies on the sexual constancy and steady salary of his partner, Norah: "He thought briefly but with no pain of the tedious office where she spent her days; with no pain because she didn't mind it, Norah never minded anything" (151). Margaret sees Jeffrey as "childlike," and his appearance is twice noted as being "like a baby's" (63, 64, 185). Later in the novel, this dynamic is made explicit when Margaret and Norah converse, describing their choices to forego childbearing at their male partners' behest—in the guise of "making some sort of protest against something"—in order to have the time, resources, and energy to spoil their men like children (305–06).

Slesinger takes pains to establish the development of the journal as structurally equivalent to developments in Margaret's pregnancy. In the following passage, for example, Margaret counts the months until the birth while Miles's friend Bruno, in a sudden burst of courage, orates.

> *December, January, February*, Margaret thought.
> "I propose," (the thing took all his strength) "oh what the hell," he cried, "what's stopping us? I propose we *have* the God damn Magazine."
> *March, April, May*, thought Margaret. (98–99)

Even the syntax of the title's chapter, "Why Can't We Have a Magazine?" cries out for the substitution of the term *baby* for *magazine*. The building hopefulness surrounding the journal's inception precisely parallels, moreover, Miles's brief renewal of love and passion for Margaret. But when Miles sees the collapse of his hopes for the journal, he responds by pressuring Margaret into an abortion she does not want.

The dream of the magazine finally falls apart in Slesinger's long implosion of a chapter, "The Party," which is, as its title suggests, an ironic take on party politics but which also describes a literal party, a cross-class gala planned by the three male characters to generate financial support for the magazine. Wealthy patrons mingle with folks off the street; everyone must purchase a ticket to enter. When Bruno, the spokesperson for the journal, rises to speak, he begins, "FRIENDS, INTELLECTUALS, FELLOW-SCEPTICS. . . . I am with message" (324). But his carefully crafted lecture has been shredded to bits by a jealous acolyte. As all Bruno's fine thoughts fall in literal fragments around him, the cynical speech he concocts on the spot damns the entire project irrevocably:

> "[A]re we going to dope ourselves and stuff ourselves, intoxicate ourselves, anaesthetize ourselves, against all decent feeling—and meanwhile miss the bus?" . . . "The answer is: WE ARE." The laugh broke out, relieved, the merry cocktail laugh, the self-indulgent, self-effulgent upper-class champagne laugh. (325)

The structural similarity of Bruno's opening statement "I am with message" to the phrase "with child" is not insignificant, for Slesinger has structured the novel so that the collapse of the magazine precisely coincides with the Flinders's decision to abort.

For Slesinger, the abortion functions to represent the collapse of the intellectual's role in socialist political change. The hope of the movement lies with the younger generation, who possess both the theories of their elders and the lived experience of labor and poverty. During a joint planning meeting of the student group and the old guard of Miles, Bruno, and Jeffrey, the passionate young Cornelia "quietly and insolently faint[s]" from hunger, making the clever arguments about aesthetics and philosophy seem a sham (222). Her lover Firman announces in terms resonant with both hunger and pregnancy: "A revolution is for a full belly. There isn't anything else. You've got a full belly or you haven't. You're in favor of them for everybody or you're not" (199).

His words argue for freedom, equality, and self-determination at the level of the body, in contradistinction to the arguments of the old guard, who eventually come to realize that their own bodies are "numb," "paralyzed" by the "academic scaling" in their minds (212). "[L]it with pity" for Bruno during his final party speech, the younger socialists rise and leave the debacle; the text describes them as "the vanguard of the newest intellectuals who, not remaining aloof with their books and their ideas, had strength to mingle with the living and bring their gifts among them" (329, 332). It is this "strength to mingle with the living" that Slesinger tropes with pregnancy; Margaret and Miles, who have no such strength, abort their personal hopes along with their political ones.

In the final chapter, Margaret leaves the hospital where her abortion has been performed and takes a taxi home with her husband. Miles and Margaret are limned in mechanized terms; the only nature present is controlled nature. Miles has sent Margaret a basket of fruit, which she recognizes as his guilty and inadequate substitute for the physical fruition of their sexuality, and Miles "seat[s] himself on the little seat, the better to watch his woman and his woman's fruit; and screw[s] his head round on his neck" (342). When Margaret speaks, she does so "mechanically," and she "forg[ets] to turn on her smile" (350); she notes her brain functioning like "an adding-machine" (357). Margaret presses a piece of fruit on the taxi driver, who refuses a peach, and then an apple.

> "But a pear, just a pear," said Margaret passionately.
> Mr. Strite wavered, standing on one foot. "Maybe he doesn't want any fruit," said Miles harshly.
> "Not want any *fruit!*" cried Margaret gayly, indignantly. Not want any fruit? —ridiculous! . . . Three days I spent in the hospital, in a Maternity Home, and I produced, with the help of my husband, one basket of fruit. . . . Not want any of our fruit? I couldn't bear it, I couldn't bear it. . . . (Italics and final ellipses original, 356–57)

Margaret's repeated phrase "I couldn't bear it" draws our attention to the syntactical ambiguity of *couldn't*, which operates here both as a conditional ("I wouldn't be able to bear it if he didn't accept my gift of fruit") and in the past tense ("I was unable to bear it," the child she wanted). The literary ambitions of the leftist intellectuals and the Flinders's relationship have both collapsed; neither has borne fruit.

"Annunciation"

How can I describe what is said by a pear tree? Karl did not speak to me so. No one spoke to me in any good speech.

The image of the pear and the pear tree function as controlling metaphors of Meridel Le Sueur's 1935 short story, "Annunciation," asserting the value of female desire for continued pregnancy in the face of male pressure to abort.[1] Le Sueur is best known for her proletarian reportage of the 1930s, particularly her explicitly feminist pieces such as "Women on the Breadlines" (1932) and "Women Are Hungry" (1934). More experimental than much literature of the American Left, Le Sueur's work bears traces of high modernism and was particularly influenced by D. H. Lawrence; Le Sueur and Latimer, moreover, were close friends who shared their work. "Annunciation" is based on Le Sueur's first pregnancy, which she refused to terminate despite the urgings of her husband, Harry Rice (born Yasha Rabonov), a Marxist labor organizer. The story is dedicated to her daughter Rachel, born in 1928.

Significantly, "Annunciation" differs from the three novels in its use of the first-person point of view, suggesting a significant investment of authority in its protagonist. The text also encodes the process of its own creation; the narrator describes her construction of the narrative as notes to her unborn child, written on small scraps of paper. In the story, the unnamed narrator is four months pregnant and has moved to the city with her husband, suggestively named Karl, in search of work. But there are no steady jobs, and they live among the destitute in a dilapidated boardinghouse. The narrator takes refuge in her identification with a pear tree and its fruit:

> Ever since I have known I was going to have a child I have kept writing things down on these little scraps of paper. There is something I want to say, something I want to make clear for myself and others. . . .
>
> There is the pear tree I can see in the afternoons as I sit on this porch writing these notes. It stands for something. It has had something to do with what has happened to me. (125)

Although the character intuitively recognizes the tree's significance, she initially must grope for the words with which to express its meaning: "It stands for *something*. It has had *something* to do" with her experience. Yet Le Sueur's narrator is able to make the connection much more explicit when she delineates her purpose: "It is hard to write it down so that it will mean anything. I've never heard anything about how a women [*sic*] feels who is going to have a child, or about how a pear tree feels bearing its fruit" (130).

It is *this* story the pear tree enables her to tell, the untold story of the subjectivity of the pregnant woman. This is doubly an act of resistance, firstly because the narrator is breaking the silence that has historically surrounded the experience of pregnancy, and secondly because the pregnancy itself is not wanted by her husband. She begins to write when Karl attempts to coerce her into aborting the pregnancy. She explains: "Perhaps [beginning to write] had something to do with Karl wanting me all the time to take something. 'Everybody does it,' he kept telling me. 'It's nothing, then it's all over.' I stopped talking to him much. Everything I said only made him angry. So writing was a kind of conversation I carried on with myself and with the child" (127). Unlike Herbst's, Latimer's, or Slesinger's protagonists, Le Sueur's narrator refuses to act against her own will, and Karl becomes increasingly furious at her refusal: "Just to look at me," she writes, "makes him angry now" (128). He shouts at her in public and frequently fails to come home at night with his odd-job earnings, leaving her to walk the neighborhood in an attempt to forget her hunger.

Withdrawing from his hostility, the narrator finds herself increasingly moved by her sense of connection with the tree. Validating her own desires and experience via this identification, she begins to reconsider the primacy of her husband's status within the marital relationship: it is her own subjectivity that now intrigues her. Associating her own pregnant body with "the gentle and curving body of the tree," she recognizes her new identification as fundamentally subversive:

> I have looked at it until it has become more familiar to me than Karl. It seems a strange thing that a tree might come to mean more to one than one's husband. It seems a shameful thing even. I am ashamed to think of it but it is so. I have sat here in the pale sun and the tree has spoken to me with its many tongued leaves, speaking through the afternoon of how to round a fruit. And I listen through the slow hours. I listen to the whispering of the pear tree, speaking to me, speaking to me. How can I describe what is said by a pear tree? Karl did not speak to me so. No one spoke to me in any good speech. (132)

Rejecting the cultural rhetoric that surrounds her as insufficient for the expression of her own experience and desire, the narrator replaces the inadequate "speech" of her social environment with an identification with nature and with her own writing, constructing a resistant female voice that draws strength from the natural world. The narrator's identification with the pear tree and the articulation of her own desire through writing fortify her to resist pressure from her husband.

The association of technology, abortion, and male domination operates in contrast to the linkage of female fertility with nature throughout the narrative. The narrator is dragged out by her husband for a walk, for example, during which "he kept talking to me in a low voice, trying to persuade me. It was hard for me to listen. My teeth were chattering with cold, but anyway I found it hard to listen to anyone talking, especially Karl. I remember I kept thinking to myself that a child should be made by machinery now, then there would be no fuss" (128). Though Karl's persuasion prompts her to ruminate upon the possibility of manufactured children (similar to that which Marinetti realizes in *Mafarka*), her acknowledgment of her body, signified by her chattering teeth, interferes with her ability and desire to listen. Her resistant sense of her pregnancy, in contrast, is allied with nature imagery—and with the working class, here figured as agricultural laborers: " . . . the many vistas of the earth meant something—the bony skeleton of the mountains, like the skeleton of the world jutting through its flowery flesh. My child too would be made of bone. There were the fields of summer, the orchards fruiting, the berry fields and the pickers stooping, the oranges and the grapes" (128).

In "Annunciation," Le Sueur's narrator contrasts the world of nature and beauty to the world of modernity and technology, which she genders male, and hopes that her unborn child will be intimate with the former. The title "Annunciation," by invoking the biblical story of the angelic visitation to Mary, functions in its employment of Christian archetypes similarly to—though less heretically than—that of Latimer's *This Is My Body*, which usurps gender privilege as well. Yet Le Sueur's "Annunciation" is not an announcement delivered by a powerful figure to a mute, acceptant woman; rather, it gives voice to the woman's own subjectivity. In this experimental appropriation of an archetypal structure to express the experience of a woman in poverty, as in its innovative style, structure, and use of symbolism, Le Sueur successfully blends modernist, feminist, and leftist concerns, resisting critical and ideological pressures to restrict her scope and strategies.

Abortion is a malleable trope. In these texts, it is nuanced in complex and shifting ways that serve to mark sites of failed promise within both the middle class and the Left. In keeping with the Left's development of the genre of reportage, with its characteristic blend of the personal and the objective, these four texts draw self-consciously from their authors' life experiences, yet each writer reserves the right to experiment with narrative style and structure, producing works closer—both in their literary texture and in their exploration of subjectivity—to high modernism than to traditional socialist realism. The many ways in which abortion is inflected in these narratives demonstrate that Herbst, Latimer, Slesinger, and Le Sueur were participating in a culture-wide conversation, responding to multiple movements in American and international society during the period. Though committed to the ideals of the Left, they were not narrowly or programmatically so. Rather, their narratives entered debates about women, nature, futurism, modernity, socialism, and sexual politics. Each carves out a space for mobility, a refusal to be pinned down to any programmatic party line.

The choice of abortion as a locus of contention is particularly contributory to larger social critiques, for the body, as Grosz has argued, "is the ally of sexual difference, a key term in questioning the centrality of a number of apparently benign but nonetheless phallocentric presumptions which have hidden the cultural and intellectual effacement of women" (*ix*).

Abortion functions in these texts and for these writers as a trope for more general kinds of loss or failed potential: the failure of the bourgeois ideal of maternity to translate to lives of political commitment and economic instability, and (most clearly in Slesinger's *The Unpossessed*) the failure of leftist politics to comprehend important aspects of women's experience. Joining economics and the body at the node of abortion, these texts resist those who would submerge women's issues within the leftist agenda or encode sexuality and politics as distinct narratives. Women writers on the Left play on abortion's metaphoric possibilities and multiple meanings, then, in order to critique capitalist culture and interrogate masculinist assumptions of the Left—sometimes simultaneously. The fact that they used modernist techniques to do so and that they published in high modernist venues as well as publications of the Left serves to complicate our understanding of the period, problematizing traditional boundaries of literary history that would depict leftist and modernist movements as discrete.

NOTE

1. In *Labor and Desire*, Rabinowitz traces the relationship of abortion resistance and maternity to working-class women's sociopolitical consciousness and collectivity in Le Sueur's novel *The Girl* (1977), which was originally published piecemeal during the 1930s and 1940s.

"Shriveled Breasts and Dollar Signs"

The Gendered Rhetoric of Myra Page's *Moscow Yankee*

ANGELA MARIE SMITH

In Christina Looper Baker's *In a Generous Spirit*, Myra Page recounts the story of Valya Cohen, whom she knew while in the Soviet Union in the early 1930s. Page describes Cohen as a "beautiful," "voluptuous," and "athletic" girl, an aspiring engineer from a family active in the Communist Party. Cohen was living with her family in Baku when one day, while she was swimming, seven members of the region's Azerbaijani minority attacked and raped her. According to Page, "In part, the rape was an expression of hostility toward the Party and all that Valya and her family stood for" (Baker 134). The attack on Cohen suggests a real violence enabled by and, indeed, implicit in the deployment of women and their bodies as icons of abstract concepts, political or social orders. Page's use of Cohen as a model for Soviet working-woman heroine, Natasha, in her novel *Moscow Yankee* (1935), indicates both the novel's attempts to envisage potent new embodied identities for a radical politics, and its ambivalent exploitation of conventions of gendered representation.

Recent feminist scholarship on the American Left of the 1930s has foregrounded the gendered stereotypes and imagery integral to radical discourse and literature, and has brought attention to women's works previously neglected within the proletarian canon. Some such studies suggest that women's radical novels of the '30s potentially challenge the erased, marginalized, or demonized women in male radical literature with active female protagonists; reveal the gendered tropes on which such literature depends; and testify to the inextricability of gender, sexuality, and class, or, as in the title of one study of 1930s women's literature, labor *and* desire.[1]

Page's *Moscow Yankee* offers a tale of labor and desire, and has been categorized by Barbara Foley as a "proletarian bildungsroman," a hybrid genre created by merging the collectivist politics of radical working-class movements with the bourgeois novelistic form that traces an individual's journey of self-discovery. First published in 1935 by Putnam, and reprinted in 1995 as part of the University of Illinois Press's "Radical Novel Reconsidered" series, *Moscow Yankee* tells the story of Andy, a Detroit auto mechanic, who flees the Depression with two fellow workers in order to earn money in the Soviet Union. Through his experiences in Red Star, a truck-manufacturing factory in Moscow, and his encounters with Russians and expatriate Americans, Andy is slowly converted to the communist cause, eventually electing to stay in Moscow rather than return to the United States. Andy's political conversion is figured through his growing romance of, and eventual marriage to, Natasha, an attractive Russian worker in the truck factory.

Like the works of other radical women writers in the '30s, *Moscow Yankee* sets out to affirm proletarian women within an American Marxist intellectual environment overtly preoccupied with the politics of literary form and content, and implicitly structured by ideas about gender. American Marxists repeatedly characterized proletarian literature as a bold, masculine enterprise. During the 1920s and 1930s, the most explicit clarion-calls for proletarian literature were issued by *New Masses* editor and radical writer Michael Gold whose ideal author had "vigor" and "guts," was "a wild youth of about twenty-two, the son of working-class parents, who himself works in the lumber camps, coal mines, and steel mills," and wrote "in jets of exasperated feeling" ("Go Left" 188). Gold contrasted this virile proletarian genre with modernist, bourgeois literature like that of Thornton Wilder, which Gold characterized as "a daydream of homosexual figures in graceful gowns moving archaically among the lilies" ("Wilder" 266), and thus, as Rabinowitz notes, "implicitly connected modernism with bourgeois decay and femininity" (22).[2]

Although this dependence of American Marxist discourse on gendered icons remained largely unexamined during the 1930s, scholars have suggested that perhaps women's proletarian texts of the period realize the implications of such imagery for gender inequity.[3] Myra Page certainly occupied the position of an active female radical writer who might produce a work that both met Gold's definition of proletarian literature[4] and rewrote the conventions of gender on which his rhetoric depended. Born into a middle-class Virginian family, Page worked with a number of unions, and received a doctorate of sociology from the University of Minnesota in 1928. In the 1930s, she traveled to the southern United States, Europe, the Soviet Union, and Mexico as a Communist Party activist and radical journalist, filing reports with a number of left-wing journals and newspapers including the *New Masses*, the *Daily Worker*, and *Soviet Russia Today*. Her 1932 novel, *Gathering Storm*, depicts the Gastonia textiles strike of 1929, while *Moscow Yankee* draws from her experiences in the Soviet Union, and is based upon her nonfiction piece *Soviet Main Street* (Baker xviii).[5]

Page's remembrance of her life in Baker's biography makes clear both that her roles as wife, mother, and activist were equally important to her, and that she sometimes felt a painful conflict between these roles. She also expresses an acute awareness of the different ways in which women's bodies were constrained at the time, criticizing both the lack of contraceptive information available to poor working women, and the negative attitudes of the American Left to activist women who also chose to be mothers. Her life exemplifies the contradictory relationship between the Communist Party USA and its female members: while the party opened up activist and intellectual roles for women, it also exploited sexist iconography in the name of the workers' revolution, and advocated the postponement of the redistribution of gender relations until that revolution had occurred.[6]

Moscow Yankee, as the work of a woman who experienced these contradictions, and as a novel set in the Soviet Union after the revolution, thus necessarily constitutes a complicated negotiation of gender ideology and class politics, one that seeks to challenge the ambivalence directed at working women, but that also chooses to harness gender to the purposes of revolution. The novel's proletarian bildungsroman form both structures and complicates its capacity to reimagine gender and class relations. While this genre suggestively yokes politicized content to a narrative driven by personal desire, Foley has noted that women writers drawing on the bildungsroman must grapple both with the traditionally masculine focus of its journey of self-discovery, and with its bourgeois "ideological baggage" (343). Such baggage includes a focus on an individualized protagonist and personal autonomy, a pretence to a neutral narrative view, and a drive toward closure, all of which directly conflict with the collective, politicized, open-ended ideology of leftist social movements. Most importantly, with its focus on the heterosexual love plot, the bildungsroman displaces political concerns onto personal relationships, thus "falsely settling issues in the 'public' sphere through the vicarious emotional satisfactions gained by resolving problems in the private sphere" (347). In maintaining this gendered division of public and private spheres, the bildungsroman inhibits women writers' efforts to emphasize and expand women's roles in the working world and the class struggle.

The conflict between proletarian content and bourgeois form is paralleled by the conflict between the effort to imagine active female characters and the reliance of the proletarian narrative on gendered tropes. Laura Hapke has demonstrated that even women writers striving to emphasize female agency in class struggles had difficulty escaping conventional tropes of femininity, often

challenging proletarian idealization of mothers and demonization of working
women through another stereotype, that of mothers as flawed, monstrous
oppressors of their daughters. The maternal trope in particular was continually
co-opted, in both positive and negative forms, in the rhetoric of the Left. Rabinowitz notes that in the early 1930s maternity was "viewed as draining, debilitating, and ultimately dangerous for the worker's struggle" (56), but that later
proletarian rhetoric recuperated the maternal as the figure of the collective,
"the mass body" (113).[7] Regardless of whether the values assigned it were positive or negative, then, the feminine remained primarily an iconic resource in
the effort to theorize and represent the materialist project, a resource marked
with ambivalence.

An initial exploration of *Moscow Yankee* does not immediately discover the
symbolic deployment of gender that impels it. The novel fervently endorses the
Soviet project, although, as Foley points out in her introduction to the text's University of Illinois Press edition, it also frankly acknowledges the bureaucratic
muddles, incompetence, and the poor quality and limited quantity of staples
and consumer goods that accompanied the Soviet Union's changing work and
political structures. Red tape makes procuring necessary materials at the factory
a time-consuming business, and lengthy queues for basic supplies greet Andy
as he wanders Moscow. There are even hints that not all is well in the new state:
a mysterious stranger draws Andy aside in the street to tell him of suffering and
destitution in Ukraine and Georgia: "Ah, ugly, ugly things are going on in my
Russia" (60).[8]

Mostly, however, these inconveniences are presented as "crazy hangovers
of an old system" (93), which Andy and his colleagues must work to overcome.
Drawing on her experiences as radical writer and traveler, Page incorporates, in
documentary fashion, a range of Western responses to the Soviet situation: the
self-righteous arrogance of Andy's friends Tim and Morse who continually crit-
icize the Soviet Union and soon return to the United States; the reluctant realization of the "professional revolutionist" (13) couple Gus and Freda Heindrick
that socialism is hard work; greedy engineer Henry Crampton's bourgeois
resentment of the breaking down of class and racial divisions; and in contrast to
these, Andy's gradual, warm acceptance of communism. As the novel proceeds,
Americans sympathetic to communism, like Scottish-born Mac and engineer
Philip Boardman, and a number of good-hearted Russians like Andy's workmate, Sasha, and his foreman, Mikhail, convince Andy of communism's worth,
while his encounters with African American Ned Folson dispel his inbred
racism. By the time former aristocrat Alex Turin threatens the factory with sabotage, Andy is as invested as the others in preserving the factory and the Soviet
order it represents.

As Foley notes is typical with the proletarian bildungsroman form, the novel displaces Andy's political dilemma—United States or Soviet Union, capitalism or communism—onto a choice between his American girlfriend, Elsie, and his Russian workmate, Natasha. It is not irrelevant that the characters' struggle to create a new state from old structures through mechanical production offers a model for Page's welding of conventional forms to radical concepts, and the potential therein for a reimagination of the relationships between gender and class. In its marriage of conventional gender tropes to radical concepts, *Moscow Yankee* carries out what Wai Chee Dimock has characterized as a specifically materialist practice of metonymy that generalizes "from a physical body to a political body, from an individual to a class" (74). The novel's tropes of maternity, prostitution, and mechanization thus offer potent figurings of the intersections of class and gender politics, but in so doing conduct a precarious negotiation between those politics, risking the circumscription and metaphorical exploitation of female bodies.

In its adroit use of images of bodies—male, female, and mechanical—*Moscow Yankee* is a genuinely materialist text seeking to represent the embodied experiences of workers in a communist state. For Marx, particularly in *Economic and Philosophic Manuscripts*, capitalism alienates workers from sensory, bodily experience. Under the division of labor and the accumulation of capital, the worker is dependent on a "very one-sided, machine-like labor," and "is thus depressed spiritually and physically to the condition of a machine and from being a man becomes an abstract activity and a belly" (68). However, in an ideal, post-communist-revolution world, the emancipated individual is sensuous and substantive: "All history is the preparation for '*man*' to become the object of *sensuous* consciousness, and for the needs of 'man as man' to become [natural, sensuous] needs" (143). Marx's vision here invokes the sensual engagement with a humanized world denied to the worker under abstract systems of alienated labor. Dimock suggests that this nineteenth-century concept of materialism as an epistemology grounded in the corporeal subject has been overlooked in defining materialism solely as a theory of economic determinism (61).

Moscow Yankee thus seeks to envisage the collective, sensuous body of a postrevolutionary world, integrated in its physical, laboring experience within the factory. In the Red Star truck-manufacturing plant, Page creates a mechanical world used in the service of collective human enterprise. The first depiction of the factory sets the scene with a portrait of a new kind of body, worth quoting at length:

> The shop was a thundering vortex of machines and men. Through its
> wide skylights the pale yellow sky of a Russian winter drifted down

through cranes and pulleys and finally settled on the swinging arms of workmen and the broad asphalt aisles. Amid the hoarse and strident clamor the persistent click-click of the steel-tread conveyor rhythmically dominated all. Nothing could halt it: everything was timed and controlled by its speed.

The grotesque skeletons which it picked up and carried were transformed under the eye into coherent high-geared mammoths; gawky ribbed metal sprouted axles, steering gears, gray fenders. Black shiny motors and double-tread tires descended on endless revolving lines from floors overhead: bodies and hoods smelling of fresh paint swung down and fastened into place. Dozens of blue caps and women's red kerchiefs moved along the line, climbed over the monsters, pried into their vitals, fitting screwing mastering the vast mechanism of assembling two-and-a-half ton trucks.

The main line was the beautiful quivering nerve center of this automobile plant, its hard final testing ground, where all the synchronized movements of countless parts of metal rubber lumber engines and men were registered and every misfire courted disaster. . . . Day and night through the shed's unceasing labor, the steel-tread conveyor thrust hungrily forward.

Andy was part of it. (22–23)

This factory contrasts with the alienation of the Detroit Ford plant where Andy worked; Red Star's collective ownership and communal investment is clear in the novel's image of a collective body, which all are equally invested in protecting and nourishing. The factory is a microcosm of communist interaction and equity, wherein machines become extensions of workers' laboring bodies, emblematic not of dehumanization and oppression, but of empowerment through cooperative, equitable labor and ownership. As the workers fashion the bodies of trucks, they simultaneously refashion themselves, in a manner that counters the alienation of the laborer under capitalism.

In its materialist vision of the working body, *Moscow Yankee* contests the gendered division of a feminine, decadent bourgeoisie, and a virile, masculine proletariat, by imagining a female proletarian: Natasha, the independent, intelligent communist worker. On this level, *Moscow Yankee* challenges the sexisms of male proletarian literature delineated by Hapke: its idealized mothers, submissive wives, and branding of female workers as sexually promiscuous. Where male-authored texts largely fail to imagine positive roles for working women, *Moscow Yankee* affirms the new Soviet woman as a skilled and intellectual laborer, such that Andy must acknowledge Natasha's freedom and dedication to the proletarian cause: "The man Nat hooks up with'll never be the

center of her universe. Not her. Always come second, her damn work first"
(220).

Undeniably, then, the novel's characterization of Natasha imagines a role
for femininity within the new order that is not consigned to the negative. But
Moscow Yankee's use of individual bodies to image materialist concepts rests on
a series of gendered conventions, both materialist and modernist, that necessi-
tate a more nuanced reading of the novel's gendered tropes. For Dimock, Marx's
repeated use of the organic, individual body as an image for immaterial concepts, such as the collective, ties his materialism to a practice of metonymy
dependent on "generalizations, especially generalizations from part to whole,
from the tangible to the intangible" (61). This practice is both productive in its
representative power, and potentially limiting in its gender politics:

> What especially concerns me is the status of gender when it is harnessed
> to this practice, when 'woman' is invoked as a representative sign, and
> constructed as a signifying body to serve that purpose. Such a practice is
> both clarifying and obfuscating, I argue, clarifying, because the force of
> the indictment here is obviously considerable, but also obfuscating,
> because the mapping of class upon gender not only flattens out any pos-
> sible nonalignment between the two, but also flattens out the figure of
> 'woman' into a categoric unity, a signifying whole that, in its very singu-
> larity of feature, might end up being emptied of its claim to attention. (86)

The novel's symbolism both powerfully incorporates the female body into its
vision of class politics and, in the very act of emphasizing and foregrounding
the female body, diminishes female specificity and agency, eliding the materiality of women's bodies and gender difference by abstracting and subsuming the
feminine to the revolutionary cause. In this sense, a very proletarian literary use
of the feminine risks slippage into the chauvinistic elements of bourgeois modernism, wherein female sexuality and subjectivity are indexed to the feminized
decay of modern capitalist culture.

Natasha's body thus serves double duty in *Moscow Yankee*. She is not just a
working woman, but an emblem of the new social and political order, an embodiment of the health, vigor, and beauty of the new state. When we first see her,
her body is emphasized in relation to the factory's machinery: "Lights overhead
threw her figure into bold relief against the whirring machines in the aisle
beyond" (43). Soon after, she pulls on a "black, close-fitting" bathing suit which
emphasizes her "firm breasts" (66). As she joins "the swishing spank of bodies"
(66) in the local pool, she is eyed by Andy and his friend Morse while they compare the physical attributes of Russian, American, and German "girls" (67).
These two glimpses of Natasha introduce her as a young, beautiful, and energetic representative of the communist order, whose physical attractiveness,

fitness, and strength are cultivated in the name of the factory's productivity. Natasha's sexual and bodily difference is at once foregrounded and absorbed by the narrative so that Andy's eventual marriage to her may represent a marriage to the new order, the social body to which her own body repeatedly refers.

That such iconic use of the female body potentially enables violence against that body is indicated by the rape of Natasha's real-life counterpart and, more obliquely, by Andy's first encounter with Natasha, which, like the attack on Valya Cohen, occurs while she is swimming. Having seen and desired Natasha, Andy introduces himself by deliberately colliding with her in the pool. This painful physical encounter is reflected in the pair's subsequent awkward conversation and walk to the bus, in which Andy clutches the reluctant Natasha's arm, and clumsily rejects her communist beliefs. The swimming pool collision, it seems, is intended to parallel the characters' initial political and cultural clash. But the use of this literalizing technique means that Andy's first engagement with Soviet culture and politics is enacted violently on the body of a woman who, throughout the novel, stands as an icon for the new order, and for the role of women within that order. In illustrating Andy's rejection of the Soviet worldview through his physical collision with Natasha, the novel underwrites a symbolics of femininity that circumscribes the liberations communism provides for women. Although the narrative itself and Page's other writings indicate that Page is well aware of the symbolic value invested in women's bodies, the connections between such "real" acts of violence and the rhetorical violence that structures female bodies in the name of an ideal world are marginalized in *Moscow Yankee*.[9] And, insofar as such radical rhetoric indulges this iconography, it risks tacit complicity with high modernism's usages of the feminine and thus with its bourgeois underpinnings.

The representative function of Natasha and her body plays out across the novel's panoply of female characters. Like the men with whom Andy is compared and contrasted, a host of women within the novel serve as counterpoints to Natasha's character. As Foley comments, the proletarian bildungsroman tends to conflate the material with the bodily, investing "the concrete, in the crudest sense . . . with the rhetorical power to generalize about class-defined essences" (345); it thus fully exploits the metonymy critiqued by Dimock. This tendency is not restricted to female characters. Certain men in the novel are characterized by features that indicate their failure to embody the masculine proletarian ideal: Foley cites Henry Crampton's large girth as a signifier for management's greed, while Gus Heindrick's shortness and red hair indicate a certain unfitness for the Soviet way of life.[10] But the representations of women in *Moscow Yankee* more overtly draw upon particularly female stereotypes, and further erase female subjectivity by deploying each character as a microcosm of a specific social or economic order. It is female bodies that are primarily burdened as "fully *representative* of the immaterial body" (Dimock 71) of capitalism or the Soviet state.

Thus, *Moscow Yankee*'s women are, on one level, negative stereotypes of the feminine: burdened, ignorant and oppressed mother-figures; grasping, selfish bourgeois wives who compromise themselves for material comfort; weak-natured prostitutes. But, in their role as counterpoints to Natasha, they high-light her embodiment of the new state only insofar as they themselves embody other, discredited social orders. Thus, Natasha's mother's body differs dramatically from her daughter's sleek athleticism: "Veined hands clasped across her stomach which bulged permanently with child. . . . Bent for decades under heavy loads of wood and fodder, her spine had molded when Natasha was still a little girl, into the patient curves of the burden bearer" (193). Natasha's mother manifests the organic body's suffering under heavy farm labor and thus indexes feudalism more generally; in repudiating her body, the text repudiates the oppression of peasants under feudalism, and commends instead a strong young body emblematic of collective industrial labor. Through its distaste for this maternal body, the novel implies a fear of organic, uncontrolled nature, particularly in its generative form, and favors the supercession of the mother's procreative body by the factory's productive one. The trope of the maternal is again recuperated by materialist discourse.

This is not to deny the realistic motivations behind such a depiction of maternity. Page's *Gathering Storm* relentlessly portrays the ways in which repeated childbearing drains and further impoverishes poor millworkers, and is rendered pointless by high infant mortality. But maternity, in *Moscow Yankee* as in American Marxism more generally, proves a malleable and potentially misogynist trope. In addition to imaging feudalism, the maternal is also co-opted in the name of capitalism and its corruptions, as in the novel's brief encounter with the mother of Elsie, Andy's American girlfriend. Andy, who has named his potential mother-in-law the Old Woman, recalls: "The Old Woman had stared through him, hinted broadly. He'd swear her shriveled breasts were marked with dollar signs. Throwing up to him how Elsie had turned down swell chances, and couldn't he work in the insurance line. . . . Puking old hag!" (10). The Old Woman is only the first of several mothers in the novel demonized as harridans who perpetuate capitalism through their mercenary, ladder-climbing outlook. Most notable amongst these mothers are the wives of the two American engineers at Red Star: racist, greedy Edith Crampton, and miserable, socially ambitious Mary Boardman, a nagging burden on her communist-leaning husband Philip.

These images of maternity powerfully and productively convey these women's unhappiness as a result of their entrapment in bourgeois marriage and motherhood, the suppression of their own interests and careers.[11] Yet the rhetorical deployment of the maternal, even as it gestures to the potential space of women's liberation, also forecloses the complexities and agency of women, refiguring 'woman' as a "signifying whole" (Dimock 86). A comrade of Andy's reads him a poem, from a Russian magazine, entitled "A Matter of Honor," in which the maternal is appropriated to the cause:

> Across our vast land
> History has strewn
> > Her dragon teeth
> > Of Revolution—
> We her offspring,
> Youth of a young day
>
> Good old Mother
> You are fertile
> > Freeing the mind
> > Gripping the will.
> Travel far!
> Bear often and boldly
>
> Until all men know
> *Ours and the world's April!* (197)

Natasha's mother's organic generativity is sublimated into an abstract "bearing" of revolution itself, which leaves little space for maternal subjects. Small wonder that Natasha's approach to childbearing, seen through Andy's eyes in the closing pages of the novel, is careful, planned, and measured: "She wanted three kids but not right off. Not until they got further along in their course. . . . They were young enough. Plenty of time. But maybe in two years" (287–88). The quote suggests a controlled, maternal productivity dictated by the needs of the factory and the state.

The maternal is not the only category of femininity co-opted by *Moscow Yankee* in its inscription of the new order. As noted by Hapke, a number of male social protest and proletarian novels proffered women only two subject positions: idealized mother or denigrated prostitute. *Moscow Yankee*'s image of the Old Woman's dollar-marked shriveled breasts metonymically merges female sexuality with money and commodities, indicating both the negative elements of femininity that Soviet women must abjure, and the socioeconomic models that the proletariat must overthrow. This conflation of maternity with money also invokes the prostitute, who, like the repudiated mother, functions as a conscripted figure in the radical cause.

The characterization of the bourgeoisie and of mass consumer culture as effeminate is salient in both modernist and materialist thought. As Andreas Huyssen has shown, "In the late nineteenth century, a specific traditional male image of woman served as a receptacle for all kinds of projections, displaced fears, and anxieties (both personal and political), which were brought about by modernization and the new social conflicts" (195).[12] This usage of female imagery permeated high modernism, which constructed itself as "autonomous," "self-referential," "experimental," and a "rejection of all classical systems of representation" (197) in opposition to the culture of "the proletarian and petit-bourgeois masses [who] were persistently described in terms of a feminine threat" (196).[13] As Janet Galligani Casey points out, then, in proletarian discourse such as Gold's, "the metaphorical use of the feminine as a means of devaluation is not fundamentally challenged, but merely reappropriated in the service of a reversed, but equally sexist, aesthetic" (27).[14]

Modernist and material tendencies to construct commodity culture as feminine and feminizing converge powerfully in the figure of the prostitute. In modernist thought, the prostitute encapsulates, on the one hand, modernity and commodity culture. For example, in Baudelaire's poetry and Walter Benjamin's readings of Baudelaire, the prostitute, in her status as "mass article" (Rauch 86), embodies the mass production of the modern age and literalizes the transformation of bodies into commodities implicit in capitalist culture. Materialist thought shares this employment of the trope of prostitution: Marx found prostitution an ideal figure for "the *general* prostitution of the laborer" and of the capitalist (133). On the other hand, the prostitute figure of modernist thought ostensibly offers transcendence of this superficial commodity culture: in discussing modernists such as Flaubert, Karl Kraus, and Otto Weininger, Laurie Teal contends that in their work the prostitute offers "a new 'ideal' femininity defined as pure flesh" (82).

The ambivalence of the prostitute figure recalls the co-optation by proletarian rhetoric of the maternal trope in both positive and negative forms. Seemingly, the prostitute figure can both assuage the fears and impotences of male intellectuals by taking onto herself all the artificial and denigrating aspects of mass culture, and also function as "an apparent holdout of the 'real,' a place to encounter bodily experience at its most immediate" (Teal 83), thus seeming to offer transcendence of the spectacles, artifices, and commodifications of modern life. Importantly, however, the association of the prostitute with both the "real" of the body and the artifice of mass culture reveals as a mirage any potential transcendence through this trope: the prostitute becomes a cipher, a hollowed-out and alienated object "made to signify whatever the consumer chooses (including the illusion of direct access to the real)" (Teal 84). Writes Rauch, "The stress on the body in the prostitute inevitably also makes visible the body's mortality, thus undermining illusions of eternal life, forcing acknowledgment that beauty is a myth of femininity" (87).[15] It is this ambivalence, this potential for the prostitute both to *embody* capitalist culture and to *critique* it, that suggests the prostitute image might split open gendered discourse in her status as "saleswoman and wares in one" (Benjamin "Paris" 157), as *the miscegenation of the natural and the cultural*" (Seltzer 66).

However, Marxist deployment of the prostitute as a symptom of capitalist culture rather than a source of its critique seeks to rein the trope back into a masculinist discourse. On the one hand, in *The Economic and Philosophic Manuscripts*, the prostitute is, as noted above, an image for "the *general* prostitution of the laborer" and capitalist (133): what Susan Buck-Morss has called "the ur-form of the wage laborer" (184), embodying capitalist alienation of one's labor and sensuous being from oneself.[16] She is thus "the political rubbish thrown up by urban society," clearly a victim of capitalist violence (Wilson 55).

On the other hand, also in the *Economic and Philosophic Manuscripts*, Marx uses the prostitute figure, as woman made "a piece of *communal* and *common* property," to represent a crude communism that institutes "*universal* private property" rather than transcending private property altogether (Marx 132).[17] In figuring the deformation of the communist state in this way, the prostitute is also a woman whose "painted [face] concealed duplicity and evil" (Wilson 55). In these contradictions, the prostitute indicates the nexus of sexual desire and class politics that both materialism and modernism depend upon rhetorically but fail to acknowledge fully; as such, the prostitute figure must either be embraced in all its capacity to reveal the intertwined logics of sex, gender, and class, or restrained in the service of an ideology that seeks to fix the category of class through the obscured manipulation of gender.

Moscow Yankee, in seeking to constrain the body of the prostitute in the name of both the new industrial order and narrative resolution, thus obscures some of the gendered assumptions through which its new world is envisioned. The former prostitute, Zena, is indicted within the novel for failing to fulfill her role on the factory line. Significantly, we first glimpse her in the sexual embrace of Alex Turin, the former aristocrat, or White Russian, who eventually tries to sabotage the factory and the new order. In a heated meeting, the factory workers confront Zena for shirking her work, and denounce her for continuing her old ways. But Natasha insists on holding accountable the men involved with Zena, and in turn, all the workers: "Who's guilty? That's the point. Only Zena? Nonsense. Shame, shame on us all! Fourteen years after our revolution, think of it! And one of our workers selling her body! Shame! Rotten shame!" (191). Thus, as in Marx, the prostitute embodies a deformation of the communist state, and disrupts the "natural" relations the proletariat seeks to construct, depicted most clearly in Natasha and Andy's equitable relationship.[18] The novel resolves this dilemma somewhat creakily: Natasha challenges Zena to a "socialist competition" "[f]or good work and rate of progress in studies" (192), and Zena's bodily energies are redirected to the collective cause.[19]

As a figure for the pre-revolutionary world, for capitalism, and for a wrong-headed form of communism, then, Zena constitutes a political disruption re-configured as a sexual disruption: a reconfiguration enabled by anxiety over the female body and its uncontrolledness. Her actions endanger the communist ethic through her failure to adequately fulfill her role as an organ in the col-lective body. She is a metaphorical wrench in the works of the factory and the communist state; her use of her body as a commodity that does not contribute to collective production thus disturbs the functioning of the collective body, and the new order it represents. While we should not simplistically understand Zena as the joyful figure of individuality and sexuality in the face of communist repression, we must acknowledge that the reshaping of her body along the lines of Natasha's is part of a worldview in which women, if they are not to be pros-titutes or mothers enslaved by the burden of their bodies, must be part of a mech-anized, collective, mass-producing body.

We will turn to the gendered implications of that mechanized body shortly. But first, it is important to note how the novel links female sexuality and the commodity to create the taint of the prostitute, which the novel's female char-acters must avoid if they are not to be condemned. The label of prostitute is not restricted to Zena but, as noted above, hovers around those women whose shriv-eled breasts are marked metaphorically/metonymically with dollar signs, who seek to consume rather than to work. Page's depiction of American wives as embodiments of the degradations of American capitalism and bourgeois life sets up parallels between bourgeois wives and prostitutes. Her text is thus consistent with communist thought of the period in suggesting that bourgeois marriage is merely a form of prostitution sanctioned by capitalism. Elsie, Andy's girlfriend in the States, is a typist who desires upward mobility, and is "always planning, always urging [Andy] on" (7). She tells her fellow typists that Andy is a bonds salesman, rather than a mechanic, and nags him to learn law. Together they plan the furnishings they'll have, and Andy wonders whether he'll be able to buy her the clothes and jewelry she desires. Their future together, and the insti-tution of bourgeois marriage more generally, is represented in the union of the Old Woman and her henpecked husband: "That old saying like-mother-like-daughter gave [Andy] the willies" (10). Elsie's love of fine clothes and high fash-ions embodies her enslavement to the commodity and her view of marriage as an exchange of her body for commodity comfort.

The powerful way in which metonymy operates to link women to prostitu-tion, and to index female sexuality to the taint of modernism and commodity culture, can be seen in *Moscow Yankee* through the motif of silk, a feminized commodity that connects Zena, Natasha, and a third Russian woman charac-ter, Katerina (Katia). At a narrative level, the three women are interrelated in one chapter by the predatory attentions of Alex Turin. When Natasha stumbles

upon Zena and Alex kissing in a corner of the factory she scolds them both, but
her own proximity to objectification and prostitution surfaces in Alex's response:
"No instincts of your own, eh? Maybe you need some loving up yourself!" followed by his inner thought, "Pretty bitch. . . . He'd like to give her pretty shoulders what for" (120). The third woman subjected to Alex's leering in the space
of two pages is Katia, herself a former aristocrat or "White Russian." When Katia
surreptitiously passes Alex a note, connected to a sabotage plan revealed later
in the novel, Alex grasps her hand and tries to delay her, but she hurries off.
Again, his thoughts construct the female as inherently prostitutional: "So, Katia,
my pretty one, you think you can spurn me? Be careful, my hour will strike.
Honor, Civilization demand it. Do you think the upstarts can ride the saddle
forever? Illiterate swine. My lovely witch, some day you'll come fawning back
to me. Shall I take you? Be careful" (121).

The novel condemns Katia, who hopes to escape the Soviet Union through
an affair with an American engineer. She is introduced through the eyes of Philip
Boardman, who contrasts her with the "nice girl" Natasha: "[Katia] never worked
overtime, that girl: not unless there was a pair of silk stockings in it" (39). Another
scene references Katia's "silkclad hip" (230). Katia's liking for luxurious commodities underscores her status as femme fatale. Although she is confident in
her seductive talents—"She had yet to meet the man she couldn't subdue"
(122)—her charms fail on Boardman, and she turns to Crampton, a capitalist
through and through, in a manner that emphasizes her self-prostitution: "She
endured his kiss, throwing back her head in a pretty submissive gesture. This
man was a boor, really" (123).

Katia's willingness to purchase her escape with her body and to offer overtime for a commodity marks her as a prostitute, and thus aligns her with both
the American capitalist system and the persisting corruptions of the old Russian order. Soon after, Natasha is overtly threatened with the mark of prostitution when Andy woos her in his room, in an increasingly lecherous and
aggressive manner, and by means of his store catalogue:

> She didn't understand his words, yet their meaning flamed from his
> eyes, eager body. His arms closed about her. "Honest Nat, you sure are
> sweet." He thrust the book at her. "Silk and whatever you want—"
>   She slapped it against his face. *Durak*! Fool! Did he treat girls in
> America like this? "What you take me, eh? A bitch? You fool! . . . Sell
> myself for a pair of silk stockings, eh?" (128)

The pair of silk stockings for which Katia would work overtime, the silk stockings which Andy offers Natasha, and the silk scarf for which Zena is later
accused of selling herself, link the three women.[20]

Silk is thus a mobile signifier of a prostitution relentlessly associated with class betrayal and corrupt capitalism. The prostitute's position at the threshold of the natural and the artificial is paralleled in silk's conflation of the organicism of nature and the artifice of the commodity. It is an association which Natasha angrily rejects; as Philip Boardman has noted in comparing Natasha to his bourgeois wife, Natasha is as different from Mary "as steel from silk" (186). Natasha thus not only has to distance her body from the organic body of her mother, subject to pregnancy and ageing, but also from the sexualized and debased body of Zena, and from her figurative counterpart, the prostituted bourgeois wife.[21]

Moscow Yankee's demonization of prostitution, like the demonization of mothers it shares with other women's proletarian novels, is certainly a strategic move designed to make possible a positive image of the working woman. In order to affirm the working woman in a materialist context, Page counters the concept of the factory as the site of women's degradation by relocating the threat of prostitution into the bourgeois home and the marketplace. But her reenvisioning of the factory testifies to the commonality of gendered structures in bourgeois and radical depictions of the modern, working world and to the consequences of such unacknowledged gender politics for the new, materialist order.

The vulnerability of *Moscow Yankee*'s female characters to charges of prostitution does not merely hold significance for those characters, and by extension for "real" women as constructed by materialist discourse, although it undeniably constricts their lives and identities. The fact that both modernist and socialist texts reinscribe this gender politics suggests that materialist imaginings of new worlds are delimited by the same conditions that determine class inequity under capitalist industrialism. We have seen that in order to avoid maternal organicism and sexualized commodification, Natasha must model herself after steel, and after the factory's streamlined machinery. This image of the mechanized body denotes the diminishing and flattening effects of materialist gendered rhetoric on women. In its images of the mechanized body and its counterpart, the gendered, sexualized machine, we can perceive the sneaking authoritarianism of the novel's bodily "metonymies." At the same time, while the mechanical imagery in many ways continues to rhetorically and politically delimit female identity, and to echo the sexisms of the novel's female stereotypes, the industrial rhetoric used to describe these Soviet bodies also conveys the radical potential of *Moscow Yankee*'s effort to reimagine embodied and politicized identities.

When *Moscow Yankee* disavows the bodies of mothers and prostitutes, and imagines instead a Soviet Union of women like steel, it constructs a gendered, technological body complicit in what Foley depicts as the novel's uncritical admiration of Soviet "fetishization of technology" (xviii). The gender dynamics that traverse the novel's repudiation of the organic in favor of the mechanical are suggested in Philip Boardman's Soviet industrial fantasy: "To build! To build! What engineer had not dreamed so—to clear wastes, drain swamps, plumb depths, risk hides—to build!" (80); his fantasy suggests a masculine industrial conquering of an untamed and feminine Nature.[22] This fetishism of technology and machinery indicates an uneasy slippage between Page's mechanized vision of communality and the conflation of fascism and machine aesthetics most often associated with the Italian futurists in the World War I era.

Clearly there *is* a distinction between Marxist and fascist imaginings of a technological world and its working bodies: Hal Foster, in analyzing the philosophies of futurist F. T. Marinetti and vorticist Wyndham Lewis, contrasts "a [M]arxist project to *overcome* technological self-alienation dialectically (for all)" with "a protofascist desire to *elevate* this self-alienation into an absolute value (for a select few)" (8). In the context of the—certainly conflicted—intellectual and political relationship between Marinetti and Mussolini, the futurist embrace of alienation and destruction of the organic makes way for fascism: "the (masochistic) drive to self-destruction at its core may also be turned into the (sadistic) drive to master others" (26). In contrast, in delineating a Marxist vision of a technological world in his "The Work of Art," Walter Benjamin, while welcoming the mechanical interpenetration of reality in the form of film, condemns mankind's futuristic/fascistic ability to "experience its own destruction as an aesthetic pleasure of the first order" (242). Distancing his stance from the futurist manifesto and its acclamation of war, Benjamin asserts that war constitutes the outcome of a failure to adequately integrate the mechanical into society, "to incorporate technology as its organ" (242).

Within a Marxist worldview, then, technology offers an extra "organ" for a collective social body; for the futurists, it heralds organic death and mechanical resurrection in the form of war. In the former, the mechanical is organically incorporated, in service to collective production; in the latter, it is technology that enlists, and ultimately subsumes, organic bodies. But critics such as Caroline Tisdall and Angelo Bozzolla suggest that Benjamin offers a reductive picture of relations between futurism and fascism, "overlook[ing] the radical aspects of Futurism that led to Marinetti's split with Mussolini in 1920, and equat[ing] Futurism and Fascism as part and parcel of the same tendency" (17).[23] Tisdall and Bozzolla also point out, for example, that "the aestheticization of city life" envisaged in Luigi Russolo's futurist-influenced manifesto "The Art of Noises" was most fully realized "not in Futurist or even Fascist Italy, but in the hopeful days of young Soviet Russia. In 1920 the *Concert for Factory Sirens* was performed: work was beautiful, and the sweetest noise for the workers was the orchestrated unison of the sirens that summoned them" (115). The tractability of the machine-body aesthetic thus both serves different political causes, and links them by potentially "infecting" them (to use a somatic metaphor) with its contradictory political implications.[24]

It is in the slippery ground between these two models of technologized and embodied identity that *Moscow Yankee* operates in promoting its radical politics with gendered concepts. As it seeks to envisage a collective, industrialized body in which the mechanical is organically incorporated, the novel's advocacy of the Soviet state and its industrialization clearly depends upon a metonymic and synecdochal use of individual bodies that, particularly with female bodies, violently indexes them to social, political, and economic orders. The figure of Natasha's mother, the organic, aged, maternal body, representative of the feudal order, is superceded by Natasha's sleek, working body. Organic, maternal reproduction is displaced by male-controlled industrial production, as indicated toward the end of the novel when Andy and his workmate, Sasha, race each other to produce a record number of trucks: "The first day they made twenty-two babies, the next seventy-three" (276).

In this generative union of men and machines, not only are women elided from the (pro)creative process, but factory machinery is invested with conventionally feminine attributes. Clearly, because Natasha must distance herself from her mother's past and the maternal role, that reproductive capacity is relocated within the industrial machinery; similarly, Natasha's necessary abjuration of any expression of sexual or commodity desire that might align her with the prostitute suggests that the machinery is also eroticized, in a kind of sublimation of the creativity and power of communism. At one point, Andy's relationship with Natasha is virtually displaced onto the machine at which she works:

> Hands thrust into his side pockets, he neared her machine. Deserted. . . . He touched the gleaming side of her lathe, stroked its curves. Gorgeous creature. Even when still, you felt its power. Trim, set to go. What was the use? He couldn't help it. Come what may. . . . Swinging her dust-cloth and humming a new air, she came full on him. . . . She leaned one arm over her machine, her palms pressed against her hot cheeks. He gripped the metal. Hard. (236–37)

Page's text thus reworks tropes of femininity; in order to imagine a young working woman who is not a prostitute or an idealized or monstrous mother, she has Natasha embody the youth, energy, and athletic beauty of the new order, and seeks to sublimate female sexuality and sensuality, conventionally understood as both attractive and dangerous, through the productive work of factory machinery.

The dynamic of attraction and danger characteristic of traditional representations of female sexuality plays out in men's relationships to the machinery. We see Scottish-American Mac, who repairs the factory's machinery, become engrossed in the workings of an operation lathe: "He watched the machine churning, revolving, cutting, feeding, everything timed in perfect rhythm. A wonder! MAG, as Misha and he affectionately termed her. . . . Just look at her, with what precision she was cutting teeth in this screw. Like a human, was MAG, with brains, nerves, eyes. Little darling" (101).

Female sexuality is reconstituted as a productive energy under the control of men in the name of the state; and that control is required to counter both female voracity—one worker's fingers have been "chewed off by a greedy unguarded machine" (104)—and the machinery's tendency to feminine fragility and unreliability. This fragility, and the partial displacement of women by machines in men's affective lives, becomes explicit in Mac's angry altercation with the careless turner operating MAG: "This namby-pamby entrusted with such a beauty! . . . Furious, the turner threw on the power. 'Say, who do you think you are! This is my machine, ain't it?' Mac danced with anger. Did he think he was going to let him spoil her! 'Listen, you boob, I told you before about letting her pound on her end like that. Oh, you'll wreck her!'" (101). The two men's possessiveness, and Mac's certainty that he knows how to treat "such a beauty" without "spoil[ing]" her, suggest a male rivalry over a desirable woman. Mac's anxious paternalism toward the machine is later validated, and Mac devastated, when the worker's carelessness breaks the machine: "Mac ran a tortured hand over MAG's stilled body" (102).

Such imagery has the conservative effect of reinstalling a heterosexual narrative, in which female energy is predominantly under the control of men,[25] and indicates the difficulty of conceiving a radical world in which the operation of gendered rhetoric is at once so oblique and so deterministic. If modernist texts about women and the industrial economy render the female body mechanical, and thus controllable and useful, partly to "deny the progressive dehumanization of the male body under industrialism" (Stubbs 150), Moscow Yankee's feminization of machinery is a complementary rhetorical function, which replicates the modernist deployment of a feminized trope in the name of male transcendence.

At the same time, although certain similarities between modernist and materialist uses of gendered rhetoric are unarguable, such rhetoric is also used deliberately and variously both within and between modernist and materialist canons. Moscow Yankee thus perhaps consciously invokes modernist, bourgeois, and masculinist rhetorics of femininity in order to rewrite them, particularly in relation to factories and machines. For example, Dimock notes of Melville's short story "The Paradise of Bachelors and the Tartarus of Maids," that "the scene of labor is consistently imaged as a highly sexualized landscape, mechanical production here being dramatized as a kind of mechanical violation of the female body" (Dimock 86). The factory is a space which nurtures "deviant female sexuality," for as the unmarried working girls tend phallic machines that "vertically thrust up a long, glittering scythe . . . look[ing] exactly like a sword," they seem to be "unnaturally coupling with machines" (86), and to be "giving birth, not to babies but to industrial products" (87).[26] To subvert this capitalist vision of the factory as the stage for "the drama of perverted womanhood" (Dimock 87), and to absolve her female workers from charges of deviance, then, Page perhaps chooses to resexualize the machinery as feminine. Her text thus constitutes a very specific practice of materialist rhetoric that diverges from both modernist and conventional male materialist practices of gendered rhetoric in important ways.

Moreover, in Natasha, *Moscow Yankee* does achieve a female character who both embraces her technologized role within the laboring body and expresses a willful, humorous, and active sexuality on her own terms. It is in Natasha, perhaps, that the organic and the industrial coincide most successfully: rather than read her decision to delay childbirth as a fear of organic procreation and a subservience to the industrial collective, we might see it as the active procreative choice of a liberated communist woman, a choice which will facilitate conjoinment of a working and a maternal life. That Natasha rewrites normative gender concepts in uniting the organic and the industrial is suggested in her outfit when she takes Andy to a Beethoven concert: "Her blue silk and wool sweater brought out all the copper glints in her skin and hair" (244). Associated at once with metal and with the silk that has signified degraded female sexuality in the novel, Natasha models a female Soviet subjectivity that can adapt conventional gendered associations to her own identity.

Indeed, further examination of the novel's technologized imagery suggests that it is ultimately in the insidious determinism of bodily metonymy that *Moscow Yankee*'s most radical critique may lie, consciously or otherwise—a critique that confronts both the empowering possibilities and structural flaws of the new Soviet state, and that is intimately connected to bodies, machinery, and the desire for male transcendence. The feminization of machinery, and the association of Natasha with steel, both necessary strategies in constructing a positive, nonprostituted female worker, disrupt the conventional opposition of the natural, organic, and traditionally female to the mechanical, industrial, and traditionally male. Foley has suggested that the novel's displacement of political conversion onto the love plot between Andy and Natasha elides Soviet structural problems—such as overemphasis on fast, efficient production, and the unresolved issue of the relationship between mental and manual labor—in favor of a focus on individual voluntarism as the engine that propels the state. But in the novel's gendered imagery and corporeal logic—the latter striving to imagine an empowering union of the organic and the mechanical—those structural problems reappear. In particular, the mechanization and malfunctioning of *male* bodies in the novel testifies, on the one hand, to flaws in the Soviet experiment and in the materialist effort to exploit gendered rhetoric and, on the other, to the difficult, risky, and daring nature of the text's grappling with a new kind of embodied and political subjectivity.

Clearly, Page wishes to challenge a fear of technology discredited by Boardman toward the end of the novel: "The bigwigs in Europe and the States were saying science and technology were a joint Frankenstein. . . . It wasn't so, and here they'd been proving it!" (281). The novel seeks to present machinery in the same romantic light previously reserved for natural wonders, as in its depiction of "rows of stilled machines which glistened like a forest of oak trunks after a quick spring rain" (85). Here, Page overtly adopts conventional natural imagery in the service of a radical celebration of technology under communism, ultimately elevating the technological above the natural—itself inevitably a strategy with gendered implications. The devaluation of the natural is explicit in the narrative's frequent depiction of threats to the state and hangovers from the old order through natural metaphors: Alex Turin is repeatedly characterized as a rat and a "wolf in overalls" (269); Henry Crampton is a "fat buzzard" (259); Natasha's much-maligned mother is a "[p]oor little mole" (194) with a "pumpkin stomach" (240); a priest selling icons is an "anti-government skunk" (82); Natasha castigates Zena's clients as "skunks" (191); and Edith Crampton is a "sour apple" (258).

But the corresponding implication, that right-thinking workers—especially men who are less conventionally marked by association with the organic—are mechanized, undermines simplistic confidence that technology functioning in the name of a communist state will inevitably create an equitable world. The proliferation of mechanical metaphors for bodies and body parts throughout the narrative suggests that gendered rhetoric might not effectively and obediently serve any political agenda. Like the figure of the prostitute whose contradictions reveal the vulnerability of male bodies to mortality, these mechanical images suggest the alarming equivalence of bodies and machines, and the violent effects of the "fetishization of technology." Not coincidentally, such mechanical images often traverse romantic and sexual encounters: Andy's desire for Nat gets his "sparkplugs going" (86); Alex's arm is "a tightening vise about [Zena's] waist" (119); and when Andy takes Natasha's arm at the height of their courtship, "[i]t was like a current pulsing through them, she was welded fast" (242). Mechanical imagery becomes particularly insistent toward the novel's conclusion: as if to belie Boardman's denial of Frankenstein, Andy's heart is a "triphammer" on his nervous walk to receive an award, while "his brakes were jamming" (282). Factory supervisor Mikhail, galvanized by the threat of sabotage, is a "supercharged battery, crackling between his timed, resolute moves" (261); soon, however, exhausted from overwork, he is depicted as "stripping his gears"

(279): "He had turned into a machine, was killing himself" (204). The metonymic morphing of these men into component parts of the trucks they build suggests, against the text's narrative thrust, the dehumanizing elements of the new order, the danger of what Foley terms "productive forces determinism" (*Radical Representations* 243–46; "Introduction" xxiii), and the traces of futuristic fascism in the glorification of mechanization. Like the mysterious man Andy encounters on the streets of Moscow, this mechanization darkly, obscurely, but nonetheless definitely gestures toward the interrelated breakdown of gendered metonymy and the communist vision of the Soviet Union.

At the same time, the conscious effort to reconceive both political and sexual identity with the active, "charged" language of electricity, machinery, and the industrial workplace draws attention to the ambitious nature of Page's literary enterprise. Her effort to imagine new, nonsexist forms of embodied identity is suggested also by other occurrences of male bodily breakdown in *Moscow Yankee*—as when Andy and his American friends are struck with hives, and when Andy breaks his ankle leaping from a streetcar. These instances both parody and challenge the concept of male invulnerability, and go some way toward mitigating the effort to transcend such vulnerability through the image of a strong, collective, mechanical-organic body that carefully circumscribes female bodies.

Finally, in celebrating technological advance, the novel does not lose sight of either the practicalities of agricultural production or the enduring significance of nature and landscape in the new social and political order. *Moscow Yankee* concludes with Natasha, Andy, and several of their workmates helping out on a state farm on one of their free days, in a chapter that emphasizes nature in the midsummer heat: "Looking up from the row of potato plants he was hoeing, Andy caught the gentle roll of the chocolate brown earth heaving its slow breath under the torrid glare of high noon" (286). It is a deliberate effort to reassert a materialist merging of industrial and organic: "The new life they were making would unite city and country and everybody would enjoy the best of both" (287). And the novel's closing sentences insist on the possibility of selves shaped simultaneously by their relationships to sexual partners, coworkers, industrial progress, and natural beauty: "From ahead came warning cries, the whirr of an approaching train. Pulling Andy's arm, Natasha ran with him over the moist earth, between flecked birches, toward their workmates gathering in the station" (290).

Writing of Dos Passos's *U.S.A.*, Casey asserts that it "attempts simultaneously to historicize women—to give them voice, and therefore validity, within a literature and a society that have silenced them—and to use woman as a symbol for radical ideological alternatives" (16). For Casey, this effort displaces female agency and subjectivity—she cites Alice Jardine's question, "If everyone and everything becomes Woman . . . where does that leave women [?]"—but simultaneously locates women in "cultural margins" that are a "vital source of sociopolitical regeneration" (16). Similarly, multiple forces are at work in *Moscow Yankee* as it struggles with the conventions of both the capitalist order it challenges and the materialist order it wants to realize. Undoubtedly, through its realism and proletarian bildungsroman form, the novel offers an engaging, vibrant narrative with quirky characters (male and female), an energetic and hopeful vision of a new world, and most of all, a pointed, timely challenge to the horrors of capitalism playing out in America's Depression. It simultaneously offers a powerful example of how the gendered dynamics of literature—prole-tarian and modernist—permeate the constructions of political orders and the material lives lived within them. Clearly, the new collective laboring body depicted by the text depends upon a fetishization of machinery and mass pro-duction which assigns traditional fantasies of female sexuality to the machines; this collective body depends also upon a liberal reform of the prostitute, an exclusion of aged and maternal bodies, and an increasing mechanization of all laboring bodies. Yet, from the contested space between the desire to imagine an active role for women and the desire to deploy powerful gendered imagery in the name of radicalism emerges a telling vision of men and women striving to shape themselves and their lives, despite their enmeshment in rhetorics that structure their very bodies.

NOTES

A version of this paper was presented at the Inaugural New Modernisms Conference, Pennsylvania State University, October 1999. For their insightful comments and sugges-tions at various stages of this paper's development, I would like to thank Matthew Basso, Janet Galligani Casey, Paula Rabinowitz, and the anonymous readers for University of Iowa Press.

1. In its attempt to understand the complex aesthetic and political interplay in *Moscow Yankee*, this paper owes much to what Alan Wald has termed "a genuine critical renaissance of critical studies of the 1930s applying the new methodologies that grew out of the 1960s, especially feminist literary theory and a more sophisticated Marxism" ("1930s Left" 21); Wald includes in this renaissance Cary Nelson's *Repression and Recovery: Mod-ern American Poetry and the Politics of Cultural Memory, 1910–1945*, Paula Rabinowitz's *Labor and Desire: Women's Revolutionary Fiction in Depression America*, and James Bloom's *Left Letters: The Culture Wars of Mike Gold and Joseph Freeman*. Other semi-nal texts which revisit and rearticulate the cultural and political expressions of the Left in the 1930s and have informed this paper include Constance Coiner, *Better Red: The Writing and Resistance of Tillie Olsen and Meridel Le Sueur*; Barbara Foley, *Radical Rep-resentations: Politics and Form in U.S. Proletarian Fiction, 1929–1941*; James F. Murphy,

The Proletarian Moment: The Controversy over Leftism in Literature; and Caren Irr, *The Suburb of Dissent: Cultural Politics in the United States and Canada during the 1930s*. For feminist rediscoveries of women's literature of this period, and analysis of the role of gender in both men's and women's radical literature, see Coiner; Foley; Rabinowitz; Charlotte Nekola and Paula Rabinowitz, eds., *Writing Red: An Anthology of American Women Writers, 1930–1940*; Laura Hapke, *Daughters of the Great Depression: Women, Work, and Fiction in the American 1930s*; Janet Galligani Casey, *Dos Passos and the Ideology of the Feminine*.

2. The masculinist rhetoric of leftist critical discourse was reinforced by a visual iconography that, in the *New Masses*, opposed hyper-masculine, muscular workers on the cover to "cartoons of big-bosomed leisure class women" (Foley 220).

3. See Rabinowitz; Coiner; Foley; Hapke. Foley notes that "[n]ot all leftist male writers considered testosterone a necessary component of proletarian selfhood" (233) and lists works such as James Steele's *Conveyor*, Thomas Bell's *All Brides Are Beautiful*, and Jack Conroy's *A World to Win* as male-authored texts that critique "[i]deologies of male dominance" (234). In *Dos Passos and the Ideology of the Feminine*, Casey contends that Dos Passos's attention to "gender as a component of political analysis" and his ideological use of the feminine align his works with radical women authors such as Josephine Herbst (41).

4. As Rabinowitz notes, "*Proletarian literature* was the term officially sanctioned by the CPUSA for the new writing of the late 1920s and early 1930s" (72). For various contemporaneous definitions of "proletarian literature," see Walter B. Rideout, *Radical Novel* 166–69; for Rideout's own definition see Rideout, 209; for Josephine Herbst's preference for and definition of the term "revolutionary fiction," see Rabinowitz, 73. For a recent working critical definition of "proletarian literature" see Casey, note 4, 194.

5. As well as numerous journalistic pieces, proletarian pamphlets, and short stories, published and unpublished, Page also wrote a third novel, *With Sun in Our Blood* (1950), which was republished in 1977 by Persea Press as *Daughter of the Hills*, and published again under the same title by the Feminist Press in 1986. For a compilation of oral interviews with Page in the form of a "first-person biography," see Christina Looper Baker, *In a Generous Spirit: A First-Person Biography of Myra Page*.

6. For more detailed analysis of the roles of women within the CPUSA, see Coiner, "Women and the American Communist Party in the Depression" in *Better Red*; Foley, "Women and the Left in the 1930s" in *Radical Representations*; Robert Shaffer, "Women and the Communist Party, USA, 1930–1940"; and Casey, *Dos Passos and the Ideology of the Feminine* 35–40.

7. In both instances, maternal imagery is deployed in the name of male self-actualization, and elides female subjectivity: the trope precludes "the presence of a female body that has not become a maternal body" (162), and the mother-figure remains "both menacing and erotic" (113), as giving birth is portrayed as both "productive" and "horror-filled, a monstrosity" (92). Rabinowitz does suggest that the contradiction in the maternal trope potentially "produces gaps in the conventional narrative of proletarian fraternity" (91). For the most part, however, the maternal metaphor in the proletarian narrative effectively "produces difference in order to erase it" (162).

8. Of her time in the Soviet Union, and her ignorance about the dark side of Stalin's regime, Page has this to say: "I didn't look into the matter of the purges, because the Soviets were covering up the facts. I believed them, and I was wrong. An American journalist, Louis Fischer, tried to raise the issue of the purges with me. 'You should know what's going on down there,' he said, trying to persuade me to go down to the Ukraine and see for myself. . . . We didn't know about the horrors of collectivization because we chose not to know. Fischer was right, but we didn't believe him" (Baker 124). Despite Page's continued lack of knowledge about the purges at the time of writing *Moscow Yankee*, she has this stranger offer a voice of warning not unlike that of Fischer.

9. Page's conscious engagement of the relationship between the iconographic deployment of the feminine and violence against women is conveyed, for example, in the traumatic and brutal scene of *Gathering Storm* in which a white mill-owner's son rapes and murders the young black woman who works for his family as a maid.

10. Henry Crampton is by far the most "embodied" of the novel's male characters: he is variously depicted as a "[b]loated squash" (36), a "fat buzzard" (259), the owner of a "ponderous body" with shaking jowls (263), and a "bulging figure" (264). As noted below, this characterization is an example of both the novel's denigration of the organic as feminized and bourgeois, and one of several instances of male bodily vulnerability that indicate the breakdown of gendered rhetoric and the possibility of an equitable model of embodied subjectivity.

11. Toward the end of the novel, Mary Boardman's character is somewhat recuperated as she is invited "to serve on a committee . . . to inspect children's nurseries" (229) and Philip realizes that she may need only "work, new interests: to be a person on her own" (228).

12. See also Alice Jardine, *Gynesis: Configurations of Woman and Modernity*.

13. This essay uses "modernism" to encompass both the kind of high modernist literature referenced in the proletarian literary debates carried out by the *New Masses*—the works of Eliot, Joyce, and Pound, for example—and a chronologically broader field of thought and art characterized by the self-referentiality, linguistic and formal experimentation, and rejection of verisimilitude iterated by Huyssen.

14. For a delineation of the relationship between the gendered rhetorics of modernism and proletarianism, see Casey, "Critical Legacies," in *Dos Passos and the Ideology of the Feminine*.

15. For Benjamin, the prostitute offers this kind of transcendence; he depicts her as representing the crossing of a class threshold, enabling for the male customer "an obstinate and voluptuous hovering on the brink" of a frontier beyond which "lies nothingness" ("A Berlin Chronicle" 11). But Benjamin also insists upon the "shock" that disrupts this modern, commodity-driven "dream state" (Rauch 83) and that forces him to confront the "real and mortal nature" of female *and* male bodies (Rauch 88).

16. Writes Marx: "Prostitution is only a *specific* expression of the *general* prostitution of the *laborer*, and since it is a relationship in which falls not the prostitute alone, but also the one who prostitutes—and the latter's abomination is still greater—the capitalist, etc., also comes under this head" (*Economic and Philosophic Manuscripts of 1844* 133). Prostitution is thus a metaphor for the inherently dehumanizing operation of capitalism.

17. The quote derives from "Private Property and Communism," in the Third Manuscript (an appendix Marx wrote for a missing page of the Second Manuscript), in which he theorizes an early and crude stage in the movement toward communism:

> The task of the *laborer* is not done away with, but extended to all men. The relationship of private property persists as the relationship of the community to the world of things. . . . [T]his movement of opposing universal private property to private property finds expression in the animal form of opposing to *marriage* (certainly a *form of exclusive private property*) the *community of women*, in which a woman becomes a piece of *communal* and *common* property. It may be said that this idea of the *community of women* gives away the secret of this as yet completely crude and thoughtless communism. Just as woman passes from marriage to general prostitution, so the entire world of wealth (that is, of man's objective substance) passes from the relationship of exclusive marriage with the owner of private property to a state of universal prostitution with the community. (Marx, *Economic and Philosophical Manuscripts of 1844* 133)

18. See n. 16. Marx asserts that the crude form of communism which he likens to prostitution contradicts people's natural relations to one another: "the relation of man to woman is *the most natural* relation of human being to human being" (*Economic and Philosophic Manuscripts of 1844* 134).

19. That the maternal and prostitute figures may be conflated, and that positive and negative versions of the mother may collude equally in the sexism of gendered rhetoric, is confirmed by Zena's partial redemption through her status as a mother, as indicated by Natasha's succinct plea, "Zena, your boy . . ." (192).

20. The meaning of silk is further entrenched by its several brief appearances in the text: for example, Andy witnesses the arrest of two exiled *kulaks* who have stolen "miscellaneous finery" including "a heavy silk shawl" (235). *Moscow Yankee*'s Russian glossary defines *kulak* as "a term used to denote the rich farmer who opposed the collective farm movement" (291).

21. Even Australian physician Dr. Agatha Lloyd, who appears briefly twice in the novel, grapples with this restrictive dogma, in which a woman's failure to toe the party line invites characterization as a prostitute. Agatha has been rejected by her anthropologist husband because her socialist opinions will not stretch to communism: "'Hopelessly bourgeois,' he had finally called her. And to him, she knew, a streetwalker was more deserving of tolerance, pity. She, a good liberal, wellknown for her medical social work, dubbed hopelessly bourgeois! Nonsense! Simply because she loved him was no reason for committing mental prostitution was it? She must be genuinely convinced" (113). The prostitute metaphor occurs twice here, once as a figure awarded greater tolerance and pity from Agatha's husband than herself, and once as a figure for an unqualified and uneducated acceptance of communism; Agatha must travel to the Soviet Union to avoid an intellectual prostitution deemed lower than its sexual counterpart.

22. Foley notes, as the title of Gold's editorial piece "Go Left, Young Writers" suggests, that "[t]he West metaphor was one of Gold's favorites," which constructed "the project of proletarian literature as an expansion of the frontier." While Foley disagrees with Rabinowitz's assertion "that the party's outlook for proletarian literature can be conflated

with 'invasion, exploration, and rape,'" she acknowledges the problematic sexual and racial implications of the image, referring the reader to "[t]he locus classicus for analysis of sexual conquest in the American iconography of the frontier," Annette Kolodny's *The Lay of the Land: Metaphor as Expression and History in American Life and Letters* (Foley 223).

23. In providing a more nuanced view of the relationship between futurism and fascism, Tisdall and Bozzolla do acknowledge important shared tendencies, including "romantic and uninformed glorification of the machine (technology) in society, the use of physical violence against opponents, and infatuation with youth" (200).

24. On the continuities between Russian futurism and Marxist ideology, see Irina Gutkin, "The Legacy of the Symbolist Utopia: From Futurism to Socialist Realism." Another example of the potential blurring between mechanical imagery used in the service of Marxism and that used in the service of fascism comes in Benjamin's assertion that Marx "early recognized it as his task to forge the amorphous mass, which was then being wooed by an aesthetic socialism, into the iron of the proletariat" ("On Some Motifs" 166).

25. Toward the end of the novel, Philip Boardman laughingly tells Andy how Natasha "razzed" him recently about the lack of women on machines (288).

26. Hapke notes that "the fallen woman myth" associated with Victorian warnings of "the morally corrupting effect of the factory" on women (45) is reconstituted in, for example, Erskine Caldwell's eroticized female millworkers of *God's Little Acre* (1933) who flourish while their male counterparts wilt and apparently "prefer the machines to men as sexual surrogates" (21).

Monstrous Modernism

Disfigured Bodies and Literary Experimentalism in *Yonnondio* and *Christ in Concrete*

JOSEPH ENTIN

One of the central reasons for the tortured tone of the textual portion of James Agee's and Walker Evans's celebrated 1941 portrait of three Alabama tenant farming families, *Let Us Now Praise Famous Men*, is Agee's expressed frustration with the incapacity of language to convey the full materiality of the sharecroppers' existence. "This is a book only by necessity," Agee states. "More seriously, it is an effort in human actuality in which the reader is no less centrally involved than the authors and those of whom they tell" (xvi). How, Agee asks, can "human actuality" be represented? Asserting that "language cannot embody . . . it can only describe," Agee contends that he would do better to provide a variety of extra-textual evidence that would bypass the inability of language to render the "actuality" of the real: "If I could do it, I'd do no writing at all here. It would be photographs; the rest would be fragments of cloth, bits of cotton, lumps of earth, records of speech, pieces of wood and iron, phials of odor, plates of food and of excrement" (13). And then, in a sentence given the significance of a full paragraph, Agee declares: "A piece of the body torn out by the roots might be more to the point" (13). The grotesque image Agee paints here is designed both to signify the limits of any "book" to capture the materiality of lived existence and to represent a figure that, although delivered in words, gestures beyond language toward the actuality that language inevitably fails to embody.

Although Agee's image of the torn tenant farmer's body is striking, it is by no means unique—images of wounded proletarian bodies litter the literature of the '30s. Early in *The Disinherited* (1934), for instance, young Larry Donovan's aunt takes him to the home of a miner who has been crushed by falling rock. The man "lay trussed like a blue fowl, his feet protruding beneath a cheap cotton shroud"; his "scarred hands," coal dust-blackened nails, and lips, "glued in a hideous grin," serve as a gruesome and foreboding specter of life in the mines (68). The middle-class narrator of Meridel LeSueur's short story "I Was Marching" (1934) is moved to join a local strike when she is confronted by the bodies of picketers who have been injured by police: "whole men suddenly spouting blood and running like living sieves, another holding a dangling arm shot squarely off, a tall youngster, running, tripping over his intestines" (159). Dalton Trumbo's novel *Johnny Got His Gun* (1939) channels its critique of industrial warfare through the body of his protagonist Joe Bonham, who returns from the battlefield without legs, arms, or a face. "He was nothing but a piece of meat like the chunks of cartilage old Prof Vogel used to have in biology" (63), nothing but "raw material" (82); "a side of beef" (109); a "stump of a man" (162). Like Agee's "piece of the body torn out by the roots," these graphic images of disfiguration signal the complex negotiations between social existence and literary representation that characterize much Depression-era working-class literature. For proletarian literature, a genre frequently dedicated to conveying the immensely extra-literary quality of physical harm inflicted on working-class persons, images of disfigured bodies serve as potent symbols both of the limits of literary representation and of experimental efforts to transcend those limits, to create what Agee calls "illusions of embodiment" (13).

This essay examines two novels from the '30s, Pietro di Donato's *Christ in Concrete* and Tillie Olsen's *Yonnondio*, that employ images of wounded working-class bodies to mediate traditionally distinct literary and epistemological modes. Using tropes of the body, especially the injured body, to fashion literary representations, these two novels interrogate and ultimately destabilize hegemonic boundaries between social "experience" and literary aesthetics, political critique and formal innovation, producing highly self-reflexive works of literature that employ modernist techniques to narrate social injustice. Both novels represent monstrous modernisms, hybrid literary forms that fuse a modernist emphasis on rhetorical experimentation with a materialist focus on bodily harm.[1]

In 1940, historian Caroline Ware, author of an innovative 1935 book on the ethnic and working-class culture of early twentieth-century Greenwich Village, wrote the introduction to a collection of new historical essays entitled *The Cultural Approach to History*.[2] In her introduction, Ware issued a bold call for history "from the bottom up," insisting that scholars should turn their attention to the overlooked experience of America's urban immigrants. Placing ethnic life and labor at the forefront of historical research, Ware suggested, requires a radical reorientation of the landmarks through which historical time and experience are marked: "[I]t is to Ellis Island rather than to Plymouth Rock that a great part of the American people trace their history in America. More people have died in industrial accidents than in subduing the wilderness and fighting the revolution. It is these people, rather than the frontiersmen, who constitute the real historical background and the heroic tradition of the mass of urban Americans" (73). Perhaps no modern American novel speaks more directly to Ware's concerns — especially her emphasis on industrial accidents — than Pietro di Donato's *Christ in Concrete*, which narrates the story of Paul, an Italian American whose father, Geremio, a master bricklayer, is killed when a building he is working on collapses on Good Friday when Paul is twelve years old. The oldest of six children, Paul takes up bricklaying to support his family after they are denied compensation from the construction company and aid from the Church and the city government. In the course of the novel, Paul's uncle, Luigi, loses a leg during a construction accident, and Paul's godfather, Nazone, falls off a scaffold to his death. Paul abandons the Catholic Church, much to his mother's dismay, but she blesses him and entrusts her younger children to his guidance as she passes away in the novel's final pages.

   Christ in Concrete is a disjointed novel, a text that patches together multiple and at times conflicting voices, styles, and ideological registers. To narrate the lives of its working-class immigrant characters — the "cheated fragment selves" of the "polyglot worker poor" (234), the "calloused and bruised bodies" living in "shabby railroad flats" (5) — the novel combines allegorical, naturalist, and modernist modes. Structurally, the novel is divided into five sections. The first and last, "Geremio" and "Annunziata," are named for Paul's parents and narrate the transference of generational authority. In the opening section, Geremio is crushed beneath the rubble of a collapsing building, leaving Paul as the oldest male in the family; the final section records Annunziata's death and her commission that her other children obey Paul, despite his rejection of the Church. The middle three sections represent the central aspects of Paul's existence — "Job," the construction industry in which he earns his living; "Tenement," the multi-ethnic space where his family makes its home; and "Fiesta," the symbol of the Italian Catholic traditions shared by the community in which he grows up.

   Through literary fusion, di Donato creates a monstrous modernism, a form of narrative experimentalism designed to narrate both the horrid conditions under which the text's working-class characters live and a utopian potential for political and spiritual redemption. The monstrosity of di Donato's novel captures the fundamentally contradictory, even perverse quality of the social world seen from the perspective of the Italian American workers who are the text's protagonists, the sense that American "reality" undercuts the nation's "promise," that, as Nazone asserts, "this land has become a soil that has contradicted itself" (211). As Paul explains near the end of the text, "my toil has been used against me" (230). The overwhelming power of social and political contradiction places

Paul and his family in an untenable position in which, as Geremio explains, "to rebel is to lose all of the very little. To be obedient is to choke" (13). Lacking meaningful political or social agency, the laborers are literally crushed beneath the weight of industrial capitalism, twisted and deformed into inhuman figures embodied in the monstrous image of Christ in concrete, of workers buried in industrial mud. Through this hybrid figure, an image that condenses bodily destruction and spiritual redemption, the novel asks us to see "Christ" in "concrete," to recast the Christian ideal of brotherly love as pagan identification with the "polyglot worker poor," to ground spiritual outrage in the inequities of material existence, to link spiritual salvation to social revolution. The model for this fusion of spirit and politics is the text itself, which uses high modernism's language of abstraction and consciousness to underscore material forms of degradation and oppression.

Christ in Concrete employs a variety of experimental narrative techniques that we typically associate with modernism, techniques that resist or subvert the immediate contact with "reality" that the codes of realism appear to supply.[3] However, *Christ in Concrete* differs significantly from conventional examples of high modernism. If, as many critics have argued, high modernism generally attempts to seek refuge from a social world that is in the process of being industrialized and organized bureaucratically by constructing an autonomous aesthetic space, *Christ in Concrete*'s aesthetic innovations derive from the attempt to narrate the very processes of industrialization that high modernism typically seeks to avoid. *Christ in Concrete* renders modernity not by achieving what Quentin Anderson calls, in his description of high modernism's aestheticizing tendency, "secular transcendence" (704), but rather by employing modernism's formal devices to underscore the materiality of modern experience, performing what Fredric Jameson characterizes as "a materialist regrounding of the dominant ideology of modernism" ("Reflections" 206). The "modernism" of *Christ in Concrete*—its stream-of-consciousness, its fragmented narrative form, its often unorthodox syntax—represents not sublimation, the transformation of the social world into the private languages and aesthetic productions of the psychological self, but rather an effort to render the contradictions of material and social inequities. To narrate the vicious rhythms and the transformative power of industrial labor, both the world-making and world-destroying power of capitalist production and the way that power is siphoned through the human body, the novel combines several different literary registers: a sensationalist rendering of gratuitous gore, a Catholic-inflected materialism, a naturalist attention to graphic detail, and the bilingual inflection of its Italian American author. The result is a unique brand of radical modernism that combines flights of experimental and lyrical excess with a materialist focus on quotidian realities of exploitation and struggle.

The primary manifestation of the text's monstrous modernism is its representation of labor and laboring bodies. In *Capital*, Marx underscores the contradictory forces to which industrial capitalism subjects working bodies. On the one hand, capitalism's ceaseless drive to improve the speed and flexibility of production requires creative, adaptable workers. "Modern industry never views or treats the existing form of a production process as the definitive one. . . . By means of machinery, chemical processes and other methods, it is continually transforming not only the technical basis of production but also the functions of the worker and the social combinations of the labor process" (617). Large-scale industry, Marx asserts, "necessitates variation of labor, fluidity of functions, and mobility of the worker in all directions." At the same time, however, the relations of production remain hierarchical, rigid: "On the other hand, in its capitalist form [large-scale industry] reproduces the old division of labor with its ossified particularities . . . [T]his absolute contradiction does away with all repose, all fixity and all security as far as the worker's life-situation is concerned" (617–18). As David Harvey has recently argued, Marx's analysis suggests that "the exigencies of capitalist production push the limits of the working body—its capacities and its possibilities—in a variety of different and often fundamentally contradictory directions": "While subservience and respect for authority (sometimes amounting to abject submission) is paramount, the creative responses, spontaneous resources, and animal spirits necessary to the 'form-giving fire' of the labor process must also be liberated and mobilized" (103). The combination of flexibility and discipline that characterizes the system of production, Harvey contends, is complex and unstable.

The experimental semantic forms that di Donato employs to narrate the labor process convey these contradictions. On the one hand, the novel's descriptions of labor suggest the brutalizing force of industrial production, the power of work to twist, cripple, and exhaust the body, draining every ounce of human productive capacity. On the other hand, di Donato describes labor as an avenue of self-expression, bodily fulfillment, and empowerment. To convey the significance of labor, the novel personifies it, describing work as a figure of immense power and persuasion, a personality, "Job," that dominates Paul's psychological and emotional vistas. Paul's relationship to Job is fundamentally ambivalent: Job is both the site where Paul's primary energies and ambitions are expressed and a space where uneven social relations, in which workers risk their bodily health for the profit of owners and managers, take material form. In *Christ in Concrete*, labor is a realm of both pride and exploitation; it is also a primary locus of the novel's most innovative, experimental prose.

Di Donato describes Job in language that blends both desire and decimation, excitement and danger, coordination and confusion in "an inferno of sense-pounding cacophony":

Compression engines snort viciously—sledge heads punch sinking
spikes—steel drills bite shattering jazz in stony-stone excitedly jarring
clinging hands—dust swirling—bells clanging insistent aggravated warning—severe iron cranes swivel swing dead heavy rock high—clattering
dump—vibrating concussion swiftly absorbed—echo reverberating—
scoops bulling horns in rock pile chug-shish-chug-chug aloft—hiss roar
dynamite's boomdoom loosening petrified bowels—one hundred hands
fighting rock—fifty spines derricking swiveling—fifty faces in set mask
chopping stone into bread—fifty hearts interpreting labor hurling oneself
down and in at earth planting pod-footed Job. (36)

This passage's vigorous stylistics illustrate the text's ambivalence about the shape
and force of industrial labor. Through a cubistlike explosion of the scene into
an array of perspectives, the sequence suggests both the enthralling dynamism
and the overwhelming violence of large-scale construction work. The long, broken sentence conveys speed and energy, forces that converge in a bebop rhythm
("shattering jazz," "vibrating concussion," "bulling horns"); di Donato's use of
alliteration and onomatopoeia give the passage momentum and punch. But the
scene's vitality is both rigidly orchestrated and extremely violent. The first half
of the passage is devoid of human figures—engines, sledgehammers, drills,
dust, bells, cranes animate the site, providing the motion and action that make
Job run. When workers do appear, they figure as segments, as pieces rather than
organic entities—hands, spines, faces, hearts. Laborers have become component parts, much as the individual phrases di Donato uses to describe the
scene—incomplete or broken sentences on their own—are embedded in a
larger, multifaceted image. And if the human elements of Job have been dehumanized, the inorganic elements take on animal-like characteristics—they
snort, bite, punch.

   To convey Job's speed, tension, and pressure, di Donato constructs a unique
brand of narrative experimentalism—a labor modernism—that strips the
description of work and the construction site of conjunctions and punctuation
to craft crowded, confusing sentences that overwhelm standard syntax. Di
Donato describes Job as a "symphony of struggle" (8): "The men were transformed into single silent beasts. Snoutnose steamed through ragged mustache
whiplashing sand into mixer Asses-ass dragged under four-by-twelve beam Lean
clawed wall knots jumping in jaws masonry crumbled dust billowed thundered
choked . . ." (9). Here, the modernist explosion of the sentence is used to convey proletarian exploitation. The absence of punctuation underscores the
relentlessness of labor's pace; Job does not hesitate, does not rest, but moves with
a seemingly self-perpetuating and overpowering momentum ("billowed thundered choked"). Like Job, di Donato's prose is a "balanced delirium" (180), com-

bining naturalism's emphasis on gritty details and anonymous forces with a Joycean-like stream-of-consciousness. Here, as elsewhere in the novel, the deformation of conventional syntactical arrangements dovetails with the rewriting of labor and laboring bodies; the narration of work as a dual process of not only production but also destruction and death facilitates the dismantling of normative semantic patterns.

Throughout the novel, di Donato outlines the ways in which Job compels and consumes laborers, dismantling and subsuming their bodies, their voices, and their desires into its seemingly inexorable workings until "our bodies are no longer meat and bone of our parents, but substance of Job" (142). In *Christ in Concrete*, labor is an enduring state of struggle, a daily contest in which the laborer's body is twisted, contorted, deformed. Job wounds and splinters Paul's skeleton, stripping his nervous system bare: "His neck was split and yet connected. . . . He rolled over on his side, his lower back shooting fire all over him and screaming of a spine of broken cords connected by a thread that would sever any second" (82–83). In another scene, "His back . . . broke and seemed to come apart. The bending point severed and became a gap connected with trickling, shocking electrical flashes" (143). Near the end of his first week of work, Paul's young body begins to disintegrate under the strain of Job's relentless pressure: "He thought he could convince his body to accept his duty, but now everything within had broken apart and was trickling away" (93). In these passages, Paul's corporeal integrity dissolves as the pain of labor transfigures him into a monster—an industrial cyborg, a bundle of "broken cords," "split" and "severed" components, linked by "shooting fire" and "shocking electrical flashes." As elsewhere, the form of di Donato's experimental prose underscores the thematic thrust of the text: snapshots and violent images strung together by loose syntactical connections and conjunctions, di Donato's writing echoes the physical fractures caused by the backbreaking labor.

Although Job is a dominant, coercive force, workers' relationships with their labor are not one-sided or uniformly negative. Job not only crushes, but paradoxically sustains and empowers the bricklayers: "Brick and mortar was to become for Paul as stuff he could eat, and the constant motion from brick pile and tub to wall was to become a motion that fed upon itself" (142). Job has a dual impact—it is a source not only of pain but pride, not only of impairment but empowerment. Labor is the process of worldbuilding, of transforming hope and desire into concrete reality: "It was an actual corner. It was real" (70), Paul thinks to himself, surveying his work. Although performed within the matrix of Job's coercive system, laying brick "thrilled him. It felt like one of his dreams where he had raced an incredible distance at terrific speed on a road that stretched beyond the earth" (142). Here, labor seems to offer, however temporarily, the possibility of transcendence, of stretching "beyond the earth." Paul "gloried in his body's labor" (169); work is an "Olympic contest" (177) that Paul finds "thrilling" (179). Within Job's repressive regime, then, the working body is not only fractured but also extended and empowered. Bricklaying is skilled work and di Donato's novel displays a craftsman's labor aesthetic.[4] Paul's "first fleshy sense of Job" (69) signifies not merely his entrance into the logic of capitalist production but also a sense of personal power: "Dabbing mortar on the head of another brick he laid it down and pressed it up against the end of the first brick and tapped it down into the soft mortar until it seemed level with the first brick; and then he did the same with four more bricks" (70). The experience is a revelation: "O God you have heard me—*I have laid brick!*" (70). For Paul, Job is both the brutalizing extraction of human energy—the "soul's sentence to stone" (143), "a brick labyrinth that would suck him in deeper and deeper" (142)—and a metric of personal power, a potentially revolutionary realization of spiritual and physical energy: "Paul was now bricklayer worker . . . welded to the hands whose vibrations could shatter the earth" (143).

The quotidian trials and triumphs of work are punctuated and contextualized by violent catastrophe; all the scenes of daily labor occur within the shadow cast by scenes of deadly accidents. As a whole, the novel is framed by two deaths: Geremio's death at the novel's beginning, which prefigures Nazone's death near the text's end. Paul gazes with "ghastly fascination" at Nazone's broken body, which resembles a shattered, bony melon:

> A brilliant red wet overalled pulp splotched over broken terra-cotta. . . .
> His head, split wholely through by a jagged terra-cotta fragment, was
> an exploded human fruit. His top skull was rolled outward, with the
> scalp, underlayers, and cartilage leafing from it, and his face halved
> exactly down the centerline of nose, with the left nostril suspended
> alone at the lip-end, curled out and facing the right nostril. . . . The cres-
> cent of his mouth and teeth was wide askew, and mingled over the sweat
> of his stubble were the marine contents of his blood and brains that
> spread as quivering livery vomit, glistening on the burning flesh a tenu-
> ous rainbowed flora of infinite wavering fibrins. . . . (218–19, last ellipsis
> in original)

This passage is remarkable for the tensions embedded in the prose. On the one hand, di Donato describes Nazone's burst body in lyrical turns, phrases and images that lend the scene a virtually inspirational quality. Di Donato narrates this moment of physical and epistemological collapse with remarkable prosaic mastery: in sharp contrast to the frenzied tone that characterizes much of di Donato's prose, this scene is rendered slowly, in painstaking detail. The narrative gaze lingers on each disfiguration, delineating them in highly aestheticized terms. The rhetoric of illumination ("brilliant," "glistening," "rainbowed") and of organic metaphors ("fruit," "flora," "pulp") lend the scene an ironic splendor and suggest the possibility of finding literary "beauty" or transcendence amidst the pain being described. On the other hand, however, the lyrical potential of the prose is undermined by its very excess. Nazone's physical being is here reduced to the base, organic materials of which it is composed—not only nostrils and lips, each separate from the "face" they join to create, but also "cartilage," "fibrins," "blood." Nazone's "body" has been destroyed, his physical integrity blasted into a kaleidoscope of fluids and tissues. This scene of exceeding violation—not only death but complete physical obliteration—reinforces Job's power to literally "unmake" the world, to reverse the process of human development.[5] Each detail of Nazone's fractured body reverberates in Paul's consciousness: "Every disfigurement of his godfather echoed in Paul with lightning flashes, shuddering and crushing him" (219). Di Donato's prose is stretched to the breaking point, loaded with such excessive detail that the sentences begin to unravel into a brand of experimental writing that suggests the absurdity of calmly rendering such a scene in romantic terms. As material production (the construction of a building) has become destruction (the death of a laborer), so literary production (the writing of coherent sentences) veers toward rhetorical dissolution (a surplus of horrific sights and textures that overwhelms the very language employed). The density of rhetorical figures, minute details, and abstract language ("a tenuous flora of infinite wavering fibrins") begins to collapse under its own weight, reinforcing the very bodily collapse the scene describes.

The scenes of violent industrial accidents and wounded working bodies that serve as the narrative's dramatic highpoints—Geremio's death beneath a collapsing building; Luigi's leg crushed by falling stone; Nazone's shattered corpus lying at the base of a scaffold—"embody" the novel's political and rhetorical critique. Politically, the bricklayers' torn limbs signify the workers' acute physical vulnerability and the indifference of capital to the well-being of the laborers who build the steel and stone monuments that give physical form to the triumph of corporate power. Rhetorically, the descriptions of bodily harm are the highpoints of the novel's lyricism. In contrast to the punctuationless stream-of-labor descriptions of work on Job, the depictions of Geremio's and Nazone's deaths by industrial accident are written in a more conventional syntactical structure and are marked by an almost mellifluous prose, rich in organic metaphors and florid descriptive terminology. However, the romantic qualities of the prose are pushed to the breaking point, creating a kind of gothic lyricism, a form of elegant description weighted with such excruciating attention to gory detail that the prosaic "beauty" turns obscenely sour, augmenting the reader's sense of horror and revulsion. The immense rhetorical twists and turns through which

Nazone's crushed body is described suggest the immense irony, or even impossibility, of an aesthetic rendering of bodily violence.

The novel's use of disfigured bodies as emblems of political critique suggests not only di Donato's Marxism but also the influence of Italian Catholicism. Although ethnicity informs several aspects of the text—its language, the scenes of fiesta and ritual—the most deep-seated element of ethnic culture in the novel is religion, which forms the grounds upon which Paul's generational narrative is told. For Paul's father, Geremio, the religious faith that forms the backbone of the family's ethnic identity provides the personal and spiritual power to persevere in the face of oppression. "Who am I to complain when the good Christ himself was crucified!" (4), Geremio announces after a hard day's work. Geremio's religious convictions provide resources for adjustment, methods and narratives from "outside" capitalism's ideologies for persisting within a capitalist economy. "[W]ith the help of God I'll see this job through" (5), Geremio reassures himself. For Paul, however, a logic of sacrifice based on deferred religious promises offers an insufficient narrative for dealing with Job's monstrosity. "I want justice here! I want happiness here! I want life here!" (23), he proclaims to his mother, denouncing the crucifix hanging on her wall.

But *Christ in Concrete* is not, as Paul's vehement condemnation of the crucifix might suggest, a wholesale rejection of Catholic-inflected values; rather, the novel recounts—and itself represents—a complicated refashioning of those values. In particular, di Donato's text affirms a central component of Catholic ideology, its materialism. Catholicism in general—and Italian Catholicism in particular—has long been condemned by Protestants for its emphasis on elaborate ritual and its use of material representations of divinity.[6] Di Donato described himself as a "sensualist" who "respond[ed] to the sensuality of the Holy Roman Catholic Church, its art, its music, its fragrances, its colors, its architecture, and so forth—which is purely Italian. We Italians are really essentially pagans and realists" (Von Huene-Greenberg 36). Responding to what historian Robert Orsi describes as the "graphic, material" (xvi) quality of Italian American Catholic worship, di Donato crafted a hybrid figure of revolutionary hope akin to the composite symbolic forms described by French critic and surrealist Georges Bataille. Writing shortly before the publication of *Christ in Concrete*, Bataille contended that in certain instances, the dispossessed have conjoined symbols of immense degeneracy and filth to symbols of purity and brilliance, creating "myths [that] associate social ignominy and the cadaverous degradation of the torture victim with divine splendor. In this way, religion assumes the total oppositional function manifested by contrary forces, which up to this point had been divided between the rich and the poor, with the one ground condemning the other to ruin" (127). Like the myths that Bataille describes, the novel's figure of "Christ in concrete" grounds "divine splendor"

in "cadaverous degradation," recasting Annunziata's longing for spiritual transcendence "in the next world" as Paul's cry for "justice" and "salvation now!"
(230). The novel's image of "Christ in concrete" constitutes a pagan, sensualist
transfiguration of the central Christian image of redemption. In di Donato's
recasting of this myth, salvation becomes a question of worldly, political justice;
through the figure of "Christ in concrete," the text turns Christianity's
metaphoric vehicle for transcendence into an allegory of material pain and a
demand for social equity. The challenge the text offers to its readers is to comprehend this blending, to understand that the contradictions of Paul's world
demand an alternative, hybrid epistemology, one that can recognize the
redemptive in the degraded, the demand for revolution in figures of revulsion.[7]

     In 1932, at the age of nineteen, Tillie Olsen began work on the
novel that would become *Yonnondio*. Unfinished and lost until the early 1970s,
when it was edited and finally published, the novel narrates the story of the Holbrooks, a working-class family searching to find a stable living during the
Depression. Over the course of the narrative, the Holbrooks migrate from a
Wyoming mining town to a South Dakota farm to the slums adjacent to a packing house in an unnamed midwestern city. The first third of the novel—in the
mining camp and on the farm—is narrated predominantly through the eyes of
Mazie Holbrook, age six. The latter section of the text, which recounts the Holbrooks' struggle to carve out a living in the packing house ghetto, is told primarily from the perspective of Mazie's mother, Anna, who, after being raped by
her husband, Jim, falls ill and nearly dies.

  Like *Christ in Concrete*, *Yonnondio*'s "monstrousness" refers to its resolutely
unorthodox formal character—its fusion of proletarian protest and modernist
experimentation—as well as to its use of images of bodily disfigurement as emblems of political critique and rhetorical innovation.[8] Like di Donato, Olsen
focuses on the contradictory forces coursing through the bodies of working-class
individuals. In Olsen's fiction, bodies are texts; as critic Mara Faulkner observes,
for poor people like the Holbrooks, who have been historically silenced and
culturally marginalized, "one must read the stories of lives transcribed on
bodies or miss them altogether" (134). In large part, these stories are tales of
terror. Consistently, the text insists on the power of industrial capitalism to cripple, wound, and exhaust the Holbooks and their neighbors, to drain their bodies of productive power and personal resources. Men are injured at work,
women by domestic abuse and rape as well as by labor, children by hunger and
neglect. Describing a mine accident early in the novel, the narrator emphasizes
the horrid impact of industrial violence on laboring bodies and counters the
potential for readers to transform such images of pain into objects of aesthetic
pleasure:

And could you not make a cameo of this and pin it to your aesthetic hearts? So sharp it is, so clear, so classic. The shattered dusk, the mountain of culm, the tipple; clean lines, bare beauty. . . .

Surely it is classic enough for you—the Greek marble of the women, the simple, flowing lines of sorrow, carved so rigid and eternal. Surely it is original enough—these grotesques, this thing with the foot missing, this gargoyle with half the face gone and the arm. In the war to live, the artist, Coal, sculpted them. It was his master hand that wrought the intricate mosaic on this face—splintered coal, inlaid with patches of skin and threads of rock. . . . And inside it carve the statement the company is already issuing. "Unavoidable catastrophe . . . (O shrink, super's nephew, fire boss that let the gas collect) . . . rushing equipment . . . bending every effort. . . ."

(*Dear Company. Your men are imprisoned in a tomb of hunger, of death wages . . . Please issue a statement; quick, or they start to batter through with the fists of strike, the pickax of revolution.*)

A cameo of this, then. Blood clot of the dying sunset and the hush. No sobs, no word spoken. Sorrow is tongueless. Apprehension tore it out long ago. (20–21)

This passage contains many of the formal and thematic elements that characterize the text's monstrous modernism. First, the passage is both didactic and experimental, employing techniques associated with both proletarian and modernist modes of narration. Like a classic proletarian novel, the scene delivers an explicit critique of industrial violence and corporate power, tracing the workers' injuries to the coal company's malignant neglect of dangerous working conditions. However, this social critique is presented in the prototypically modernist form of a montage, in which the narrator's voice is interspersed with excerpts from letters to and from the company. In a kind of Brechtian estrangement effect, the narrator interrupts the flow of the story, pausing to offer the audience an experimental metacommentary on the conditions under which the action is taking place. The form of the passage, like the text as a whole, represents a combination of conventionally distinct and discrete literary forms, what Fredric Jameson calls a "modal heterogeneity of narrative registers" (*Unconscious* 192). Furthermore, the passage critiques not only the literal violence inscripted on the bodies of the miners but also the representational violence inherent in what the text calls "classic" aesthetics. The passage suggests that the "classic" mode transforms a horridly mangled body—"this thing with the foot missing"—into "simple, flowing lines," reducing and recontaining the terror of the scene, transforming injury into art, turning "gargoyles" into "bare beauty." In addition, the "classic" extracts and abstracts the accident from its immediate temporal con-

text, rendering it "rigid and eternal," timeless rather than timely, thereby elim-
inating the event's political urgency.

In contrast to the "classic" rendering of the scene in static, eternal, rigid
terms, Olsen's rendition offers a far more "grotesque" view that, like Agee's image
of a "body torn out by the roots" and di Donato's image of Nazone's shattered
corpse, refuses to diminish the horror and the conflict of the situation. The dis-
figurements of the wounded body that the scene describes—"this gargoyle with
half the face gone and the arm"—are echoed in the experimental shape of the
passage: the "broken" quality of the text—the interlacing of textual fragments that
give the passage its montage effect—mirrors the "broken" quality of the damaged
body the passage describes. Like the wounded body, described as an "intricate
mosaic," the scene itself is an unresolved patchwork of elements (the letter to the
company, the company's public statement, the narrator's voice) that do not,
finally, cohere. *Yonnondio* is, as Christopher Wilson has suggested, a resolutely
anti-cathartic text, a work of art that refutes the tendency of classical aesthetics to
obtain ideological closure, to "fix" an event for all time, to turn political injustice
into "flowing lines of sorrow," offering emotional release and consolation.

As the cameo scene suggests, the novel's addresses to the reader are mani-
fold and varied. In five interpolations in the first half of the text, such as the
cameo scene, the narrator intervenes to provide pointed political commentary.[9]
At other moments, characters' inner thoughts are rendered in stream-of-
consciousness monologues, unmediated by a narrative voice. In one instance,
as Mazie flees the house after her mother's miscarriage, she is overwhelmed by
a stream of violent associations, memories of incidents and sights that run
together in a bizarre tangle: "Running, so much ugliness, the coarse hair, the
night bristling, the blood and the drunken breath and the blob of spit, something soft, mushy, pressed against her face, never the farm, even baby's cryin,
get away from me ya damn girl, the faint vapor of river, run, run, but it scares
you so, the shadows the lamp throws in the wind" (77–78). Here, Mazie's
thoughts flash before her like a disjointed roll of snapshots, an undigested montage of painful memories. A series of damaging, frightening events converge in
a flow of horrible associations—Anna's miscarriage, the "blob of spit" that grazes
Mazie's cheek as she falls in the street (69), the anxiety encoded in baby Bess's
cries, Will's harsh rejection of Mazie that crystallizes for the first time the gender difference between them ("get away from me ya damn girl"). The reader
here is positioned to act as a witness, challenged to decipher the unconnected
series of images, to actively participate in the construction of the meaning by
recollecting scenes that have preceded this moment.

Like *Christ in Concrete*, *Yonnondio* turns the traditional structure of modernism on its head, inverting high modernism's tendency toward social isolation and autonomy. Several critics have contended that modernist writers

typically "dislocated the primary site of subjectivity from the realms of politics
and everyday life to that of highly stylized literary works" (Miller 176), "bracket-
ing off the real social world" and imaginatively isolating themselves in an "imper-
meable space" (Eagleton 140) of psychological interiority. In contrast, *Yonnondio*
employs modernist techniques—stream-of-consciousness, sentence and narrative fragmentation, interior monologues, surrealist descriptions—to narrate precisely the material aspects of modern, industrial existence—the pain of physical
labor, the dirt of economic destitution, the determining power of economic structures—that modernists frequently sought to avoid. What makes the world Olsen
depicts "unreal" (58) is not the distance or isolation of individual consciousness
from the social realm, but its very embeddedness in the social world, the very vulnerability of individuals to social violation and harm. Like *Christ in Concrete*,
Yonnondio redeploys the experimental aesthetic techniques of high modernism
to explicitly political ends, using forms of narrative fragmentation to render social
contradictions of material inequality and oppression.[10]

   Yonnondio's modernism represents a language designed to render the
immense, deformative power of industrial capitalism—the "uneven rhythms"
that rack the "shoddy houses" of the poor, "jerking the skeleton children," as
"monster trucks shake by, streetcars plunge, machinery rasps and shrieks" (47).
These violent industrial rhythms reach a crescendo during the novel's last chapter, in which a steam pipe bursts in the meat-packing plant, scorching the workers, a catastrophe narrated through the minds of one of the laborers: "steamed
boiled broiled cooked *scalded*, I forgot *scalded*" (125). The scene of disaster, in
which boiling water and steam burn the assembly line butchers, is surreal ("Is it
a dream, is it delirium?" [125]), both terrible and disorienting: "When the door
to the hog room, always kept closed against the Casings stench, the Casings heat,
is flung open, the steam boils in so triumphantly, weds with the hog-vat vapors
to create such vast clouds, such condensation, the disembodied scalded figures
of horror (human? women?) seem disembodied flickering shadows gesturing
mutely back to whence they have fled" (125–26). If surrealism is an aesthetic that
evokes the unconscious and dream world to convey modernity's hidden meanings, *Yonnondio* offers what might be called an explicitly anti-capitalist surrealism, an artistic mode that employs the language of the subconscious to narrate
the insane workings of large-scale industry, in which production (of meat products) becomes destruction (of the workers' health and safety), in which human
bodies become "disembodied scalded figures of horror."

   Yonnondio proceeds by violence and interruption, by shock, catastrophe,
and pain, interspersed by brief moments of calm and pleasure. The novel's plot
is punctuated by episodes of violence: Jim's abuse of Anna and her subsequent
abuse of the children; Sheen McEvoy's attempt to throw Mazie into the mine;
Jim's rape of Anna and her ensuing miscarriage; the bursting of the steam pipe

in the factory where Jim works. Echoing the scenes of violence, disfigured bodies litter the text: "the hunchback" miner, Andy Kavertnick, "stretched and tense as a corpse" at the bottom of the mine shaft (5); the "skeletons of starved children" (6); the Holbrook children, bruised from beatings by Jim and Anna; McEvoy's "writhing" "jelly face," deformed by a mine explosion (11); the body of young Erina, who haunts the dump, with "bad bruises" and a "stump arm ending in a little knob" (120, 112); Anna's body, bloated, violated, and ill from pregnancy, rape, and miscarriage. More than a coherent, fluid narrative, the novel is a series of scenes or set-pieces, what the novel calls, at one point, "a frieze" (77), flashpoints of struggle and agony. Like Walter Benjamin's angel of history, the text seems to "progress" through the accumulation of debris. These piles of debris—the junk heaps that dominate the landscape of the packing house slum—become the resource ground for the children of the poor who sift through and redeem the neglected material ("Theses" 103). Likewise, the novel itself was pulled from the scrap heap, revived after forty years of abandonment, cobbled together from what Olsen describes as "odd tattered pages, lines in yellowed notebooks, scraps" (v). Like the voices of the poor, drowned out by the immense clamor of industrial production and omitted from the pages of official history, the novel itself was nearly lost forever, written in the early 1930s, but "long thought since destroyed or lost" (v). "Only fragments, rough drafts, outlines, scraps remain," Olsen states in a note at the end of the text, "to tell what might have been and never now will be" (135).[11]

A central aspect of the violence the text depicts is the power of the industrial environment to rob the Holbrooks of their capacity for verbal expression. In the cameo scene, the narrator asserts that the workers' "sorrow is tongueless," muted by "apprehension," the constant fear of death on the job. Elsewhere, the novel suggests that the capacity for articulation is limited by the material conditions of working-class life. "[T]he day at Cudahy's has thieved Pop's text. . . . And when Anna comes out, her apron front still wet from doing dishes, it is too late for texts" (110). The ability to compose and communicate, to form their experience into narrative, has been disrupted by the exhausting labor at the packing house and in the kitchen. The environment in which the Holbrooks live, dominated by the noise of mechanized production, drowns out the power of human speech: "far underneath" the industrial din "thinly quiver human voices—weeping and scolding and tired words that slip out in monosyllables and are as if never spoken" (47). Repeatedly, the text notes the discursive power of the industrial infrastructure, its capacity to produce texts, sounds, and voices that overpower the speech of those whose labor makes the factories and packing houses throb with noise. "That stench [from the packing house] is a reminder—a proclamation—*I rule here*. It speaks for the packing houses, heart of all that moves in these streets; gigantic heart—pumping over the artery of

viaducts the men and women who are the street's lifeblood . . . " (47–48, emphasis in original). The system of production is described as a body writ large—the
mine a throat, the packing house a heart. The architecture of production is also
a discursive power—the stench "speaks," proclaiming the dominance of the
packing house over the neighborhood, over the "voices" of the persons who live
in its shadow and labor in its midst. The interior of the packing house is marked
by thundering sounds, a harsh mechanical "music" that articulates a chilling
message: "Music by rasp crash screech knock steamhiss thud machinedrum.
Abandon self, all ye who enter here. Become component part, geared, meshed,
timed, controlled" (114). The noise and fury of the packing house drowns out
the voices of the persons who work inside it: "Clawing dinning jutting gnashing
noises, so overwhelming that only at a scream pitch can the human voice be
heard" (115).

Although the preponderance of bodily images in *Yonnondio* represent bodies wounded or incapacitated, the text does contain several glimpses of potentially redemptive or resistant bodies. If the bodies of the poor are objects of
capitalist subjugation, the source of exploitation from which corporations
extract profit as well as the surface on which the immense violence of industrial
production is inscribed, those same bodies, the novel suggests, also constitute
potential resources of hope and pleasure. The images of revolution the text contains, for example, are cast in corporeal terms: the "fists of strike" (21) that
threaten the mining company's indifference; the "day millions of fists clamped
in yours, and you could wipe out the whole thing" (64); "the day that hands will
find a way to speak this: hands" (79). These speaking hands, images of an impossibly corporeal language—a language that could, as Agee says, "embody"—are
echoed on the novel's final page, as baby Bess slams a jar lid on a table. Her
action, a sign of creativity and persistence amidst the squalor of the Holbrooks'
house and the heat of the 106-degree weather, constitutes a form of self-realizing
expression: "I can do. Bang! I did that. I can do. I!" (132). Likewise, when Anna
caresses Mazie as the two sit under a catalpa tree, the novel offers a utopian
image of the body's expressive potential. Anna's touch soothes the pain of physical and psychic harm, lending Mazie a renewed sense of security and selfhood.
"The fingers stroked, spun a web, cocooned Mazie into happiness and intact-
ness and selfness. Soft wove the bliss round hurt and fear and want and shame—
the old worn fragile bliss, a new frail selfness bliss, healing, transforming" (102).
Not only Mazie, but Anna is transformed: "Mazie felt the strange happiness in
her mother's body" (101). The text suggests that this restorative mother-
daughter touch is an alternative mode of expression that counters the power of
the factory and the city to stifle verbal communication. However, the healing
contact is disrupted when wind shifts, bringing the stench from the packing

house, a reminder of the economic conditions that dominate their lives. The scene of healing that Olsen depicts here is brief, but compelling, suggesting the presence of a transformative power residing within the bodies of modernity's victims.

Stripped of the capacity to create a consistent culture of resistance through speech, the Holbrooks and their neighbors produce the meaning of their lives in unusual, unorthodox ways, crafting an alternative world within the lacunae and interstices of capital's dominance. The children who live in the shadow of the packing house transform the local dump into a realm of imaginative creation, crafting improvised structures from the detritus of industrial production: "Children—already stratified as dummies in school, condemned as unfit for the worlds of learning, art, imagination, invention—plan, measure, figure, design, invent, construct, costume themselves, stage dramas"; "On the inexhaustible dump strange structures rise: lookout towers, sets, ships, tents, forts, lean-tos, clubhouses, cities and stores and train tracks, cabooses, pretend palaces" (103). Here, the novel delineates an alternative epistemology that requires an alternative mode of recognition to be adequately understood—the "creativity" and "intelligence" of these children can only be comprehended *outside* the conventional parameters of scholastic achievement and measurement. Their "strange structures" are allegories of the novel itself—a series of provisional forms and "designs" that fail to meet normative expectations of aesthetic integrity and wholeness.

Yonnondio's aesthetics of contingency and disfigurement strike a noted contrast to the dominant epistemological tendencies of high modernism. In his narrative of the "lost generation," Malcolm Cowley contends that the goal of modern art was to transform conditions of squalor into monuments of aesthetic perfection, to transcend the sordid, oppressive density of material life. He writes: "And although our lives might be dingy and cluttered, they had one privilege: to write a poem in which all was but order and beauty, a poem rising like a clean tower above the tin cans and broken dishes of their days" (101–102). In sharp contrast to the phallic "tower" of literary transcendence that Cowley offers as the apotheosis of modernism, *Yonnondio* offers a modernism built out of "broken dishes"—a modernism of discarded objects, neglected people, wounded bodies. Early in the novel, the narrator surveys the packing house landscape and sees what we can read as an allegory of Olsen's own aesthetic. "Yes, it is here that Jim and Anna Holbrook have come to live. . . . Over the cobbled streets . . . past the human dumpheap where the nameless FrankLloydWrights of the proletariat have wrought their wondrous futuristic structures of flat battered tin cans, fruit boxes and gunny sacks, cardboard and mother earth" (48). Like the twisted structures patched together from the refuse of industrial society by these neglected working-class architects, the novel's own modernism is unorthodox and provisional, a testament of perseverance and hope forged from images of poverty, disintegration, and decay.

The images of disfigurement that di Donato and Olsen place at the center of their novels constitute what critic Patricia Yaeger calls "figures of condensation" (26), literary emblems that contain multiple meanings. On one level, the images of corporeal disfiguration—Nazone's shattered corpse, workers scalded by steam, Anna bruised by Jim's beating—signify the material and epistemological violence inflicted on working and working-class bodies. These figures are monsters of the everyday, images designed to denaturalize the quotidian routines and regimes of proletarian oppression—of unsafe industrial labor, and for Olsen, of the domestic sphere, which her novel suggests is not "private," but in fact highly permeable by "public" forces. Similar to the grotesque bodies of southern women's writing that Yaeger analyzes, these "highly embroidered bodies," rendered in language that blends highly abstract and immensely concrete images, represent literary attempts to render the ordinary "terrorism that is both surrealistic and all too real" (Yaeger 237). On another level, the images of disfigurement provide an allegory of the texts' own formal compressions, combinations, and experimentations. The fractures of the bodies maimed by machinery and eviscerated by strain echo the stylistic ruptures that crisscross these texts, which combine diverse literary modes in ways that compromise the integrity of each individual form. Mixing naturalist emphases on oppressive social forces with proletarian insistence on the politics of class and labor with avant-garde techniques of rhetorical innovation, these two novels represent monstrous incarnations of modernism that deploy experimental formal techniques to narrate the material contradictions of history that high modernism typically seeks to transcend. By focusing on the disfigured body as a multivalent metaphor, we can see the formal heterogeneity of working-class literature—its ability to negotiate and combine narrative forms from diverse traditions—as well as the complexity of these writers' social critique, which emphasizes both the power of material forces to shape the lives of the poor as well as the often clandestine, provisional forms of hope and resistance crafted in the face of oppression.

NOTES

1. My sense of these texts' category-violating formal qualities and radical political preoccupations is indebted to Michael Denning's notion of the proletarian grotesque (see *The Cultural Front*, especially chapter 3). However, I have elected to use the term "monstrous" rather than "grotesque" to emphasize the especially horrific aspects of bodily disfigurement presented in these novels. The grotesque may be, as Kenneth Burke contends (and Denning after him), "revolutionary"; however, it is a relatively established and tra-

ditional category of aesthetic analysis. The monstrous, I hope, conveys the limits of the "aesthetic," of representation itself, to which these texts gesture. These novels, I argue, suggest the limitations of their own efforts to depict and delineate the world of their working-class characters—especially the horrific forms of harm and injury to which the impoverished and laboring figures in these texts are subject. The concept of monstrosity is meant to signify an element of atrocity and horror that extends beyond the weirdness of the grotesque. For more on monstrous aesthetics, see Cohen, which provides a provocative, if trans-historical, theory of cultural monsters.

2. For more on Ware, see Fitzpatrick.

3. On modernism as the breaking of realist codes, see Eysteinsson.

4. The novel's ethos of labor, in which work is conceived as a realm of self-expression and self-sufficiency as well as a medium of exploitation, represents a particular reworking of Catholic ideologies of labor value prevalent in many ethnic American communities during the 1930s. Although not nearly as radical as various forms of socialism advocated by left-wing labor advocates during the decade, the Church's doctrine explicitly condemned capitalist greed and exploitation and praised the social and moral value of labor. See Gerstle, 247–59.

5. On labor as the making and unmaking of the world, see Scarry, esp. chapter 4.

6. In his history of Italian American devotion to la Madonna del Carmine—which culminated in an annual procession of the statue of the Holy Mother through the streets of Italian Harlem—Robert Orsi highlights the deeply material way in which the community represented its faith, the "sensuous, graphic" quality of the people's piety (*Madonna* xxii). Blessings and prayers were offered to the Virgin in material form— money, candles, jewels, and most relevant to *Christ in Concrete*, wax body parts. Orsi notes that booths were set up on the sidewalks the day of the procession, selling "wax replicas of internal human organs and . . . models of human limbs and heads" to be offered to the Virgin as signs of which part of the body a person needed to be healed (3). Until the late 1930s, the Madonna's altar would be piled high at each year's festival with wax body parts, melting in the heat of the abundant candles (10). The image of disintegrating body parts, offered as tokens of prayer and healing, resonates with di Donato's vivid, graphic description of the shattered bodies of Nazone and Geremio. Although the similarity is most likely unintentional, it suggests a link between di Donato's narrative and his Catholic heritage, between his monstrous modernism and his ethnic community, between concrete and Christ. If di Donato, like Paul, ultimately rejected Catholicism, he seems to have retained a sense of the particular materialism of his immigrant community's faith.

7. For more on strategies of "degradation" in proletarian literature, see Libretti. We should also note that the novel's uneasy combination of Marxist and Catholic-inflected tendencies is crystallized in the term "Job," which connotes a proletarian insistence on the determining power of labor through reference to the biblical tale of Job's suffering and redemption.

8. Several critics have mentioned, but not fully explored, *Yonnondio*'s modernist qualities. See, for example, Lauter. My argument about the novel's use of experimental language to articulate bodily sensation and injury is indebted to Paula Rabinowitz's

provocative and insightful reading of Olsen's text. According to Rabinowitz, the novel suggests that language use is generally different for working-class men and women. For men, it is largely abstract; for women—and for the text itself—language is "embodied," inextricably embedded within the body and its desires. "The bodies of mothers and daughters removed from the factory encode language," Rabinowitz asserts; "their experiences are constructed by learning to read and to interpret signs unspoken by their men, inscribed on men's hands" (133). *Yonnondio* implies that the body is not prior to or opposed to language, history and culture; rather, the body becomes in Olsen's novel the very medium through which language and power are filtered and acquire meaning.

9. For an astute reading of these narrative interventions—and of Olsen's strategies of textual "resistance" more broadly—see Coiner.

10. Modernist devices and strategies enabled many radical writers to challenge and rewrite hegemonic notions of "reality," placing emphasis on voices and perspectives that had been absent from the pages of "serious" American literature. On the intersection of modernism and radicalism see, for starters, Schoening; Denning; Dawahare; Browder.

11. For more on the implications of the text's recovery, see Christopher Wilson, "'Unlimn'd They Disappear': Recollecting *Yonnondio: From the Thirties.*"

The Objectivity of Nature in Josephine Herbst's *Rope of Gold*

CAREN IRR

Literature of the Great Depression of the 1930s has remained distinctive and important in American culture because it so powerfully illustrates the effects that economic change can have on a society. The severe economic downturn of 1929–1933 rattled and reorganized American social life — including the culture of literary intellectuals.[1] Although the causes of profound social change are often complex and obscure, in this period they appeared with great clarity. During the 1930s, objective conditions altered the substance and form of subjective life, and American novelists responded to this alteration.

Commonly, these objective economic conditions are represented through the shorthand of "the crash." To represent the drama of the crash, important novelists of the day often employed convention learned from the newsreels of the period; for instance, in the last Biography section of his monumental trilogy, *U.S.A.*, John Dos Passos anticipates the transition from the 1920s to the 1930s by introducing a chilling sketch of the unscrupulous financier Samuel Insull.[2] Such narratives identify the cause of social change with a single event (the crash), and they often leave the cause of that event unexplained. At most, they associate the cause with a small and untrustworthy element of the population (devious stockbrokers). With the establishment of the Securities and Exchange Commission, such narratives implicitly assure us, public scrutiny has contained and shamed unusually scheming profiteers. The economy is important in this sort of Depression-era narrative because it can be subjective. It is subject to biased and overly self-interested manipulations that should be prevented by a neutral form of regulatory supervision. In this kind of narrative, then, objective conditions are ideally disinterested and impersonal, while subjectivity is purest when left to its own devices outside the economic realm. In other words, famous American narratives of the Depression acknowledge the effect of objective conditions primarily in order to urge a more rigid separation of objective and subjective elements. For this reason, Depression-era novels often exaggerate either the objective style (as Dos Passos does in his imitations of journalism) or the subjective style (as John Steinbeck did so effectively in *The Grapes of Wrath*). Novelists used style to illuminate the consequences of what seemed to many observers during the 1930s a chaotic and dangerous reorganization of social life.

Not all writers of the period, however, were as convinced of the need to separate subject and object as were Dos Passos and Steinbeck. To understand how this problem in Depression-era literature was also approached differently, we need only look at some of the more politically radical writers of the decade. Fundamentally concerned with the deep and ongoing entanglement of subjective and objective processes, radical writers worked within the literary forms they inherited to convey what they saw as the essential character of social transformation. Famously, the proletarian novelists experimented with various means of communicating the past, present, and future of working-class consciousness as they thought it was taking shape during the period. Many of these writers depicted the social and emotional challenges involved in the organization and centralization of the labor movement, but they also described the life of homeless travelers, shop girls, and young lovers as well as the hopes of immigrants and aspiring writers.[3] For these radical writers, describing the Depression meant describing the emergence of a new way of looking at the world and a new way of treating its subjective elements. Although some of their contemporaries scoffed at the aesthetic results of proletarian novelists' efforts to capture the experience of dramatic social changes from the point of view of the working classes, these writers could not and did not thoughtlessly insert a new and isolated working-class subjectivity into the inherited genres of middle-class self-discovery. Instead, with varying degrees of success, they attempted to reinvent the basic relationships of the novel: the relations between hero and environment, author and reader, text and author. Ultimately, many of their efforts (although very different at the sentence level) were consistent with those of their high modernist contemporaries. Like modernists such as Ernest Hemingway and William Faulkner, the proletarian novelists often conveyed the causes of social change during the economic depression by emphasizing authorial perspective over other elements.[4] They paid special attention to the narrator's role in balancing objective and subjective elements within the genre of the realist novel, and ultimately they transformed that genre from within.

Of course, as mentioned above, the project of the proletarian novelists was not always well received. For example, in his analysis of so-called tendency or proletarian literature, Georg Lukács asserts

Our literature . . . does not always succeed, by a long chalk, in portraying what the class-conscious section of the proletariat wants and does,
from an understanding of the driving forces of the overall process, and
as representative of the great world-historical interests of the working
class, portraying this as a will and a deed that themselves arise dialectically from the same overall process and are indispensable moments of
this objective process of reality. In place of the portrayal of the subjective factor of revolutionary development, we find all too frequently a
merely subjective (because unportrayed) "desire" on the part of the
author: i.e., a "tendency."[5]

That is, instead of producing a more complex objectivity that re-enacts the
process by which people make the circumstances that make them, Lukács
points out that proletarian novelists frequently perpetuated habits of subjectivism that they had learned from earlier novelists. Too often, says Lukács, the
proletarian novelists ended up displacing all the action to a mystical terrain of
undefined longings. In such cases, the psychology of characterization remains
that inherited from nineteenth-century realists such as Charles Dickens—writers who often described characters at odds with their environment but unable
to act upon it. For Lukács, a better strategy is for novelists to reveal the desire
for change as both a "will" and a "deed." Lukács's ideal is for a novel to do two
things: stand outside objective conditions (in order to describe and understand
them) and reproduce the subjective experiences essential to social life (to show
how desires arise from and are indispensable to society). The accomplishment
of this double task is, for Lukács, the highest achievement of a socially conscious
writer, and this is an accomplishment that is often thought to be beyond the
reach of most American Depression-era writers. In fact, many accounts of twentieth-century fiction assume that Lukács's ideal version of social realism could
only produce narrow-minded, aesthetically displeasing, and tedious results.

    In this essay, however, I argue that in her expansive, pleasing, and engross-
ing 1939 novel *Rope of Gold* Josephine Herbst comes very close to fulfilling
Lukács's goals. Hers is not by any means the only work from the 1930s to do so;
it may not even be exceptional in this regard. My view is that we need not isolate Herbst from a crowd of lesser and more tendentious writers in order to recognize her achievements; rather, by foregrounding the problem of dialectical
objectivity in Depression-era novels as a group, I wish to suggest that radical
writers might share an approach to the objective/subjective question that is distinctive. Visible in varying degrees of thoroughness in various works, a radical
and dialectical objectivity treats the Depression not as the result of a single
event, triggered by unscrupulous and exceptional financiers (i.e., as a moral failing) but rather as a relatively fuller expression of long-term structural crisis, a

crisis prefigured by the farm problems of the 1920s, the standardization of industrial labor since the 1870s, the waves of proletarianization of the labor force accompanying the transitions into and out of merchant capitalism, and more broadly the project of imperial domination in the New World. For radical novelists such as Josephine Herbst, the Great Depression of the early 1930s was more concretely related to the structure of capitalism and more mysteriously and subjectively evanescent than it was for many other literary observers. Her novel is thus worth recovering and analyzing precisely because it exemplifies the distinctive and sophisticated world-historical vision of radical novelists concerned with the Depression of the 1930s.

I

When *Rope of Gold* appeared at the tail end of the Depression, its critical reception was mixed. Although all reviewers agreed it was the strongest volume of the trilogy it completed, they were divided in their assessments of its merits in relation to a broader field of literary accomplishment. Admirers claimed the novel's characters were "sensitively drawn," asserting that Herbst wrote "about them with a nervous intensity that carries its own compulsion," and that "she succeeds in suggesting very richly something of the inner life of her characters . . . convey[ing] a profound feeling of the pity and brevity of life, the pathos of experience, the mystery of time and memory."[6] Meanwhile, detractors objected to what they read as the novel's sociological qualities, citing Herbst's "mechanical joining" of individual drama and documentary, the "strange effect of newspaper headlines of four years telescoped into a book," and a fear that "the ambitious chronicler . . . is rapidly sinking under her load of sociology."[7] Typically, negative reviews attributed what they identified as the inadequate artistry of the novel to the author's excessively ideological commitment. That is, the division of opinion on the novel broke down along political lines, even though both sides agreed that a good novel ought to be "human" and involve rounded characters with the type of emotional depth and internal complexity typical of earlier realist writers. At the time of its first publication, Herbst's novel was either charged with insufficient depth or defended on the grounds that the historical context of the family epic constitutes depth. Since the novel, in effect, disappeared from literary history for the duration of the twentieth century, the former judgment seems to have predominated.

Since 1984, when the Feminist Press republished *Rope of Gold* as part of their excellent series "Novels of the Thirties," and with the benefit of Elinor Langer's passionate and engagingly readable biography of Herbst, the terms of critical reception have remained much the same. Although important biographical revelations (primarily to do with Herbst's same-sex relationships) have provided new explanations for the resistance to the exploration of subjective depth in Herbst's writings, most critical discussion of her work still accepts the premise that more subjective writing is better and that sociological objectivity indicates a failure of literary and perhaps also political imagination. If anything, feminist approaches have enhanced the emphasis on independent subjectivity in Herbst criticism by unveiling the nuanced and intimate relation between Herbst's own political and personal lives.[8] Despite the enormously significant effort to reconsider Herbst as a woman writer concerned positively with family life, romance, and the home, contemporary feminist critics have, like reviewers during the 1930s, persisted in isolating *Rope* and the Trexler trilogy from Herbst's earlier bohemian novels, while also considering them separately from her later novels and memoirs, as well as from her biography of Pennsylvania naturalists John and William Bartram, which she wrote toward the end of her publishing career.

By way of contrast, I argue that the objectivist features of Herbst's work are positively linked to her political project, and that *Rope of Gold* exhibits important continuities with the concerns of her other works (notably *New Green World*, the Bartram biography). Reading *Rope of Gold* with an eye on the role of nature in particular reveals a dialectical objectivity at work and, furthermore, heightens attention to the critique of property relations that structures the novel's political vision. Focused in part on the emergence (and blockage) of revolutionary subjectivity (in the persons of dissenting farmers, union organizers, and bohemian intellectuals), Josephine Herbst's *Rope of Gold* portrays these subjective "wills" also as "deeds" constrained by social relations organized around property in land. In this context, nature operates as (a) a nostalgic fantasy of a utopian space before property, (b) a dangerous threat to the exercise of revolutionary will, (c) a total and communal utopia of future relations, and (d) the stimulus for a negative critique of a desacralized world in which both action and imagination are required. These several conflicting representations of nature are necessary because it is by slowly shifting the themes and descriptive styles of the novel that Herbst reveals the emergence of a new objectivity.

II

Before outlining the several properties of nature in *Rope of Gold*, we should examine the ways that a dialectical objectivity is manifested in the tone, themes, and structure of this little-known novel.

Tonally, the novel is characterized by that affect that Russian filmmaker Aleksandr Sokurov has elegantly described in a film of the same title as "mournful indifference" (1987). The opening scene of the novel introduces Jonathan and Victoria Chance, the central characters. They are radical intellectuals and are more or less directly based on Herbst and her husband, John Herrmann:

> For the first time, the living room in his father's house seemed to Jonathan Chance small and stuffy. He remembered it as a sumptuous room with heavy brocaded curtains and chairs that stood in their places, year after year, waiting for company far more elegant than had yet appeared. Only a year and a half ago his mother's coffin had stood in front of the fireplace with the little alabaster urns on the mantel. Shoals of relatives had turned up, uncles and aunts unreconciled for years wept on each other's necks, and Jonathan had stood erect and unbending trying to erase the disapproval from his last memory of his mother's living face.[9]

Beginning, in other words, with a setting that recalls the passions and bonds of mourning as well as the pretensions of social ambition, the novel describes the radical intellectual in the process of his emergence from the middle class. Jonathan's negations — "trying to erase the disapproval" — require an indifference to the claims of family sentimentality, even though this oppositional coldness on his part is presented as, in part, a continuation of the indifference to actual social situations displayed by the room itself. Like Jonathan, the living room exhibits a form of sumptuous patience and refuses to acknowledge the family's desire for upward mobility, even though it is utterly dependent on this desire.

In addition to placing the radical intellectual subjectivity in and against the conditions that produced it, the narrative distance established at the novel's outset insistently disorients the reader's effort to create a supposedly natural and transparent psychic life. That is, instead of climbing into Jonathan's heart and empathizing with him, the narrator reports his impressions and memories and responses from somewhere in the range of five feet away. The narrator does not rhetorically recreate the full range of sensory and cognitive material from which "Jonathan" as a psychological pattern emerges. We as readers are not mired in his feelings; we follow them, tracking them, noting their logic without inhabiting or necessarily understanding them. Insofar as readers remain "with" the narrator (and there is little in the novel of the famous modernist unreliability to suggest that we should not), we hover in the vicinity of subjectivity, straining perhaps to enter the familiar terrain of identification, mourning perhaps our inability to succeed in that task, and ultimately experiencing in ourselves an enforced indifference to Jonathan, an attitude much resembling his own affect.

This refusal of the conventions of subjective identification has, of course, often been reviled. Most of Herbst's critics, as mentioned, objected to the lack of emotional depth much as contemporaries commented on the hollowness of

Dos Passos's protagonists and antagonists. Instead of treating this quality of Herbst's prose as a necessary failure or even as modernist generic miscegenation (transporting qualities of reportage over to the terrain of the literary), however, I would like to treat this effect as a specifically aesthetic quality in its own right. Though there is not space to do this fully here, we might—for instance—read this quality of "vicinity" as continuous with the officially objectivist poetics of some of Herbst's more celebrated contemporaries such as Louis Zukofsky or George Oppen.[10] Over the long haul of the novel, reporting and registering effects, treating the psychological event as an object not an experience, produces for the reader a critical exhaustion with "feeling," an exhaustion that ultimately allows social totalities to glimmer through the weakening screen of subjectivity.

This emergent objectivist tone reappears in the themes of Herbst's novel. Overall, her trilogy concerns interlocking generations and conflicts over inheritance. But, since we are concerned here only with the final volume, it is not so much the long waves of historical vision that matter for us as it is the distribution of inherited roles and problems among members of the same generation. In this respect, the proper distribution of property represents in the novel the presence of family history within the living generation. Conflicts over property thus replay the emergence of a new political objectivity from the subjective terrain of the family. For example, Jonathan's discomfort in his parents' parlor derives both from his siblings' reactions to his radical views of the plight of farmers and from his father's ownership of the house Jonathan and Victoria occupy. The division between an ownership predicated on care for the house (or, for the farmers or the land) and an ownership predicated on wealth and legal title recurs throughout the novel. Jonathan's father consistently uses control over property to reward familial fidelity and punish political deviation, while Jonathan and Victoria operate on an economy of need, distributing property and their limited funds to those they perceive as most deprived (sickly neighbors, Victoria's sister and unemployed husband).

Strains in this needs-based economic logic provide material for the second and more obviously subjective theme of the novel: romantic attachment. Testing the boundaries of sexual and emotional fidelity, Victoria and Jonathan ask themselves throughout the novel if they still belong to one another and what the consequences of being romantically unattached might be. Their romantic anxieties complement and offset the objectivist themes concerning property relations, although the two issues are never far apart. For example, Jonathan and Victoria's marriage (we learn several times) was required by his family, constrained by their dependence, as tenants, on Jonathan's father, and dissolved with difficulty in part because of their complicated stewardship of the house. Although Victoria (like Herbst herself) retains the use of the Bucks County house owned by her ex-father-in-law after the dissolution of her marriage, this quasi-proprietary status is a mixed blessing—requiring her further investment of labor, money, and love in a context that seems likely to impoverish her further on all fronts. Love, in other words, appears in *Rope of Gold* as both a will and a deed, a cause and an effect—reproducing the objective conditions that contain its subjective expression.

Structurally, *Rope of Gold* plays out the interrelation of the property and love themes across a range of relationships. Initially, Victoria and Jonathan's marriage directly correlates to the political plot. Their anxieties about one another, their trouble staying in love and staying together mirror the farmers' union and its difficulty forming and acting. When Victoria decides, midway through the novel, to contribute to the labor movement by moving to New York City and writing reportage, her plot line diverges from that of Jonathan, the Communist Party organizer. Each represents an alternative for intellectuals within politics.

The separation of the main characters' paths reflects their apparently incompatible family backgrounds. Jonathan's wealthier family (controlled by a domineering immigrant father and a profascist entrepreneurial brother-in-law) sketches a dangerous upward trajectory, while Victoria's optimistic wandering sister and her religious, hardworking husband move further west and further into economic decline. These two lineages thus offer opposing paths through the late Depression, although Herbst also integrates them to some extent to prevent readers from over-identifying with the political tendencies of particular subjective or familial positions. The fascist brother-in-law, for instance, presents ideologically charged descriptions of the aimless public ("It's just a bunch of sheep, following the winner. If we make the moves fast and win, they follow us" [420]), while Victoria's relatives idealize a local entrepreneur, ironically allowing themselves "Great Expectations . . . from their old friend the now important Banker" (172). Together, the mirror-image fantasies that each type of family has about the other complete Herbst's map of the Depression-era middle class.

At the edges of the middle class are two other complementary figures: the fiery working-class orator Steve Carson and the traumatized and declassed intellectual Lester Tolman. The former's narrative begins, like Victoria and Jonathan's, with family history, notably the cyclone that killed his mother and triggered in Steve a terrified longing for feminine comfort, a longing that influences his Wobbly father's courtship and later his own. Steve's involvement with urban industrial organizing and farm conditions, as well as his euphoric observation of brothers leaping into the struggle at the close of the novel, position him as the heroic version of Jonathan and Victoria's political commitment; he synthesizes their concerns and puts them into action. By contrast, Lester represents the dark side of Victoria and Jonathan's bohemianism; he repeatedly retells his experiences in Germany as the fascists took power, and dabbles aimlessly with a shallow actress who neither loves nor respects him. Initially associated more closely with Victoria (as a fellow journalist and traveler to Germany), in later portions of the novel his narrative converges with a disenchanted Jonathan. Where Steve unifies the main characters, Lester separates them.

At the close of the novel, then, Jonathan and Victoria's marriage no longer mirrors their political fortunes. The couple separates—leaving Jonathan isolated among the wealthy ladies, trapped by his own eloquence and forced to listen to "poetic" readings of Joyce's story "The Dead." Victoria, on the other hand, is (as I will explore further below) renewed with fresh and self-sufficient political vision. A drunken Lester enters a bar and, preoccupied with his own powerlessness, is aligned with Jonathan, while Victoria's plot line veers closer to that of the active Steve. The romantic couple dissolves, distributing itself across a structure of political options.

In the novel's afterword, Elinor Langer argues that this structural distribution—including the italicized intersections discussed below—suggests that the force of events described in the novel diverges from the subjective experience of them, thus saving the novel from an unearned revolutionary optimism.[11] Because I see the range of subjective expressions as being very broad, I reach a slightly different conclusion. As I see it, rather than substituting an objective truth of events for misguided subjective experience, *Rope of Gold* affirms structurally the dialectical objectivity that is also characteristic of its themes and tone.

III

If the dominant elements of the novel stall and situate subjectivism, then the subordinate elements activate and enliven the novel's objectivism. In particular, Nature operates in the novel as considerably more than a setting—that is, as more than the mechanical and abstract environment in which atomistic subjects move around, or onto which these subjects project their restless interiority. Yet, despite the novel's concern with farmers and urban/rural alliances, Nature rarely attains an active centrality for the narrative; it does not behave like a theme but rather, as a subordinate element, it enhances and expands the central concerns with momentary flashes. These accumulate and ultimately converge to form a sort of subrational nonsubjective other world in the final sections of the novel. Nature ultimately provides a utopian alternative in the novel, though a negative one that emerges only at the fringes of stalemated subjectivity.

Initially, it is Victoria and Jonathan's narrative line that most strongly employs the imagery of the natural world. Jonathan recalls his boyhood summer vacations when "he spent days in a sailboat knowing sun tan, wind drift and cloud formation, the shine of fish as they were lifted from the lake, the clear red eye of a fire burning on sand, the flash of a jackknife and the smell of resin as it hit the flame. One did not need to conquer or impress a world like that; it had only to be lived in" (20).

Similarly, Victoria remembers "the home of her childhood when she and her sister used to sit tranquilly on the front porch at evening time, breathing up the scents from the newly watered grass and listening to the singsong of the katydid that seemed to promise some dazzling happy future" (44). At other points, the sensual images of these two nostalgic idylls fuse, recalling the couple's happier days. For instance, in a passage anticipating Victoria's solo journey to Havana, she revisits a memory of sitting with her husband, "looking across that dark expanse of water toward Cuba, watching the tiny lights of ships passing at sea and coming back through the silent moonlit streets when all the dogs would start up out of the glistening white coral dust to bark, and the moonflowers would give forth such an overpowering fragrance, they could not go to bed, but sat on the front porch watching the sky lighten, smelling the lime tree by their gate, and hearing the rustling of the palm as a breeze began to stir" (38).

The sights, sounds, and smells of flora and fauna introduce a soothing and hypnotic register to the novel in these early passages. As the narrative unfolds, however, such visions are more clearly marked as backward-looking fantasies. Increasingly, images of Victoria gardening alone supplant these inter-subjective sensual assimilations: Jonathan "was afraid there were tears in her eyes and remembered how she had looked planting their first garden, in her bare feet, with her hands in the earth as if they loved the very feel of the soil. What would she do in the city, where could she go?" (116). Victoria briefly recovers a sensual idyll when teaching her German student the English names of fish ("bonita, yellow tail, king fish, pomparo, wahoo, amberjack, grunt"), but these names are based on memories of trips taken with Jonathan, and the emphasis on words here invokes one of the worrisome sub-themes of the novel — intellectuals' tendency to substitute a fascination with words for involvement in experience itself (163).

At the other end of the tonal spectrum is Steve Carson's anxious, even terrified response to the dry midwestern plains. His narrative begins not with distant and pleasurable memories siphoned into the present but rather with a recapitulation of his farm family's ideas about the land as these change over time. "No digging up of sweet bones here," Steve's father stoically concluded, "the earth was full of worms" (96). Similarly, Steve's stepmother watched how "the land frayed out; it dried like a cut apple and shriveled up and they stared out on crops fizzling. The grasshoppers came . . . gumming up the radiators of the cars, stripping the foliage of the trees and vines like hail" (105). These ominous images prepare the way for Steve's account of the "gorgeous green and yellow of the field, the blue sky like a shiny platter . . . one of the last pictures he had to remember of the family before the cyclone came"; for Steve "the land . . . was so bright and luring and took so much" (130–31).

This dangerous and barely contained nature thus has an appeal as well as a threat, and as Steve's narrative progresses it acquires associations with passion and ambition—as he dances his pony "clear to the edge of the buttes looking down coolly into the boiling water, yellow and muddy and wild with rage" (136). Transcending and gathering up that natural fury leads Steve to the intense class-conscious sense of power evident in his—and the novel's—final pages: "'I'm a lucky man,' he thought, seeing his whole life spin out. . . . He thought of himself in the cyclone cellar and his mother's cold hand growing colder, then his father's voice with its indignation against the wrongs in the world" (428). Waking up in the early morning during an industrial sit-in, understanding his life as a whole and feeling himself fully a man ("A job belonged to a man, more than a wife or child or mother"), he finally looks out the window and completes the world from this point of view: "The fire outside had made a big black scar in the white snow. . . . The snow was white and crunchy the way it looked in the picture at home called "Snow Scene," only the world didn't look like that any more with a peaceful house resting on a hill and smoke like warm fur pouring from the chimney" (429). A tarnished, anti-sentimental world (is it even nature anymore?) forecasts in Steve's narrative a fearsome but lively future.

As the masculinist frame of Steve's vision suggests, the novel also offers a dialectical contradiction to this moment, pushing forward and totalizing even further the revolutionary zeal of the novel's close and the utopian sensuality of childhood memories. Using passages drawn from Herbst's reportage, the affective climax of the novel occurs in the mountains of Cuba, where Victoria interviews the sugarcane workers and arrives at a fully internationalist view of the farm crisis. From the painful tropical poverty of Havana ("Her eyes, shielded form the sun by the brim of her hat, saw the feet of the passersby, in good snappy shoes, in torn rope-soled sandals, bare and scarred" [335]), she proceeds to an analytical and economistic internationalism ("this was a feast of all nations. She had only to check on the railroads, the bank, the various sugar mills" [339])), until finally Victoria pictures the "giant trees, the sharp mountains, the ring of light and far below the circle of sugar mills that pressed covetously closer and closer to the Realango line" (361). Finally, the members of the secret union of sugar workers agree to take her to their mountain retreat: "Up and up they went, through virgin timber with vines as thick as huge snakes, and tall ferns strong as trees. A deathly hush was in the air. The low cry of some bird, now and then a flash of wings, was startling as the report of a gun. Strange flowers dripped from trees, and the sweet fresh smell of mosses was pungent as spice" (370).

Awakened to what seems to her this alien exotic nature, Victoria is no longer reviving subjective emotive memory. Instead, like Steve, on this ride she has a totalizing historical vision in the present: "All the lives of all the people she had known joggled and pressed as if they were beams of light and she would not have been surprised to see riding by her side a strange company of faces she had never seen" (371). The engorged fullness of the tropical jungle thus finds its match in an international and historical totality. Independent ownership of the land is the political slogan for this vision and it is shared by the workers at Realango as well as Victoria's own family and many others throughout the novel.

Vaguely sexualized and certainly mystical as this revolutionary *tropicalismo* is, it fades when Victoria re-enters the United States. Completing the logic, then, of nature as a lost property, a threat to security of inheritance, and a utopia of free communalism, is Victoria's independent and negative account of denatured nature. On her bus ride back north through Florida, she pledges to herself not to forget the men of Realango. She sees the roads and fields at this point as "solid ground" and observes that "the objects of the earth like sleepy animals were rising to their knees" (406). This is a less magical view, and its only real equivalent in the novel is the collective anonymous voice of the six italicized intersections.[12]

Geographically and temporally specific, these sections range over many of the famous leftist locations of the '30s—Harlan County, Barcelona, Washington, D.C., during the Hunger March, and Paris during the antifascist rallies. Perhaps the exception is a passage set in "Vineland, New Jersey, 1935." A work song crossed with a lullaby and, perhaps, an allusion to the controversial 1930s play *The Cradle Will Rock*, the passage concludes "sleep, sleep the cradle rocks, soon it's five and you'll have to get up. Beans, peas, asparagus, and cucumbers. The garden spot. The wondermaking garden. Shubbel, shubbel, keep movin'" (142). Turning underground the bounty of the wondermaking garden state, the workers experience the basic irony of the Depression: poverty amid plenty. That this irony is figured here by the destruction of farm produce and property is more than an impressionistic coincidence. Rather, here, as throughout the periphery and substructure of *Rope of Gold*, Herbst reminds her readers of the active unfolding of a world outside the ken of more severely alienated and narcissistically subjective consciousnesses, such as those figured by Jonathan and Lester in the later sections of the novel. The nature of the "garden spot" is, of course, not an uncultivated wilderness, nor a lush snake-filled Eden. It does not operate mechanistically and independently of human agents; it is interwound with human social and working life as well as human sustenance. In this sense, this image—the garden shoveled under—collects and coordinates all the preceding roles for nature, reproducing symbolically the processes of a dialectical objectivity in Herbst's imaginary. It is an effect and an action, invoking negatively the prospect of a past and future organized otherwise and bringing to mind the wasteful conditions that produce what is perhaps too subjectively called hunger.

IV

Nature, then, especially plant life, becomes in Josephine Herbst's *Rope of Gold* the sign of conditions resulting from human effort and forcing subjective reactions from the farmers, cane workers, labor organizers, and others alienated from the land. "Nature" is depicted as being in disarray because of property relations (shoveled under) while also creating persons who create (and are themselves disorganized by) economic crisis. Thus, in the novel, we find a counter-crash account of the Depression, an account emphasizing the long haul of the origins of this event and also its enduring consequences—with a special emphasis on the way those consequences are written into family life.

These concerns are, I assert, continuous with Herbst's iconoclastic approach to the economics of love and family in her pre-Depression writing. *Nothing Is Sacred* (1928), for instance, is a family drama organized around the adult children of an elderly petit-bourgeois couple located somewhere in the Midwest. Mrs. Winter (who has a greater narrative presence than her husband) has three daughters, all of whom are married. The novel sets the Winters's marriage against the marriages of their daughters. Mrs. Winter had experienced devoted love with her husband and, earlier, with another man. She is described as a strong woman who believed in romantic love, but her daughters do not inherit this faith. Julia, the eldest, married an unsatisfying banty of a man, who plunges the family into debt in his efforts to gain her attention. Because she has little respect for him, she cheats on him repeatedly, which only exacerbates his behavior. Hazel, the second, married a good, churchy man who bores her; but rather than cheat on her husband, she adopts the airs of a put-upon childless self-sacrificer. Hilda, the youngest, married quickly and for love, but her husband is not ambitious and he scorns respectability, including fidelity to his wife. Like Jonathan in *Rope of Gold*, he causes his wife much heartache, and she does not feel secure with him.

Written shortly after Herbst returned to the East Coast after caring for her dying mother, *Nothing Is Sacred* is framed by two disasters—a debt crisis, and Mrs. Winter's illness and eventual death. Upon her death, the daughters burn her most treasured and hoarded possessions (children's clothes, a piano, love letters), the very objects they are struggling so hard to acquire for themselves. The portrait here is one of perpetual frustration: life is a longing for goods and persons that one hopes will satisfy, but never do in this novel. Death is a pointless, sad affair, leaving the survivors empty and alone. People are so full of anxiety and longing that they can barely speak, and they use commodities as a substitute for love in their relations with one another. This is a world full of fitful sentiments, and its social conventions are simply shams; there is no God, no future, no politics, no friends, no redeeming nature. Nothing is sacred, as the title says. It is an almost purely negative book. The author seems solely interested in exposing illusions and asserting that the standard reasons offered for perpetuating social formations such as the family are insufficient; such illusions are not effective even for people who believe in them. Although in the 1930s Herbst's writings were enlivened by her political commitment, the quality of negative critique articulated in her *Nothing Is Sacred* remains a distinctive and consistent feature.

Similarly, the last book Herbst published during her lifetime, *New Green World* (1954), develops elements of the critical theory of nature evident in microcosm in *Rope of Gold*. Exploring the world of Quaker naturalists John and William Bartram, *New Green World* opposes nature and progress to the ages of reason and romanticism, seeking harmony between social and natural concerns. The biography traces the relationship between father and son, offering delicate commentary on their social visions (for instance, in relation to the Native Americans) as well as enjoying the effects of Quaker plain speech and simplicity on their observations. Did Herbst turn to the eighteenth century and the Bartrams as part of a political retreat when the FBI was investigating her and when many of her former associates were rethinking their attachment to Stalinism, as some have suggested?[13] Perhaps, but in assessing Herbst's work overall it may be worth bearing in mind her own comments on historical memory: "We are not only what we are today but what we were yesterday and if you burn your immediate past there is nothing left but ashes," she wrote in the *Nation* in 1956.[14]

Taking seriously Herbst's assertion of a necessary continuity in one's concerns, then, I have focused in this essay on elements of her radical period that recur and appear even more centrally in her even less well-known works. Nature—especially an abundant plant life—is associated in Herbst's work with a radical and utopian objectivity, and it seems to me that one might find in her work as a whole the grounds not only for rethinking the Depression as a social event but also for narrating the origins of back-to-the-land movements in the 1960s and, later, eco-feminism. Novels of the 1930s, such as Herbst's, are beneficial to study not only for what they reveal about the complex and ideologically charged issues of that decade but also for the alternative trajectories of American radical movements that they sometimes suggestively prophesize.

NOTES

1. I attempt to demonstrate this point in the introduction to *The Suburb of Dissent: Cultural Politics in the United States and Canada during the 1930s*, 14–18.

2. John Dos Passos, *The Big Money*, 523–28.

3. In *Labor and Desire: Women's Revolutionary Fiction in Depression America*, Paula Rabinowitz discusses many of the variations on the worker novels of the period.

4. So argues Barbara Foley in *Radical Representations: Politics and Form in U.S. Proletarian Fiction, 1929–1941*, 87.

5. Georg Lukács, "'Tendency' or Partisanship?," 43.

6. Dorothy Van Doren, "Toward a Better America"; Rev. of *Rope of Gold*; Rebecca Pitts, "The Trexler Trilogy."

7. Edgar Johnson, "Three Proletarian Novels," 245; Fred T. Marsh, *Rope of Gold*; Philip Rahv, "A Variety of Fiction," 110.

8. Interesting feminist work on Herbst includes Angela Hubler, "Josephine Herbst's *The Starched Blue Sky of Spain and Other Memoirs*: Literary History 'In the Wide Margin of the Century'"; and Nora Ruth Roberts, "Radical Women Writers of the Thirties and the New Feminist Response." Hilton Kramer offered some pointed commentary earlier on feminist readers of Herbst's archival materials in "Who Was Josephine Herbst?"

9. *Rope of Gold*, 3. All further references to this work will appear in the body of the essay.

10. See, for example, Charles Tomlinson, "Objectivists: Zukofsky and Oppen, A Memoir."

11. Elinor Langer, "Afterword" to *Rope of Gold*.

12. Walter Rideout offers sensitive observations of the effect of the intersections on the novel's sense of time in his friendly essay "Forgotten Images of the Thirties: Josephine Herbst."

13. Winifred Farrant Bevilacqua, *Josephine Herbst*, 9, 73–77.

14. Cited in Elinor Langer's review of *Double Lives: Spies and Writers in the Secret Soviet War of Ideas* by Stephen Koch.

Agrarian Landscapes, the Depression, and Women's Progressive Fiction

JANET GALLIGANI CASEY

Any discussion of American agrarianism and Depression iconography must begin with *The Grapes of Wrath*, which manages to fuse the fundamentally conservative individualist values of the yeoman farmer with the ideal of collective, progressive action. Indeed, one might argue that the enormous success of Steinbeck's novel as an arbiter of Depression imagery largely stems from this very combination, through which radical social alternatives are intimated but orthodox (nationalist) characterization is reinforced. By the late 1930s, the farmer had long been established as the virtual embodiment of the American way, ensuring that the displacement of the Okies would carry a symbolic weight that could not be approached by parallel Depression narratives of urban impoverishment. And if the farmer epitomized Jeffersonian ideals of autonomy, nobility, virtue, and thrift, then his wife became the ground upon which such ideals were realized. Nowhere is this more powerfully clear than in Steinbeck's final scene, in which the young Rose of Sharon offers her breast and its milk as fortification for an emaciated man, thereby reframing the maternal body as a means of *ideological* propagation, making visible the female's assumed role as nourishment for a body politic that is inheritedly male.

To be sure, the history of American agrarianism would hardly suggest farm culture as a likely site for the assertion of truly subversive social ideals, never mind a radical theorization of women's bodies. In his romanticization of the Joads, Steinbeck was drawing upon an interlocking set of assumptions and images through which the open landscape, an agrarian (and highly gendered) social system, and the notion of "Americanness" had been compellingly conflated. Critical studies such as those of Henry Nash Smith, Leo Marx, and Annette Kolodny have illuminated the American myth-sets, including Manifest

Destiny, that both reflected and enabled this matrix; and Kolodny, especially, has shown how such symbolic patterns depended upon entrenched ideologies of masculinity and femininity. Not surprisingly, Steinbeck and other high-profile left-leaning intellectuals of the 1930s were no less likely to invoke these patterns than more conservative cultural commentators: for instance, Mike Gold, a Communist Party member and radical aesthetic theorist, famously called upon young writers to "Go Left!" and patterned his exhortation on well worn masculinist metaphors of westward expansion. Clearly, alignment with leftist political ideals did not prompt a correspondingly reflective consideration of the conservative values inherent in nostalgic invocations of the taming of the landscape—at least not for men.

Yet, a lesser known but insistent tradition of progressive agrarian novels by women in the 1920s and 1930s challenges these established iconic traditions. Novels by such writers as Ellen Glasgow, Edith Summers Kelley, Myra Page, Olive Tilford Dargan, Josephine Johnson, and even the popular Edna Ferber interrogate American agrarian clichés, often through images and metaphors of the female form that resist sentimental parallels—for instance, the parallel between the maternal body and the fulsomeness of the natural world. Collectively, these novels also force a reconsideration of ideas about work, notably by questioning the received schism, in Marxist thought as well as in the general culture, between production and reproduction. Indeed, the rich variety of ways in which these texts probe social, political, and epistemological cultural patterns reveals that the farm, rather than being a static cultural setting, offers rich opportunities for nuanced sociopolitical critiques—perhaps because rural life in the United States has resonated historically with both the prevalent spatial metaphors of a masculinist aesthetic imagination and the gendered ideologies of constructed space that shape the material lives of real women.

Before turning to two such novels—Edith Summers Kelley's *Weeds* (1923) and Josephine Johnson's *Now in November* (1934)—for closer analysis, it is important to situate these women writers within a reactionary set of agrarian-related social movements that flourished in the United States prior to World War II. The increasing urbanization of American society in the late nineteenth and early twentieth centuries, and attendant fears that traditional agrarian life would disappear, resulted in various attempts to revivify an agrarian ideal. Many such attempts fell under the umbrella of the rather loosely defined Country Life Movement—symbolically spearheaded by the Commission on Country Life convened by Theodore Roosevelt in 1908—which sought to improve rural standards of living and modernize images of the rural American family to reinforce both an "agrarian myth" (a complex of sentimental notions about the value of farm life) and "agrarian fundamentalism" (the assertion of the primacy of farming as the base of the larger economy [Bowers 35]). While the commission itself was not supported by Congress, which refused even to fund the printing and dissemination of its findings and recommendations, the Country Life Movement at large received a great deal of public attention in both the mainstream and agricultural presses, and through related agencies and events such as federal- and state-level Country Life Conferences sponsored by the American Country Life Association, an organization founded by some of the original members of Roosevelt's commission. While the movement's advocates generally supported technological advances designed to increase productivity for farmers, and thus might be said to be progressive, their most basic assumptions about rural life, including the notion that country living is socially and morally superior to urban alternatives, lent the movement a distinctly regressive cast. Country Life supporters argued that rural living, though perhaps less remuneratively satisfying than urban living, brings "intangible rewards" to those "more deeply sensitive to [non-capitalistic] values," and that "the farms and smaller towns and villages will remain the better places in which to live, to raise children and to do work that is particularly one's own" (Lord n.p.).[1]

Roosevelt's commission had identified specific rural problems in need of correction, citing such impediments to happy country life as poor roads, inferior educational opportunities, and lack of leadership. Significantly, the commission addressed directly the status of rural women, on whom "the burden of [rural] hardships falls more heavily . . . than on the farmer himself"; however, the commission took the position that the best way to improve women's conditions was not through a restructuring of the rigid gender roles inherent to farm society but through "a general elevation of country living"—the idea being that wide improvements in schools, health care, and the like would positively affect women (*Report* 104–05). (This position, notably, echoes that of the organized Left, which glossed over most woman-specific labor issues by arguing that women's lots would improve automatically as the result of better conditions for the working class as a whole [Shaffer 79–90]). Thus the Country Life Movement effectively reinforced traditional roles for women, specifically as "farmers' wives"—which, tellingly, provided the title of the single agricultural journal of the period pitched exclusively to women.[2] Indeed, objections to the lack of women on Roosevelt's commission led indirectly to the Smith-Lever Act of 1914 and the establishment of the USDA Extension Service (Fink 26–27), which provided education to rural women in such areas as canning and infant care via home demonstration agents; not surprisingly, some women decried these efforts as useless, since "[we were] raising babies and clothing them before those [extension] workers started to kindergarten."[3] Ultimately, then, most avenues of inquiry concerning the status or role of the farm woman failed to challenge in any significant way the normative, gendered division of labor in farm culture (which was even more intransigent than in the culture at large) and instead led back to a preestablished standard underscoring the rural woman's "natural" role as housewife. In 1920, Dan Wallace—editor of *The Farmer's Wife* from 1919 to 1935, son of one of the leaders of the Country Life Movement, and an influential arbiter of representations of rural American culture—stated the case without equivocation when he wrote in an editorial, "While a considerable portion of city women have given up their jobs as homemakers, preferring to live in one-room apartments to save work in order that they can follow the 'jazz' amusements of the city, [and] shirking responsibility at every turn, the farm women of America, God bless them! continue to live in the way that the normal wife and the normal mother should live."

Comments such as Wallace's appear to preclude, in more ways than one, the creation of progressive agrarian novels by women. Moreover, Kelley, Johnson, and their cohorts were no more likely to find philosophical comradeship within the literary arena, which harbored not only the Steinbecks and Golds, whose liberalism failed to transcend their reliance on masculinist agrarian paradigms, but also such conservative cultural critics as the Southern Agrarians. If anything, John Crowe Ransom, Allen Tate, and their colleagues were even more reactionary than other pro-farming contingents, arguing strenuously for a return to a specifically southern past(oral) that they conceived of as anti-progressive, anti-industrial, and even anti-American (given their alignment of "America" with urbanity, transience, and economic instability). While these critics appeared to undermine more typical masculinist valorizations of westward expansion, vilifying, for example, the "arrested adolescence" signified by an incessant desire to tame the landscape for the mere sake of adventure (Ransom), their characterization of the ideal farmer, whose more modest aspirations leave him time for contemplation, betrays their elitism, as does their generally racist discourse (*I'll Take My Stand*; cf. Karanikas 87–92).

These cultural contexts, resulting from generations of mythologized narratives and accumulated sentiment validating man's tilling of the soil as a pre-eminently American occupation, simultaneously ignore women (by placing the male farmer at the center of discussions about agrarian life) and depend upon them (through the use of spatial metaphors that draw on orthodox ideals of gender). Consequently, progressive agrarian novels by female writers in this period respond both to sociohistorical realities and artistic conventions, intervening in gender(ed) traditions that are both lived and imagined. Predictably, the landscape assumes enormous proportions in these novels, as it has vast material and psychic ramifications for the female characters whose lives unfold in it. Typically, for instance, these female protagonists spend their youths in a rural landscape that is symbolically open, playful, and evocative of both desire and promise, but the impingement of conventional domestic roles comes to reflect and enable the gender boundaries inherent in bourgeois social relations. The home becomes not simply the opposite of the "free," natural world but a defining psychosocial space that alters forever the perceived abandon of the outdoors. The result is a sustained stultification that is imagined as a search for both place and space, an acknowledgment that there is, literally, *nowhere to go*.

Edith Summers Kelley and Josephine Johnson, both of whom had strong ties to rural lifestyles and radical politics, are among those women who produced novels disrupting orthodox associations among desire, agency, women, and the land. A consideration of the means by which their works retheorize corporeality and essentialism in reference to women and the natural world contributes to established discussions of radicalism and the generative female body, as well as to the newly emerging discussion of women's agrarian writing and the reclamation of nature.[4]

Weeds

It is widely acknowledged that the agricultural depression in the U.S. preceded the so-called Great Depression by nine years (e.g., Walker 29–30; Fink 46), thus legitimizing as a Depression-era agrarian text Edith Summers Kelley's 1923 novel about impoverished Kentucky tobacco farmers. *Weeds* centers on Judith Pippinger Blackford, a disaffected tenant farmer's wife who is repeatedly thwarted in her efforts to transcend the strictures of her time and place. A financial failure, the book was out of print until 1972, and it was not until 1996 that the Feminist Press published an edition including as an appendix an originally excised chapter, "Billy's Birth," detailing Judith's first lying-in. Kelley's publishers in the early 1920s had apparently judged the chapter "exaggerated" (Kelley's word) and not sufficiently relevant to the story's Kentucky setting, thereby delineating the novel's chief audience as those seeking a realistic but nonetheless relatively tame regionalism.[5] Yet this rediscovered chapter, when considered in its intended position, constitutes a probing and original resistance on several fronts. It challenges virtually all received notions about maternity and domestic labor, responding both to previous literary constructions and "real-life" cultural perspectives, including those of Kelley's first husband, whose attitudes about women and childbearing lend a provocative biographical dimension to "Billy's Birth." It also destabilizes essentialist constructions of the natural world that have traditionally enabled symbolic alignments between women and nature.

It is hardly coincidental that Kelley spent her early twenties as the secretary of Upton Sinclair in the important period just after he published *The Jungle*. When that novel first appeared, Sinclair was widely admired for what was considered the first realistic presentation of a childbirth scene. At the time when

Kelley was most intimate with Sinclair, she was also briefly engaged to Sinclair Lewis; all three lived at Helicon Hall, the New Jersey commune established by Upton Sinclair in 1906 (destroyed by fire in 1907). The socially conscious, and even radical, sensibilities of Sinclair and Lewis, together with the specific instance of Sinclair's childbirth scene in *The Jungle*, certainly influenced Kelley's novel, as did her later experiences farming in Kentucky with her second husband, C. Fred Kelley. But also germane to Kelley's depiction of maternity in *Weeds*, and far less generally known, are the circumstances surrounding Kelley's own first childbirth in 1911, by which time she had married Alan Updegraff, yet another member of the Helicon Hall circle who was also an aspiring poet.

Though little is known about Kelley's brief marriage to Updegraff, his letters to her during her first lying-in have survived. They are condescending, melodramatic, and supremely self-indulgent, presenting almost a caricature of a man squeamish about his wife's labor, yet intimidated as well, and introspective enough to know it. Kelley had gone to Toronto—her birthplace—to have the baby, leaving Updegraff in New York to cogitate on his roles as lover, husband, and father; his lengthy missives to his wife discuss, among other things, his fear that their sex life will be changed; his preference for a boy (after hearing that the baby is a girl); his belief that his wife had "l[ain] awake and cr[ied] for [him]" during her travails; his expectation that motherhood might make her "unreasonable"; and, most tellingly, his apprehension that she will love the baby more than she loves him—all of this while admonishing her to "be a good girl," calling her "cherub" and other pet names, and frequently descending to babytalk. He occasionally ventures to ask after the physical aspects of the birth, while indulging in detailed descriptions of the debilitating hayfever that constantly interrupts his own work. Throughout these letters, Updegraff consistently refers to the baby as "that brat."[6]

Unfortunately, there is no extant record of Edith Summers Kelley's responses to these letters. (She and Updegraff eventually divorced.) Yet Updegraff's self-absorption suggests a fascinating biographical context for Kelley's representation of Judith's intense psychic solitude in "Billy's Birth," despite the physical presence of Judith's husband, Jerry. Although Jerry remains by her side, Judith is "quite cut off from all humankind" and is pointedly described as traveling through a "No Man's Desert of pain."[7] To be sure, Kelley asserted that she wrote "Billy's Birth" in response to her sense that the literary world had not produced "adequate" depictions of childbirth, which, she argued, should logically come from female writers (Goodman 361). While this statement invites comparison of her childbirth scene with Upton Sinclair's, it also implies that her own birthing experiences would have special relevance.

Two of Updegraff's preoccupations, reflective of general cultural perspectives, become especially pertinent to the childbearing sequence in *Weeds*. First,

Updegraff repeatedly invokes images of a mother besotted with love for her child. He imagines his wife "calling it 'baby'—how sickening!—and going into cute maternal raptures about its fingers and hair and disposition and toes and mouth, ad infin." Second, Updegraff argues that such intensity of maternal feeling is "natural" and expected, just as his own jealousy is also "instinctive" and therefore acceptable. The "nature" of femininity and masculinity cannot be reckoned with, Updegraff asserts, except through the "higher" act of "stand[ing] off and contemplating" such fundamental, and therefore inescapable, impulses.

These ideas are essential to the subsequent shaping of Kelley's provocative childbirth scene. Specifically, "Billy's Birth" is remarkable precisely for its insistence on the mother's birthing body as *un*natural, and for its refusal to consider maternity in any light other than that of *labor* in its strictest sense. An overlaying of metaphors suggests that Judith's harrowed body is brutally mechanistic on the one hand and subversively bestial on the other, leaving little room for conventional images of maternity as a triumph of both the mother's body and the body politic. In contrast to Updegraff, who stressed the special meaning of the terms *nature* and *labor* as they were normatively applied to women, Kelley seems bent in "Billy's Birth" on perverting these usages—or, more precisely, on affixing standard denotations of these words to the "special" contexts of women's lives. Thus birthing and raising babies becomes a *labor* no more promising, no more fulfilling, than the pointless round of planting and harvesting that circumscribes the poor farmer's existence. And the *nature* of women, specifically their assumed maternal nature, is no more fixed or predictable than the nature that repeatedly wreaks havoc with the crops.

Kelley refuses to idealize not only the domestic existence of the rural wife and mother but also the life of the farmer, especially the tenant farmer. She exposes the Jeffersonian ideal for the elitist paradigm that it is, showing that the tenant farmer, lacking ownership of the soil he works, can afford neither contemplation nor experimentation; at one point Jerry bursts into sobs of frustration over his continued inability to provide for his family, despite his year-round, backbreaking regimen in the fields and barn (226–27). Moreover, while Judith's misery is closely connected to her imposed—and bitterly resented—domestic role, Kelley is at pains to suggest that the specific context of rural life sharpens and particularizes Judith's sense of oppression. It has been asserted that the lives of farm women in the 1920s and 1930s were defined by their husbands' occupations to a greater extent than those in other professions (Hagood 5), and Kelley repeatedly shows how Judith and her neighbor, Hattie, bridle under the weight of expectations related both to the patriarchal structure of the farm community and to the specific tasks relegated to farm women (e.g., 144–45). This includes not only the general alignment of outdoor work with men and indoor work with women but also more specific divisions of labor: at one point Judith absolutely

refuses her apportioned task of cleaning a tub of pig guts after the men have
enjoyed the more satisfying job of butchering (236–37), and on other occasions
she insists that she be allowed to enjoy the pleasures, such as riding into town
for the horse sales, that are usually reserved for men (168). Kelley seems to be
suggesting first, that agrarian women's containment within domestic spaces is
especially acute, given that the rhythms of rural life are centered in the outdoors
generally; and second, that the relative lack of evolution in farming methods
over the generations (as opposed, say, to the huge changes in business and
industry) has resulted in a correspondingly extreme rigidification of sociosexual
roles in farm families, especially the poorest ones.

   In Judith, who is aligned from her earliest childhood with the open landscape—she is her father's best helpmate on the farm, "[in] harmony with natural things" (25)—Kelley creates a character who finds the domestic realm
especially confining, as she "dislike[s] the insides of houses" and is always "glad
to escape into the open where there [is] life, light, and motion" (116). But it is
in relation to Judith's maternity that Kelley poses her most provocative challenge
to women and agrarian ideals. Through Judith, Kelley not only refutes the widespread assumption that rural women were privileged, and deeply content, to
mother the nation's future farmers[8]; she also disrupts the trope of fecundity that
conventionally aligns women with the land. And Kelley's "lost" chapter, "Billy's
Birth," is essential to this dynamic.

   The first paragraph of "Billy's Birth" is devoted to Judith's extreme distaste
for her mother-in-law, "Aunt" Mary, who is likened to a "great cat that . . . purrs
by the domestic hearth and nurses its kittens tenderly and considers that the
world revolves around itself and its offspring, and spits and scratches at anyone
who approaches the kittens." Judith cannot refrain from "teasing" this "cat" by
periodically criticizing her husband, Jerry, in order to get a rise out of Aunt
Mary—who has come, portentously enough, to assist with Judith's lying-in.
Thus Aunt Mary represents nurturing as "natural" to female creatures, an end
and an ideal; her smug certainty about the laboring process contrasts with
Judith's fear, just as, immediately following the birth, her cooing over her new
grandchild will act as a foil for Judith's disinterest. Early on, as the birthing progresses, Aunt Mary goes about briskly preparing for Judith's confinement and
sagely advising her daughter-in-law not to "take on so" when the pains hit.
Above all, Aunt Mary's calm and meticulous performance of the household's
daily chores while Judith suffers with her first contractions frames Judith's childbearing as just another routine domestic task.

   Yet the protractedness of Judith's labor, and the narrative space that Kelley
devotes to it, suggest that it is extreme work indeed—even as Judith's body is
described in mechanical terms that link it to common industrial images. She is
repeatedly likened to a machine operating against its own desires or needs: the

birthing process turns her into a "steel and iron monster" that is "relentless and indomitable," and her contractions are like "the ever-recurring drive of some great piston" that grows "regular and incessant as clockwork." Perhaps most significantly, Jerry is frightened and awed by the exertions of his wife, and she appears to him to be "something superhuman, immense and overpowering," an instrument of "gigantic proportions." Her contractions turn her into an automaton with "no volition of her own," struggling "blindly . . . endlessly, endlessly, endlessly, without rest."

This metaphorical insistence on childbearing as work without agency is accompanied by an attention to the various connotations of *nature*, in terms both of sociobiological imperatives ("feminine nature") and of the natural world. Judith's confinement in "Billy's Birth" is doubly figurative, for the conjugal bedroom has become a scene of terror (the bed is described as a "grisly rack of torture") signifying the special constraints of female biology while also literally severing Judith from the natural world that has always provided her with respite: "These things [the dawn, the sounds of the animals waking, the freshness of the earth following the night's rain] in which Judith was wont to take delight were all as nothing to her now." Her distance from both the tranquil agrarian landscape as she has known it and from the sweet "feminine nature" that Jerry has come to expect is suggested by numerous references to her tortured, and distorted, brutishness. Jerry reflects that the guttural sounds she emits are not even those of an ordinary dog, but rather like the cries of "some wild, dog-like creature"; later he decides that a cow could not have endured her condition, and then is shocked by the implications of his comparison. Animals are no longer the friends and helpmates of Judith's youth on the farm, but usurpers of her body, as she is likened to "a tigress newly caged," "an angry wolf," a beast with a "fierce snarl."

Ironically, when the doctor arrives he announces that Judith's symptoms are "quite normal and *natural* so far" (my emphasis), and he exhorts Jerry to be patient, for "nature takes her own time." But Judith imagines that nature is not on her side at all, that in fact nature is her enemy: "Nature that from her childhood had led kindly and blandly through pleasant paths and had at last betrayed her, treacherously beguiling her into this desolate region, now sternly pointed her the one way out: the dread and cruel pass of Herculean struggle through tortures unspeakable." When the baby is finally born, this nest of metaphors relating (re)production to a nature made abhorrently unfamiliar is intricately rendered: "It was over, and the doctor triumphantly held out nature's reward for all the anguish: a little, bloody, groping, monkey-like object, that moved its arms and legs with a spasmodic, frog-like motion and uttered a sound that was not a cry nor a groan nor a grunt nor anything of the human nor even animal world, but more like the harsh grating of metal upon metal."

It is difficult to mistake here Kelley's emphasis on the *un*natural: on aberration, truncation, aversion. Even Jerry has a "shiver of revulsion" upon seeing the newborn child. And while the penultimate page of the chapter seems momentarily to suggest that Judith succumbs to more typically maternal emotions (after a brief recovery period she is indeed "captivated" by the baby), Kelley ends the scene on a pessimistic note. Jabez, an unattached old man of the neighborhood with whom Judith shares a peculiar sympathy, pronounces the childbirth unfortunate, as it means that Judith will become "cluttered up" with "babies in the kitchen" when she should, in his view, be out "over the hills a-stalkin' turkeys . . . or else jes' a-runnin' wild with the res' of the wild things" where she belongs. "Ah well," he tells her, "it's nater [sic]. It's nater, that must have her fun with all of us, like a cat that likes to have a nice long play with every mouse she ketches."[9]

The metaphor of the cat, of course, recalls the chapter's opening references to the maternal instincts of the catlike Aunt Mary, but Jabez's comments here suggest a significant twist. Judith's forced containment within biologically and socially determined female roles is seen as concordant with a manipulating, inconstant Nature that "plays" with humans in ways beyond their apprehensions, against their desires. (Perhaps not coincidentally, Jabez's comment echoes that of Alan Updegraff, who wrote to Kelley after their first child was born, "Natur [sic] has used the brat to change [you] into something I do not know."[10]) The excessiveness of Judith's maternal body, then, may be understood as an ironic extension of the harsh conditions—of heat, blight, flood, drought— affecting the land, showing that Nature's caprice is manifest through superabundance as well as deficiency. Similarly, Nature's restorative properties are also unpredictable and inconstant; Judith's "betrayal" by Nature during her lying-in does not so much suggest that the natural world is entirely exclusive to women's lives and concerns as that Nature's role as solace rather than avenger can be, at best, arbitrary.

Stacy Alaimo compellingly connects this thematic emphasis in "Billy's Birth" on the extremity of Judith's corporeality, and the involuntary work performed by her body, to the period's discourses about contraception (108–23). We might complicate that reading, however, by noting that the sheer space Kelley accords to Judith's labor process brackets the question of con(tra)ception for an extended fictional moment and instead underscores, as Jabez intimates, the connection between the female's loss of control over her laboring body and the vagaries of nature. Both nature and culture, it would seem, impose upon Judith's body[11]—yet ultimately Kelley works to dissociate a biological destiny over which Judith has little control from a social destiny that she can, indeed, challenge, evade, or perhaps even reject. Thus Alaimo's argument that the novel advocates "reproductive self-determination" may be complemented by an awareness of Judith's repudiation of *social* definitions of motherhood—a stance that may be, in the end, more deeply subversive.

Judith perceives children as not only "a torture to bear" but also "a daily fret and anxiety after they were born"; hence when she temporarily becomes "mistress of her own body" by denying her husband sex, she also plans to free herself from a "degradation and suffering" that she associates with motherhood rather than mere childbirth (299–300). While she eventually succumbs to Jerry's sexual demands and even bears him another child, her disavowal of traditional ideals of mothering behavior, and of motherhood as her identity, is relatively consistent throughout the novel, and is perhaps the more subversive precisely because it is *not* typically marked by crystallized moments of self-consciousness. Even a cursory reading of those scenes involving Judith and her children reveal her indifference to, and even cruelty toward, her offspring, and there are virtually no extended moments of tenderness between mother and children. Rather, Judith "slaps [the children] savagely," perceiving them as "greedy vampires working on her incessantly . . . never giving her a moment's peace, bent upon drinking her last drop of blood, tearing out her last shrieking nerve" (208). To Jerry's distress, she exhibits an unusual willingness from the very beginning to leave their first baby unsupervised (158), and on at least one occasion she completely abdicates her domestic responsibilities by walking away from house and children in the middle of the day (240). Moreover, her sense of her own "unnaturalness" is clearly connected not merely to her fear of pregnancy and childbirth but also to her distaste for the nurturing role of mother: "[W]hen the child was born it was only the beginning. She loathed the thought of having to bring up another baby. The women who liked caring for babies could call her unnatural if they liked. She wanted to be unnatural. She was glad she was unnatural. Their nature was not her nature and she was glad of it" (240).

Kelley seems determined to show that Judith's tribulations as a mother are largely *un*mitigated by the emotional attachments that are presumed to transform motherhood and domestic work from an affliction to a delight: while Judith acknowledges that she loves her children, she also wonders, in a disquieting moment of comparison with her sister, why she cannot, like Lizzie May, "serve them wholeheartedly, devotedly, joyfully." Unable to be, like other women, "a willing victim" to the children's constant demands, she longs for "the nostalgia of the fields and roads"—but the very formulation of this desire as nostalgic reiterates the newly uneasy relation to the natural world that is the apparent result of Judith's maternity. Indeed, during the long winter months of "captivity" with her children, she "forg[ets] the old nostalgia, forg[ets] even to look out of the window" (217). She can no longer extract joy freely from the landscape, but must make do with occasional moments when nature ceases to serve as a mockery of her state, and momentarily recalls to her the promises of her youth.

The restoration of "Billy's Birth," then, rearticulates Judith's relation to the natural world in terms that are closely bound up in her maternity. On the most obvious level, childbirthing initiates Judith fully into the domestic roles that sever her, experientially and symbolically, from the rhythms of the land that form the core of country life. If we understand her sensitivity to the natural world as genuine, a redeeming factor in a personality that her peers find otherwise suspect (e.g., 289–90), then the spatial and imaginative constraints imposed on her by domesticity are severe indeed. On a deeper level, however, Judith learns through the birthing process that nature is unreliable, inconstant, powerful in its beauty but also terrible in its vengeance. Whatever solace it offered before she became a mother is permanently unsettled in those hours of unwilling labor, when an alternative and deeply threatening landscape—a "No Man's Desert," a "sinister canyon"—unfolds before her, and when the (natural) product of her body "seems to the inexperienced eye a deformed abortion." Judith's connection to nature, therefore, becomes deeply ironic: through her maternity she is literally removed from the natural world, only to be reconnected symbolically in a startlingly subversive way. Just as nature itself cannot be reduced or contained, Judith cannot conform to social expectations—specifically, she cannot or will not take on the "natural" role of the nurturing mother.

The centrality of "Billy's Birth" to the novel's original design—intended as the twelfth of twenty-six chapters, it would have occurred, in terms of pagination, almost precisely at the novel's center—substantially revises our understanding of Kelley's major themes in *Weeds*, which emerges as more daring, and more complex in its treatment of Judith's relation to the natural world, than previously thought. (This is especially ironic given that Harcourt Brace originally cut the chapter on the grounds that Judith's labor was too typical to be of real interest.) A few observations will suffice to suggest how its restoration colors subsequent events in the novel. For one thing, Judith's affair with a traveling minister several years later acquires new dimensions of meaning in light of "Billy's Birth." Their trysts, which take place in an open meadow, at first seem to release Judith from domestic pressures and promise a return to innocence, signified not only by her sexual license but also by her reclamation of the landscape. (She and Jerry had engaged in sexual relations out-of-doors prior to their marriage.) Indeed, Alaimo points out that Judith's sexual pleasure at this point in the narrative seems displaced onto a natural world that "penetrate[s] Judith's being" and "sway[s] her like [a] master passion" (275; Alaimo 119). Yet it seems significant that Judith herself understands this heightened erotic state as a "dream" of which "the waking hour was at hand" (276). Somewhat surprisingly, Judith's more genuine synchronicity with Nature comes at the moment when she *breaks off* the affair, having chastised the minister for the abrupt affectation of conventional attitudes that have led him to call her a "scarlet woman":

> Now that she knew herself broad awake, she felt of a sudden glad, bold,
> and strong. A sense of freedom, of relief from some clinging burden that
> had grown clogged and foul, passed through her like a strong wind that
> scatters cobwebs and made her breath [sic] deep and lift her head high
> in the sunlight. Swinging the empty bucket with happy abandon, as a
> child its dinner pail, she strode with long, free steps across the pasture
> and along the ridge road, delighting in the sun and the sweet air, feel-
> ing clean, sound, and whole, her mind untroubled by regrets, unsullied
> by the slightest tinge of self-abasement.
>   . . . . [She] went on toward home walking like some primal savage
> woman. . . . (279)

The more significant displacement here, I would argue, is premised on Kelley's
revision of facile tropes of fecundity: the simplistic alignment of Judith's sexual
pleasure with a fulsome natural world is made transient, unreal, and is displaced
by a more complex vision in which Judith's sympathy with nature both enables
and reflects her momentary act of self-determination. But Kelley's refusal to
allow Judith to sustain this feeling of accord with the natural world points to Kelley's thoroughgoing critique of essentialist versions of both maternity and
nature. When Judith becomes pregnant with what can only be the minister's
child, her failed attempt to induce a miscarriage through wild horseback riding
reinforces her oblique relation to a natural world that apparently undermines,
as much as supports, her desires and needs. This extended scene, in which
Judith's galloping temporarily makes her "a girl again . . . happy and careless,"
nonetheless contributes powerfully to the sense that Judith's existence in nature
signifies nothing certain, nothing stable (282–85).

Similarly, when Judith finds herself unexpectedly pregnant by Jerry with yet
another child, she retreats to the countryside, which she greets "as an old lover
who has not lost his power to charm." But the diction here, too, suggests that
this power is ephemeral, or limited in its healing capacities—for instance, she
only "*half* forg[ets] the things that she had fled from" and feels "*almost* happy"
(emphasis mine). Indeed, at the height of Judith's pleasure in the landscape she
"cringes" at the thought of the baby within her, and "For a long time she sat
looking out over the winter landscape and seeing nothing" (240). Thus the connection between Judith's maternity (her conventional sexual "nature") and her
thwarted relation to the natural world is played upon again and again, disal-
lowing the potential role of communal earth mother that Judith's closeness to
the land might encourage in a more culturally orthodox text. Moreover, the
explosion of such stereotypes seems integral to Kelley's plan, for at one point the
narrator slyly tells us, "There is an idea existing in many minds that country folk

are mostly simple, natural, and spontaneous. . . . There is no more misleading fallacy" (152).

Among other things, "Billy's Birth" suggests that motherhood is but *pure* labor, an argument that seems consistent with Kelley's earliest philosophical leanings: at Helicon Hall, the job of childraising was shared by the community to free mothers for intellectual work.[12] At the same time, this chapter redirects the focus of *Weeds*, underscoring Kelley's radical revision of masculine conventions of the agrarian tradition. Kelley allows a "nonmaternal" female character who is nonetheless closely in tune with nature to play out the frustrations of that perceived opposition, exposing literary and cultural assumptions about "women's nature" and the natural world as psychosocial constructions that nevertheless impose powerful experiential boundaries. For Judith—who, as a child, was infamous for drawing derisive caricatures (25–27)—such boundaries constrain not just the body but the imagination as well.

Now in November

Before *The Grapes of Wrath* made Steinbeck a household name, helping him to clinch a subsequent Nobel Prize, Josephine Johnson had won the Pulitzer with another farm novel of the Depression, *Now in November* (1934). A compact, lyrical text about the Haldemarne family fighting the drought in Missouri, Johnson's novel faded from view relatively quickly, perhaps because its nonlinear style appears "feminine," and—a related point— because it focuses less on the economic and social forces affecting agrarian life than on the singular impressions of its female adolescent narrator. Indeed, the noted leftist critic Granville Hicks, while conceding that "isolated sentences" in the novel indicate (appropriate) leftist leanings, apparently castigated Johnson for writing a book that highlights individuals rather than the collective.[13] Thus while Johnson's novel may be read as a reframing of masculinist agrarian paradigms, it was nonetheless subject to parameters of progressivism conceived by a male critical establishment.

This is not to say that the reviews were generally unfavorable; on the contrary, more centrist critics raved about the novel's "subtly cadenced" prose (Rascoe) and its masterful depiction of "delicate and devious human emotions" (Walton). But as a progressive novelist, Johnson was most definitely working in a different vein from more overtly political writers. (She later tried her hand at a proletarian novel that failed.) Nancy Hoffmann sees *Now in November* as fusing "three usually distinct literary traditions: the autobiographical narrative of coming of age, the meditation on nature, and the novel of social protest" (267).

Johnson herself stressed her emphasis on nature as a central element of her life-long radicalism; in a brief biographical sketch written late in her life, she stated her belief that *The Inland Island* (1969) and *Circle of Seasons* (1974)—two late books that deal with ecological responsibility—were "the best and most enduring" of her works, and added that "only a <u>world</u> point of view that includes all of nature as well as human-kind will save us and our children's children for a life worth living. I believe in writing <u>green</u>."[14] It seems no accident that Johnson was also a painter of landscapes. As early as 1936, when she published *Now in November*, she was unusually attentive to class and gender paradigms as they are revealed in and extended through a community's relation to the natural world.

While not a member of an impoverished farming family herself (one journalist described her family's 110-acre farm as more of a "country estate"[15]), Johnson was nonetheless concerned with the plight of poorer farmers. In 1935 she traveled to Arkansas to research a lengthy and sympathetic article on the plight of sharecroppers following the organization of the Southern Tenant Farmers' Union; Johnson and the photographer accompanying her were arrested when they attempted to speak with Negroes, an episode that became part of her published piece ("Cotton"). An Associated Press release produced shortly after she won the Pulitzer Prize describes Johnson as "passionately interested in social justice" and notes that she "opposes the A.A.A. crop reduction policy," and a photograph with explanatory caption in the *St. Louis Post-Dispatch* pictures *papier maché* figures of a merchant, a consumer, and a farmer—all made by Johnson—"to enact a lesson on Co-operative stores."[16] Of course, her thirty-year marriage to Grant Cannon, longtime editor of the *Farm Quarterly*, also suggests Johnson's sustained interest in American agricultural issues.

Yet, while Johnson's first novel has been read from the very beginning within the context of other agrarian novels by U.S. women, it has also invited comparison with European models. A reader of the novel's first draft expressed a wish that Kerrin, the novel's most tragic character, was "less a Hardy heroine and more of an American,"[17] and Hoffmann aligns *Now in November* with a European tradition of girls' coming-of-age stories that includes works by Jane Austen and George Eliot. Such perspectives, however, threaten to obscure Johnson's acute sensitivity to specifically American agricultural contexts, to the ways that the presumed templates for girls' lives are rewritten in terms of Depression-era losses of both the farm (as sanctuary) and the marriage relation (as a means of security). Moreover, at least some readers have discerned in the text an effort to represent a specifically "American" landscape: one of Johnson's former professors at Washington University categorized *Now in November* as "the first truly imaginative interpretation of an American locale" ("Prof. Buchan"), and a biographer points out that Johnson's nature passages in the novel represent precisely the flora of the author's native Kirkwood, Missouri (Dawson 57).

To be sure, the careful delineation of nature in *Now in November* has captured much attention, especially insofar as Marget, its narrator and the middle Haldemarne daughter, perceives nature's circularity as pertaining somehow to herself: unlike her younger sister Merle, who "kept walking foot after foot down a straight path to some clear place," Marget's mind is forever "running a nest of rabbit-paths that twisted and turned and doubled on themselves" (13). Her lyricism is posited as a reflection of nature's organicism, and the narrative as a whole, which ends by circling back to its opening line ("Now in November I can see our years as a whole"), imitates the natural cycles that it also relates—even as Marget stresses that nature exists apart from the human experience, relentlessly carrying on, "enlarg[ing] without mutation" (69).

This antiteleological structure coupled with Marget's intense relation to the land invites discussions of "feminine" narrative strategies, although, as we shall see, Johnson goes beyond a conventional alignment of women with nature. For now, it is sufficient to note that the apparent suspension of temporality resulting from this narrative style—less a linear narration than a series of "fragmented memories" forming "pieces of a puzzle" (Hoffman 242)—effectively foregrounds the spatial dimension, highlighting the Haldemarnes' home as not only a precisely demarcated geographic place but also an acutely experienced cultural space. Since the Haldemarne daughters rarely leave their farm, and then only for brief but essential visits to neighboring farms, they know its spaces intimately (as evidenced by the precision of Marget's descriptions) and experience its culture as absolute and all-encompassing. The chores are incessant, Father's dictates are not to be questioned, and the general lack of diversion lends to isolated moments a visceral materiality, making "words and days and things . . . lie in the mind like stone" (9).

Moreover, this farm culture desperately attempts to continue on with traditional notions even as Johnson makes it clear that the culture itself is dying. Mr. Haldemarne refuses to let Kerrin, his oldest daughter, take on farm chores typically assigned to men (15), and Marget perceives that the family's interrelations, including her mother's constant acquiescence to her father, are premised on Mr. Haldemarne's belief that a "misty gulf" separates men and women (63), and that his daughters belong inside the house with their mother. This despite his desperate need for help on the land, which is revealed as less of a pastoral refuge than a repository of fear and grief. In the early pages of the novel Mrs. Haldemarne finds out that the farm, which "at least, she had thought, was unencumbered, and sanctuary though everything else was gone" (5), is mortgaged, initiating a repeated emphasis on the lack of security offered by farming, despite the assumption by others that "farmers have got stuff to eat anyway" (204; cf. 75). Marget is painfully aware of the family's economic tenuousness, and of the myriad ways in which the land might be lost: "a drouth or a too-wet year or even a year over-good when everyone else had too much to sell" (68). After visiting the decaying farm of the neighboring Rathmans, who had seemed relatively impervious to market fluctuations affecting other farmers but who have now come upon bad fortune, Marget wonders whether "there was peace or safety anywhere on the earth" (172). And her father cries out in exasperation, after his corn has brought a particularly low price, "God! don't they *want* a man to farm?" (224).

Like Edith Summers Kelley, Johnson stresses the inappropriateness of the Jeffersonian ideal to American farming realities in this period. As Dorothee Kocks points out, Johnson shows that the farm cannot be a democracy in miniature, for it does not guarantee the economic security on which solid citizenship depends; moreover, its primary social unit, the family, is inherently undemocratic (115). Marget specifically criticizes those who assess farm life from an external perspective, intimating that subsistence farmers lack the physical and psychological distance required to make the farm an abstraction:

> I could imagine a kind of awful fascination in the very continuousness of this drouth, a wry perfection in its slow murder of all things. We might have marveled and exclaimed and said there was never anything like it, never anything worse, and shaken our heads, recalling all other years in comparison with a kind of gloomy joy. But this was only for those to whom it was like a play, something to be forgotten as soon as it was over. For us there was no final and blessed curtain—unless it was death. This was too real. (113)

Even more important, Johnson depicts the tensions between policies of resistance, which, in theory, should be helpful to farmers in need, and the practical effects of such policies, which may serve to harm individuals. For instance, Grant, the hired man, is torn when Ramsey, a neighboring black sharecropper, is unable to pay his rent. Grant loans him the money, even though "To pay off [the white landowner] had seemed to Grant like throwing his money down in a sink or propping a wormed old shed with good new poles, but better at least than having the roof crash down on Ramsey's head. You couldn't stand by and do nothing just because you thought it was wrong for a man to be trapped that way" (100). Similarly, when Grant convinces Mr. Haldemarne to join other farmers in withholding their milk to protest the poor prices and possibly force them upward, Mr. Haldemarne asks, "What'll I do with a hundred gallons? . . . Can we eat milk? Read milk? Wear milk?" (129).

Thus Johnson depicts the Depression-era farm as a shaky enterprise indeed, threatened on the one hand by economic conditions that are beyond the grasp of the individual farmer, and on the other hand by social disruptions resulting from those conditions—notably a disruption of gender roles. These two issues come to a head in the person of Grant, whose hire is necessitated by Mr. Halde-marne's loss of his usual man, who has joined the roadwork crew in search of more money. But in the excitement over Grant's arrival Johnson also fore-grounds another material reality, namely the lack of approved social options that the recent exodus of eligible men presents for the Haldemarne daughters. Ker-rin and Marget, somewhat predictably, fall in love with Grant almost immedi-ately, but Grant prefers Merle, who will not have him; this concentration of misplaced feeling at once reifies a general sense of Depression-induced disin-tegration, and intensifies the novel's metaphoric commentary on how the nor-mative gender roles of farm culture are newly thwarted.

The novel's men, for instance, are clearly severed imagistically as well as materially from the expectations that the culture engenders. Mr. Haldemarne is in a superficial sense the classic independent tiller of the soil, tenaciously working the fields to support his brood, and "lov[ing] the land in a proud, owned way,—only because it was his, and for what it would mean to [his family]" (35). Yet he finds neither success nor even contentment in dominating the landscape and his household: he is bitter about his losses, joyless in his farming, and frus-trated by his lack of control over Kerrin, whose flaunting of all of the conven-tions of womanhood he finds deeply offensive. Perhaps most important is Marget's perception that her father, in sharp contrast to the romantic image of the American farmer, is profoundly insecure, forever striving "to keep things from making him seem ridiculous, and fearful of anything that might tip over his dignity, poor-balanced and easily overthrown" (91). Grant, who is kinder and more temperate than Mr. Haldemarne, is nonetheless equally incapable of tra-ditional forms of ascendancy in this agrarian culture, as his thwarted courtship of Merle mirrors his ineffectuality in organizing the local farmers. And Ramsey, when he can no longer maintain his tenancy, cuts through accumulated layers of symbol and myth by pointing out baldly that farming is no longer a way of life but a coldly economic enterprise: "'We ain't a farm if we can't pay up'" (156–57).

The women, too, fail to conform to type; it is especially significant that they are unable collectively to fulfill the "farmer's wife" paradigm. The kindly but ineffective Mrs. Haldemarne, for whom marriage is "a religion and long giving" (63), and whose subordinate position in the family has been challenged by Ker-rin and less openly by Marget (e.g., 15–16), dies in a fire that also destroys the land, suggesting that both the independent farm and its social matrices are being driven to extinction. None of the girls marries—not even Merle, the most domestic-minded, who rejects Grant for reasons unknown. Kerrin becomes more and more unbalanced as the novel progresses, increasingly aggressive in her pursuit of Grant and ultimately dying by her own hand. But it is Marget, whose narration focalizes the story and whose love for Grant is therefore most apparent to us, who is pivotal to the novel's revisioning of women's relations to marriage, procreation, and—by symbolic extension—the land. For Marget inadvertently undermines her own expressed desire for a typical courtship plot with herself as heroine, telling us, for instance, that there were many times when "the woods seemed all answer and healing and more than enough to live for" (68). In the end it is the land that sustains her, the land that gives her "courage somehow to face the mornings" (231), the land that is more fulfilling, and more enduring, than any lover.

Marget's touching and lyrical narrative, then, is a creative act that counterbalances presumably lost acts of (re)production. While her closeness to nature and her cyclical mode of recollection might appear stereotypically "feminine," Johnson destabilizes such trite associations by divorcing Marget from likely avenues of heterosexual love and its presumed maternity. (To some extent, the same is true of Merle, while Kerrin is presented as the truncated byproduct of a stiflingly sexist environment.) Despite her tenderness, her acute sensitivity, and her potential for creativity, Marget cannot be the sensual earth mother, the figure upon whom the farm's images of production and reproduction happily converge. Such a position depends, traditionally, on a corporeal act—not the act of mind and spirit that is signaled so forcefully by Marget's narration.

From the first page, it is clear that Marget is aware of how "shape and meaning" emerge through "looking down on things past"—that is, she perceives that her narrative *creates* as much as *relates* (3). Early on, she tells us, "Things were strange and unrelated and made no pattern that a person could trace easily" (4), and later still, certain questions are better left unanswered, for they "made the pattern of things more distorted than before" (62). The implied antidote to this confusion, of course, is the story itself, and the heightened performativity of Marget's storytelling lends her an agency that compensates for more constraining social and material realities. It is especially significant that her narrative, built upon an accretion of singular, fragmented moments, is entirely premised upon *loss*—of her mother, of the presumed security of the farm, and, most especially, of Grant. Hence this narrative, this creation, depends upon her *disengagement* from traditional agrarian and domestic roles and ideals.

The text's final paragraph appears to locate desire, promise, and even (re)birth in the land itself: "Love and the old faith are gone. Faith gone with Mother. Grant gone. But there is the need and the desire left, and out of these hills they may come again" (231). Yet it would be a mistake to read Marget here as mystifying the landscape, or as displacing conventional female roles onto an essentialized, eroticized natural world. On the contrary, Marget's refusal to sentimentalize nature has been a distinguishing aspect of both her personality and her narration, and forces us to understand these final comments as an effort to

find solace in a landscape that is nonetheless—like Judith Pippinger's—unpredictable in its healing properties. Indeed, Marget's vision of nature is even
harsher than Judith's, for she sees it as not merely threatening in its capricious-
ness but also thoroughly indifferent to human desire and endeavor: she asserts
that nature is "both treacherous and kind," always "inconstant, and would go its
own way as though we were never born" (8–9). The natural world cannot function as a projection of the human condition, or serve to justify social constructs,
for, despite its ability to provide occasional comfort, it is ultimately unsympathetic, relentless, offering peace only in "sparse moments of surrender, and
beauty in all its twisted forms, not pure, unadulterated, but mixed always with
sour potato-peelings or an August sun" (226). Nor can Marget function, in the
figurative (and feminine) sense, as a continuation of the world of nature, not
only because she is not a maternal figure but also because she is too much the
observer: her immersion in nature, marked by her descriptive detail and her
wonderfully creative natural metaphors ("We were the green peas, hard and
swollen" [59]), is nonetheless empirically based. For Marget, nature is an
entirely separate realm, to be admired and even feared but never controlled; if
she shares anything with the natural world, it is this detachment—the distance
that enables her narration.

Significantly, Marget discerns, and even stresses, the distinctions between
material realities and immaterial expectations, figurations, essentializations.
She seems intuitively aware of the gap between the physical and the metaphysical, observing, for instance, that words are inadequate and "pale" (35; cf.
145). And her desire for Grant, her longing to live out the scripted romance that
is the only sanctioned role for farm girls, collides with her acute awareness that
she is physically "plain—O God, so plain!" (56). Then, too, despite Marget's
aching for Grant, it is the straightforward Merle whom she admires—Merle,
who is secure enough to pass up Grant, who "did not fight half-heartedly with
faceless shadows, masked forms she was afraid to name, but knew things for what
they were and twisted them apart" (71). Marget's story, indeed, both performs
and explores this "twisting apart" of two realms: the romantic-mythic-symbolic
and the actual-realistic-material. Moreover, it seems clear that she finds the latter less constraining than the former: "It's a lie that the body is a prison! It's the
mind, I tell you!—always the cold, strong mind that's jailer."

While *Now in November* testifies to the material miseries fostered by the
Depression, it suggests that social and psychological constructs are even more
confining. Specifically, Marget resents the social mores that prevent her from
telling Grant that she is in love with him, prevent her from "do[ing] what Kerrin had done . . . touch[ing] [Grant] and get[ting] what sour comfort there'd be
in this" (206). Kerrin, the "mad" sister, and the one who challenged most openly
the dictates of her family, had made her feelings for Grant perfectly clear, and

Marget recognizes a certain bravery in Kerrin's apparent recklessness: "Poor crazy Kerrin! All that she did I wanted at times to do, but had more sense or less courage—I do not know which it was" (169). Instead of touching Grant—and going mad with thwarted desire, like Kerrin—Marget is compelled to narrate, and that compulsion marks her refutation of the approved roles for females in her culture. Perhaps just as importantly, it allows her to claim the landscape on her own terms, as neither its master nor its victim.

Sylvia Jenkins Cook has called *The Grapes of Wrath* "a sad elegy for an exhausted frontier" (174), suggesting that the westward trek of the Okies, in its reinvocation of American pastoral tropes (the regaining of the promised "garden"), somehow marked the passing of those tropes even as it reinvigorated them through its own existence as textual artifact. But the work of Edith Summers Kelley and Josephine Johnson, among other female agrarian writers, seems to have anticipated this commentary on the passing of traditional American farming culture—and to have done so in a more profoundly radical manner. Isolating the farm itself as a site steeped in assumptions about "American" values, and interrogating gendered ideals residing in and extending through the pastoral landscape, these writers expose the values that enable the idealization of Ma Joad and Rose of Sharon. That their texts remain less known than Steinbeck's only highlights the continued hegemony of the ideals they hoped to challenge.

NOTES

1. Lord is paraphrasing here the philosophy of Liberty Hyde Bailey, who was Cornell University's Dean of Agriculture at the time that Roosevelt appointed him to chair the Commission on Country Life. Bailey was a horticulturalist, a founder of the discipline of rural sociology, and one of the most well-known advocates of the Country Life movement.

2. *The Farmer's Wife*, published by the Webb Publishing Company (St. Paul, Minnesota) from 1906 to 1936, reached a circulation of over one million by 1930.

3. See "Is It a Joke To You?" This letter, appearing in the March 1932 edition of *The Farmer's Wife*, prompted a subsequent readers' forum on the relative merits of the Extension Service (May 1932).

4. Paula Rabinowitz's *Labor and Desire: Women's Revolutionary Fiction in Depression America* is the best known study of radical women writers and corporeality. More recently, Stacy Alaimo has written about how female agrarian writers "reclaim" nature as a "feminist space." In a similar vein, Nora Ruth Roberts argues that nature in women's radical texts becomes a neo-Marxist space wherein use-value triumphs over exchange-value. See Alaimo, *Undomesticated Ground: Recasting Nature as Feminist Space* and

Roberts, *Three Radical Women Writers: Class and Gender in Meridel Le Sueur, Tillie Olsen, and Josephine Herbst.*

5. For Kelley's comments concerning the excision, see Goodman 361. Alfred Harcourt wrote to Kelley that "the obstetrical incident . . . is what thousands of women go through, but—almost therefore—it is not peculiar to the story of Judith or the Tobacco country" (letter dated 6 April 1923, Selected Edith Summers Kelley Papers, Special Collections Research Center, Morris Library, Southern Illinois University at Carbondale [hereafter Kelley Papers]).

6. The eight letters from Updegraff, dated 1912, are in the Kelley Papers.

7. The excised scene, "Billy's Birth," is presented on pages 335–51 in the cited edition. Individual page references to this section are omitted.

8. For instance, *The Farmer's Wife* and the women's pages of men's agricultural journals paid constant tribute to the farm mother and idealized her role. "Creeds" for homemakers were a prominent feature; see, for example, "The Homemakers' Creed" (rpt. in Fink 110–11) and "The Home-maker's Compass."

9. Jabez plays a relatively minor role in the novel, but there is no question that his relation to Judith is crucial to our understanding of her character, as her response to his death—significantly, on the very last page of the text—suggests: "He had been the one real companion she had ever known. Now he was gone and she was alone. A weight like a great, cold stone settled itself upon her vitals; and as she gazed out over the darkening country it seemed to stretch endlessly, endlessly, like her future life, through a sad, dead level of unrelieved monotony" (333).

10. See the Updegraff letter headed "W.B., Sunday. [1912?]," opening with "Dear Edie" (Kelley Papers).

11. For an overview of traditional and contemporary considerations of the nature/culture divide, see Alaimo 1–23.

12. See Kelley's sketch, "Helicon Hall: An Experiment in Living" (Kelley Papers).

13. I have not been successful in locating Hicks's review, but it is summarized in a letter of 4 February 1935 to Johnson from Louis Birnbaum (Josephine Johnson Papers, Special Collections, Washington University, St. Louis, Missouri [hereafter Johnson Papers]).

14. Holograph biographical sketch, with typed version (Johnson Papers).

15. Clipping from the *St. Louis Dispatch*, 7 May 1935, n.p. (Johnson Papers).

16. AP release, dated 18 November (1934?), included in the Johnson file at the Mercantile Library, University of Missouri, St. Louis. ("A.A.A." refers to the Agricultural Adjustment Act, which was declared unconstitutional by the Supreme Court in January 1936.) The photo of Johnson's puppets is from an undated (November 1935?) newspaper clipping, located in the Johnson file at the St. Louis Public Library.

17. Letter from Clifton Fadiman (Simon & Schuster, Inc.) to Johnson, 6 February 1934 (Johnson Papers).

The Avengers of Christie Street

Racism and Jewish Working-Class
Rebellion in Mike Gold's
Jews Without Money

LEE BERNSTEIN

In 1933, Theodore Dreiser wrote to Hutchins Hapgood that "the Jew . . . has been in America all of two hundred years, and he has not faded into a pure American by any means, and he will not. As I said before, he maintains his religious dogmas and his racial sympathies, race characteristics, and race cohesion as against all the types or nationalities surrounding him wheresoever" (Hapgood 436).[1] Incensed by what he perceived as Dreiser's anti-Semitism, in 1935 Hapgood reprinted this correspondence in *The Nation*, with Dreiser's permission. Mike Gold, Jewish author of *Jews Without Money*, read these letters and voiced his outrage in the next issue of *New Masses*, the socialist weekly he edited:

> Theodore Dreiser, you will not assimilate the Jews to your 'pure' Americanism by force. And you cannot persuade four million people to leave the country where so many of them were born; it is too impractical. There are some ten million other Jews in the world, and if each country followed your plan, where is there a virgin land that could take care of fourteen or fifteen millions? They won't assimilate, they won't leave, and so what is the next step, Mr. Dreiser? Hitler has given one answer. As for the working-class Jew, the radical Jew, he has already been assimilated to a better America than the one you offer him, Dreiser: the America of the future, the America without capitalism and race hatred, socialist America! In the working-class movement there is no race problem; that is a problem made by capitalism. (Gold, "Gun" 229)

In the interchange between Hapgood and Dreiser—and in Gold's response to the goyim leftists arguing about Jewish assimilation, anti-Semitism, and Zionism—the making of a Jewish race was cross-cut with other social classifications, including nation, gender, and class. In voicing the inability for the "Jewish race" to assimilate into *any* form of European or Euro-American nationalism, Dreiser argued that Jewish racial identities have persisted while other racial identities changed. In pitting national identity against a subversive racial identity, Dreiser placed himself in opposition to the Internationalist discourse of Gold.[2] Significantly, he acknowledged the omni-national origins of the United States, but he saw Jewish people "against all the types or nationalities surrounding him." In order to "fade into a pure American," Jewish people needed to somehow lose their "racial characteristics." Agreeing with some Jewish Zionists of the period, Dreiser ultimately argued that Jewish people needed a state of their own.

Mike Gold latched on to Dreiser's use of "American" and responded with characteristic vehemence. In addition to imagining a socialist America free from capitalist exploitation or racism, Gold connected Zionism and Jewish identity to a history of colonialism (there is no virgin land), racism, and class oppression. Dreiser implied that national identity could not be multicultural and multiracial; Gold hoped to avoid these conflicts by focusing on class struggle. In hindsight, Gold's belief that "in the working-class movement there is no race problem; that is a problem made by capitalism" represents a misreading both of his political milieu and the way working-class social and political roles had been formed specifically in relation to race and gender differences throughout U.S. and Atlantic history. Given the vehemence with which Gold associated racism with capitalism, it is ironic that Gold's semi-autobiographical novel, *Jews Without Money*, provides an important case study in the way poor Jewish boys came to embrace socialist hopes for an egalitarian future via racial masquerade. In the novel, boyhood games like cowboys and Indians or cops and robbers are significant role-playing experiences. By moving between the roles of white colonizer and American Indian resister or white cop and African American robber, these boys show the options available to what some recent scholars have called "not-yet-white ethnics." By uncovering these connections, this essay seeks to explain, in the words of Toni Morrison, "the impact of racism on those who perpetuate it" (Morrison 11).

The characters Gold creates in *Jews Without Money* refute his later contention that racial oppression is merely a subset of class oppression. The boys, of course, cannot be expected to personify Gold's articulation of socialist politics. What they do show, however, are the ways that race and class, Jewishness and "Americanism," and outlaws and political radicals occupied much more complicated areas of resemblance and juxtaposition than the polarities that either Dreiser or Gold described. Gold was justifiably outraged by Dreiser's words, but his response belied the way he utilized a construction of working-class identity that always differentiated and played with racial boundaries. Similarly, while the roles of misogyny and sexuality were left unarticulated in the sword fight between Dreiser, Hapgood, and Gold, they played a crucial role in the formation of the working-class literary culture that Gold championed. In important ways, however, a language of race also shaped the oppositional consciousness of his characters. These not-yet-white ethnics were also not-yet-socialist political actors. In other words, to call his characters "racist" is not to imply that they identified with the white supremacy of the ruling class. Rather, as Rachel Rubin points out, racialized gangsters functioned as "ethnic heroes" during the Depression era: "They may have been the bad guys, and the law-abiding audience may have breathed a sigh of relief at their necessary downfall, but in the meantime, they were the ones giving orders, the ones who could take care of their own" (Rubin 85).

In combating Dreiser, Mike Gold sought solace from class exploitation while reflecting on "avenging" discourses from his childhood on New York's Lower East Side, the setting for *Jews Without Money*. Racial identities and racial masquerade—including anti-black racism, anti-Indian racism (cowboys and Indians), not to mention anti-Semitism—are at the center of his fictional autobiography about growing up in poverty on the Jewish Lower East Side at the turn of the century. The main characters in *Jews* are boys younger than twelve. They enact stereotypical notions of racialized behavior for their own enjoyment. However, this is more than just a game. These games construct oppositional standpoints whereby these poor immigrant boys can symbolically avenge anti-Semitism and class exploitation. It shows, as Ruth Frankenberg writes, that "racism shapes white people's lives and identities in a way that is inseparable from other facets of daily life" (Frankenberg 6).

The main character, also named Mike, worships his dear friend "Nigger." This pejorative nickname is assigned not because he is African American but because the boys feel he resembles a stereotypical African American man: "He was built for power like a tugboat, had the contemptuous glare of the criminal and genius. His nose had been squashed at birth, and with his black hair and murky face, made inevitable the East Side nickname: 'Nigger.' He was bold, tameless, untouchable, like a little gypsy. He was always in motion, planning mischief" (14). Gold can be blamed for reifying pathological stereotypes, but over time we learn that "Nigger" is a hero to the other boys. In ways that today's readers might associate with Norman Mailer's "White Negro" or the mass consumption by suburban young people of hard-edged music with criminal narratives, Gold's characters do not see the racism in their stereotypes of youthful rebellion. In fact, the nickname "Nigger" was relatively common—inevitable, according to the narrator—for darker-skinned Jewish criminals during the Depression. Perhaps best known was Harry Stromberg, a gangster known as "Nig Rosen." Rosen was a Russian-born and Lower East Side-reared gangster who came to dominate Philadelphia bootlegging in the early 1930s (Fox 72). But there was also New York's "Nigger Benny" Snyder and "Yoski Nigger" Toblinsky, Newark's "Niggy" Rutman, and Chicago's "Nigger" Goldberg (Rubin 157). In part, the nickname operated as a physical description, much like the good-natured "Happy" Maione, the homely "Pretty" Levine, or battle-tested "Scarface" Al Capone.

Gold makes clear that this nickname went beyond physical stereotypes. His mischief, contemptuous glare, and criminality also provide evidence for this nickname. While "Nigger" did not particularly object to his nickname, this represents just one of many racial and historical subversions that take place in the novel. It ultimately provides insight into the protagonist's triumphant embrace of radical politics at the close of the novel. Readers must constantly remind themselves that "Nigger" is an eastern European Jew like most of the other characters. It is only late in the novel that Gold tells readers that his parents call him "Abie." He is the leader of the "Gang of Little Yids" known as the "Young Avengers of Christie Street." The Young Avengers perform "Indian rituals," punch a teacher, harass Chinese shop-owners, Jewish prostitutes, and Irish police officers. Because virtually every aspect of Gold's characters' anti-establishment politics are shaped via these racial masquerades, it would be difficult to leave race behind once they—like "Mikey" at the close of the novel—embrace socialism.

First, the legal and racial transgressions associated with "Nigger" should be looked at particularly closely. Gold argued to Theodore Dreiser that his model of a messianic socialism would save the world from racism and class exploitation. However, a character constructed using the basest racist stereotypes served as Gold's John the Baptist. What was implied by these poor Jewish boys' decision to follow a Jewish boy named "Nigger"? How was his "blackness" represented? What significance does it take on in light of Gold's proletarian project? Nigger appears early in the first chapter and makes a strong first impression: "We spun tops on the sidewalks. We chased streetcars and trucks and stole dangerous rides. Nigger, our leader, taught us how to steal apples from a pushcart. We threw a dead cat into the store of the Chinese laundryman. He came out, a yellow madman, a hot flat-iron in his hand. We ran away. Nigger then suggested a new game: that we tease the prostitutes" (18).

When Mike's mother finds out, she admonishes and beats him, but not because of the cruelty with which he treated the Chinese shopkeeper: "This will teach you not to play with that Nigger! This will teach you not to learn all those bad, nasty things in the street!"(19). His mother uses the word as an epithet (that Nigger) rather than as a name, indicating that at least some of the Jews of the East Side were not awed by his appearance. While he is attractive and daring to the boys, he serves as a reminder to their parents that their own place in the racialized hierarchy remained unclear. Mike's parents clearly fit the often

repeated story of European immigrants who learn to be Americans by articulating the white supremacist assumptions pervasive in U.S. politics and culture.[3]
However, the racism of the parents and that of the children is not the same.
While Mike's mother clearly associates being black with crime and social
pathology, Mike and his playmates see being black as a source of knowledge and
social vindication. They embrace the reputed association of black masculinity
with crime, in spite of the evidence provided by the Jewish prostitutes in their
own neighborhood. They employ stereotypes of black masculinity in their
efforts to create a rebellious role for themselves. Michael Rogin argues that both
the fascination with stereotypical racialized "others" and immigrant racism
resulted from the lack of a clear racial category within the black/white binary
for Jewish immigrants in the early part of the twentieth century: "Facing nativist
pressure that would assign them to the dark side of the racial divide, immigrants
Americanized themselves by crossing and recrossing the racial line" (Rogin
1053). Rather than simply a case of rejecting U.S. racism, the boys idolize stereotypes that others—including their parents—demonize.

These characters and actions resist simple explanations. It would be tempt-
ing to say they are solely racist—learning to become American by learning to
be white supremacist. "Nigger" proves the premise of a variety of contemporary
scholars that immigrants from Europe took solace in "whiteness" in order to
carve out a place within the misogynist, racially polarized class structure they
entered. In addition, masculinity (and particularly stereotypical black masculinity) provided a language of power over women for these boys who seem to
have so little control over their circumstances. Alternatively, some might see the
boys as embracing the role of the dispossessed by resisting their parents' instruc-
tions in middle-class propriety. Gold's characters do not falsely identify with
those in power against their own interests. The boys were not racist and sexist
simply to solidify a common interest with white men who were exploiting them
across class lines. Rather, the self-conscious oppositional working class voices
could draw on racism and sexism in order to claim power within a social structure that often left them and their parents vulnerable to exploitation. In drawing attention to the self-identified "blackness" of these Jewish boys, the
characters articulate a shorthand way to understand class differences while fore-
shadowing the class revolt that never comes.

This stereotypical standard stands in sharp contrast to the one African American who does appear in Gold's novel: "Once my father fetched a Negro to sup-
per. My father beamed with pride. 'Katie, do not be frightened,' he said. 'This
black man is one of us. He is an African Jew. I met him in the synagogue. Imagine, he prays in Hebrew like the rest of us!'"(174). This unnamed man is ultra-
pious; he recites prayers after every course, kisses the mezuzah that hangs over
the door, and does the ritual washing of hands required of observant Jews before

a meal. The observation that "he prays in Hebrew like the rest of us" belies the lack of religiosity in the Gold household. Rather than a search for cross-racial religious communion, the father's praise of the African Jew could be read as evidence that Jewish Americans accepted the premise that white people should be afraid of black people. That Gold's mother need not be afraid of this African American makes clear that she should be afraid of other African Americans. There is something odd—and oddly attractive—that a black man can be "one of us." Of course, the turn to "blackness" for the Avengers of Christie Street was not a turn toward ultra-piety. The boys chose to ignore their only contact with a "real" African American Jew in favor of a stereotypical Jewish "nigger," who made them feel strong. Rather than African Americans being "one of us," the Avengers of Christie Street want to become "one of them."

The racial masquerade had clear and direct consequences on the Jewish working-class identities of the boys. Michael Rogin rhetorically asks, "Do cross-dressing immigrants buy freedom at the expense of the imprisonment of peoples of color? Or does that freedom itself look less like consent and more like the evasion of crimes, less like making a new self and more like endless disguise?" (Rogin 1072). The boys gain passing and individualized power by glorifying the association of being dark-skinned outlaws. They neither achieve nor intend to achieve assimilation into an undifferentiated "whiteness" through their racism. The working-class Jewish white boys do not identify with state power, nor are they on their way toward identifying with economic relationships that would exploit them just as they did their parents. Paradoxically, "blackness" takes on an oppositional meaning.[4] "Nigger's" "blackness" is used to avenge anti-Semitism and steal fruit from local peddlers, *not* to reify white supremacy. Rather than a route to assimilation, the racism of the boys more closely resembles Eric Lott's interpretation of nineteenth-century minstrelsy. Lott writes, "It was through 'blackness' that class was staged, and to some observers, at least, the combination could not have been more irksome" (Lott 64). Clearly, these boys know that their thefts can get them into trouble. By stealing and performing what Lott calls "blackness," they also ignore the hopes their parents hold for the upward racial, social, and economic mobility of their children. The oppositions created in their games are moves away from the immigrant identities of their parents, but not in the way their parents might hope. Instead of "whitening" their Jewish culture, these boys embrace their vision of black masculinity as a form of opposition to poverty and exploitation.

However, these resistances were circumscribed both by the larger context—one cannot overthrow capitalism by shoplifting—and by the racism and sexism of the resistance itself. The "freedom" offered by the Jewish "Nigger" was limited by a legal and economic order that sees male "blackness" as pathological, oversexed, and criminal. This belief was internalized by the East Side Jews and

stated in terms that reflected their rebellious interests, rather than those of capitalist interests. Their desire to break through the economic oppression that surrounded and permeated their lives rode on the shoulders of Nigger:

> Joey Cohen, a dreamy boy with spectacles, was brave. Stinker claimed
> to be brave, and Jake Gottlieb was brave, and Abie, Izzy, Fat, Maxie,
> Pishteppel, Harry, all were indubitably brave. We often boasted about
> our remarkable bravery to each other. But Nigger was bravest of the
> brave, the chieftain of our savage tribe. Nigger would fight boys twice
> his age, he would fight men and cops. He put his head down and tore
> in with flying arms, face bloody, eyes puffed to fighting, yet his father
> was a meek sick little tailor. (42)

While he is a Jewish boy by birth—the son of a meek tailor—"Nigger" stands
in opposition to that past even while he avenges the wrongs done to Jews on the
Lower East Side. "Nigger" clearly exemplifies (although in his permanent
"blackface") the two things Eric Lott attributed to blackface minstrelsy. First,
"Nigger" performs a set of class values in opposition to state power. Second, as
Lott writes of blackface minstrelsy, "what appears to have been appropriated
were certain kinds of masculinity. To put on the cultural forms of 'blackness'
was to engage in a complex affair of manly mimicry" (Lott 52). Through the performance of a stereotypical, racist construction of black masculinity, "Nigger"
is able to avenge the boys, who, as the narrator admonishes, "should have been
as brave." "Nigger" is valorized after hitting authority figures like teachers and
cops. He is worshipped after harassing other people whose class status is less
clear, like Chinese storekeepers and peddlers. "Nigger" stands up to the anti-
Semitic teacher who calls Mike a "Little Kike." Even before adolescence, "Nigger" clearly performs a kind of masculinity that values domination of opponents,
pride, daring, and sexual prowess. Stereotypes of black male sexuality in particular guided these preadolescent boys in understanding the Lower East Side,
including the neighborhood's red light district: "I remember another morning
in spring. I had always wanted to know what happened inside a whore's room,
when she went in with a 'customer.' That morning Nigger showed me" (25).

"Nigger," ultimately, is a contradictory figure. His offensive nickname
clearly draws on the worst stereotypes of black masculinity. He is a hyper-
sexual, criminally inclined boy seemingly devoid of any self-control. The nickname is a disparaging reminder that Depression-era fiction was informed by
criminological thinking that linked race and crime. In the response of Mike's
mother we see the desire for respectability that is often represented by a mother
or wife figure in Jewish American literature. In later characters in *Goodbye,
Columbus* or *Marjorie Morningstar*, the male protagonists respond to outside

pressures to conform to middle-class propriety with a rebellious desire to be romanticized individuals able to break free from the expectations of Cold War America (Prell). In Mike Gold's didactic tradition, middle-class respectability is not a goal. Gold utilizes a racist slur to champion a message of collective—if charismatic—struggle. The stereotype serves as the conduit for a white Jewish working-class performance of opposition. For the Avengers of Christie Street, racial masquerade forms their opposition to class exploitation and anti-Semitism.

The formation of a white, working-class, masculine opposition becomes still clearer when Gold slips from anti-black racism to anti-American Indian racism. In these passages, racism is most clearly seen as a form of retaliation against the conditions of poverty the boys played within. This retaliation is first enacted in terms of the U.S. position during the Revolutionary War. Early in the novel, the Avengers of Christie Street play U.S. colonists as they fight British soldiers and American Indians: "Nigger was a virile boy, the best pitcher, fighter and crapshooter in my gang. He was George Washington when our army anni-hilated the redcoats. He rode the mustangs, and shot the most buffalo among the tenements. He scalped Indians, and was our stern General in war" (37). In a similar episode, a local saloonkeeper, Jake Wolf, is revered by the Christie Street boys for his "expert" testimony on Indians: "He spent a year in the west, in Chicago, and saw the Indians. They looked like Jews, he said, but were not as smart or as brave. One Jew could kill a hundred Indians" (53). In both of these cases, the boys clearly feel superior to Americans Indians, despite their physical resemblance. This suggests that they identified with the colonists as both rebels and conquerors and that they hoped to join the fictionalized narrative of U.S. independence.[5]

Just as Jewish American and African American critics have noted the vari-ous alliances, conflicts, and distinctions between these groups, a growing num-ber of scholars are exploring the longstanding connections and conflicts between African American and American Indian groups and individuals. How-ever, little is written on the connections and conflicts between Jewish Ameri-can and American Indian groups or individuals. This is unfortunate, as the period of mass migration from eastern and southern Europe coincided with the imperial expansion of the United States into territory still under control of native peoples. As Philip J. Deloria points out, battles between the Lakotas, Comanches, Apaches, Miwoks, among others, and the United States followed the Civil War. The Dawes Allotment Act of 1887—which replaced extermina-tion with assimilation and individual land ownership as official U.S. policy— passed amid rapidly growing concern about the foreign tongues, alien religions, darker skin, and thicker features of eastern and southern Europeans entering northeastern cities. Rather than mere temporal coincidence, "the popular press," Deloria writes, "linked Indian people with the 'inferior' east and south European immigrants peopling the urban slums and low-wage factories"(Deloria 104).

During this period of forced assimilation and coerced allotment, many white Americans turned to their ideas of "Indian" dress and cultures as antidotes to the increasing alienation and rootlessness often associated with modernity. Elite whites set up summer camps with American Indian or "Indian"-sounding names where they could act out their visions of "primitive" traditions (Deloria 102). This practice mirrored earlier eras of white hostility toward American Indians. In the early to middle nineteenth century, for example, there was a sense of nostalgia in James Fenimore Cooper's *The Last of the Mohicans* (1826) and Henry Wadsworth Longfellow's "The Song of Hiawatha" (1855). The bloodthirsty demons of the previous century, Deloria notes, were joined by "Indian others" who "embodied crucial ideas about Americanness" (Deloria 40). The Jewish boys and saloonkeeper seek the power and privilege associated with the colonizer, rather than the Native Americans who were dispossessed of their land. However, they also recognize that they could be perceived as outsiders because to some they may have looked like American Indians. The physical resemblance between European Jews and American Indians, like "Nigger's" physical characteristics, draws attention to the fluid nature of racial categories for many immigrants from southern and eastern Europe during this period. So, while the boys (and Jake Wolf) identified with the U.S. aggressors in colonial expansion, they also acknowledged that they could only *play* colonizer as long as the game lasted.

When "playing colonizer," the boys had clear enemies in their own neighborhood. While the boys learned about colonizers, cowboys, and Indians from, as Gold tells us, "gaudy little paper books," they adapted the stories to serve their reality, as the following example shows:

> I walked down Hester Street toward Mulberry. Yes, it was like the Wild West. Under the fierce sky Buffalo Bill and I chased buffalo over the vast plains. We shot them down in hundreds. Then a secret message was sent us from a beautiful white maiden. She was a prisoner in the camp of the Indians. The cruel redskins were about to torture her. Buffalo Bill and I rode and rode and rode. In the nick of time we saved her. Two hundred cruel redskins bit the dust before our trusty rifles. We escaped with the white girl, and rode and rode and rode. So why should I fear these Italian boys? (187)

Unfortunately, Mike does not have as much luck with the Italian boys as his imagination had with the Indians. He is deluded by the rhetoric of colonialism in his Buffalo Bill comic books. By imagining himself in the position of the colonizer, Mike hopes to turn the Italians in the next neighborhood into objects of colonization. In addition, the "beautiful white maiden" shows which women are worthy of heroic deeds like venturing into Little Italy. However, even though the Indians in the comic books may be ineffectual foils for the superior power of the cowboys and colonists (allowing Mike to imagine himself the active, victorious savior), the ones on Mulberry Street certainly are not. They beat him up, yelling "Hooray, a Jew, a Jew!" and "Christ-killer!," until he can escape to civilization—the other side of the Bowery—"into my own Jewish land." By donning a form of racial masquerade (whiteface?), the Young Avengers make Italians into Indians. Once again, the Jewish boys turn to racial masquerade to safeguard their Jewishness.

Ultimately, Mike is not as successful with whiteface as he would be with "redface." He does not meet Jake Wolf's quota of "a hundred Indians" when he ventures to Mulberry Street; he more closely resembles Custer. Rather than try again, the boys "[go] Native" and form a gang with the "Indian" rituals of their dime novels and Tom Sawyer as a central feature of initiation: "Nigger, our leader, organized a secret league known as the 'Young Avengers of Christie Street.' Our object was to avenge wrongs done to a member and to hold pow-wows and roast sweet potatoes. . . . We took the Indian oath of fire and blood. We pricked our thumbs and spread the blood on the paper. Then with a burning stick we branded our forearms with the mystic star" (260–61). Michael Rogin argues that "Redface does not disguise but rather calls attention to the Jew wearing the costume" (Rogin 1074). I can't help but wonder if they are burning the Star of David, the Jewish six-pointed star, into their forearms and thus calling attention to their Jewishness while professing "Indianness." Even if they are not Stars of David, the Avengers of Christie Street are playing "Indians" in order to protect them from attacks from the Italian boys in the next block. Playing Indians serves as the symbolic mask that joins them together as Jews. That they cannot envision joining together as a Jewish "tribe" out of the Old Testament shows that Jewish religious and ethnic identities were experiencing strain and opposition from within (much of it intergenerational); in addition, it also shows the way racial masquerade provides these boys with a way to defend against external threats.

These threats were more than symbolic. Holding pow-wows, roasting sweet potatoes by the campfire—all among the tenements of the Jewish Lower East Side—are not all the Young Avengers do. They avenge. After Mike gets beat up several times by a "big Irish boy," he draws on the power in numbers offered by his gang: "The Young Avengers trailed me one afternoon. The big Irish boy, as usual, rushed at me like a bulldog. But the five of us fell upon him with whoops and cries, punching and clawing in a pinwheel of gory excitement. We defeated him" (261). Like "blackness," stereotypical "Indianness" (from the gaudy little paper books) is the oppositional position that allows the boys to challenge threats to their territory. Significantly, the Irish boy terrorizes Mike to take over the street corner where Mike sells newspapers. The Irish boy threatens Mike's ability to do his job. The boys don redface, band together, and destroy the threat. Later, a second Irish person appears, this time a cop. While the boy can be seen as a roadblock to earning wages, the cop more directly shows the limits placed on the lives of the Jewish boys. Furthermore, while all the boys are delinquents, only "Nigger" continues with his life of crime into adulthood. This is attributed to the different relationship "Nigger" has to the police. "Nigger" is bad, but he ultimately becomes a gangster because of the assumptions of the cop whom he harasses: "For months Nigger remembered to drop bricks, bundles of garbage and paper bags filled with water on this cop's head. It drove the man crazy. But he could never catch the somber little ghost. But he spread the word that Nigger was a bad egg, due for the reformatory. The cop's name was Murph. It was he who later tipped the balances that swung Nigger into his career of gangster" (44). So, while the boys are empowered by "playing Indians" and by "Nigger's" "blackness," only "Nigger" cannot "take off their mark of difference" (Rogin 1072). While they all may have seen themselves as able to move between racial categories, Nigger clearly tipped too far to the dark side of the racial divide.

Gold concludes the novel with the end of Mike's childhood and his conversion to socialism. Throughout the novel, anti-Semitism is a presence in the lives of the boys. Mike's conflicts with the Italian and Irish boys were overtly anti-Semitic. When searching for a job, the financial costs of anti-Semitism became even clearer to the novel's protagonist:

> I found a job as errand boy in a silk house. But it was temporary. The very first morning the shipping clerk, a refined Nordic, suddenly realized I was a Jew. He politely fired me. They wanted no Jews. In this city of a million Jews, there was much anti-Semitism among business firms. Many of the ads would read: Gentile Only. Even Jewish business houses discriminated against Jews. How often did I slink out of [a] factory or office where a foreman said Jews were not wanted. How often was I made to remember I belonged to the accursed race, the race whose chief misfortune it is to have produced a Christ. (306)

He drifts from job to job until he "took up with Nigger again" on the last page of the novel. Drinking, sexually exploiting women, and playing pool consume his adolescence. Repeating a pattern that defined much of his childhood, he turned to "the bad, nasty things" that his mother, and all the Avengers, associated with "that Nigger." Then, seemingly out of nowhere: "A man on an East Side soap-box, one night, proclaimed that out of the despair, melancholy and helpless rage of millions, a world movement had been born to abolish poverty.

I listened to him. O workers' Revolution, you brought hope to me, a lonely sui-
cidal boy. You are the true Messiah. You will destroy the East Side when you
come, and build there a garden for the human spirit" (309). But this messianic
moment was *not* out of nowhere. The whole book describes a process of searching for a symbolic and political realm to combat the social ostracism and economic exploitation of Jewish boys and men. The racist stereotypes that
organized Gold's oppositional viewpoint prior to his entry into the workforce
didn't stand a chance against structural anti-Semitism and class exploitation. In
Gold's opinion, socialism would.

While Gold argued in his rebuttal to Theodore Dreiser that socialism would
provide an alternative to class exploitation and racism, he also knew that the
Nazi party's National Socialism was attaining legitimacy in Germany and the
United States. *Jews Without Money* was first published in 1930. Its second printing occurred in 1935. Much had changed in the five years since its release. In
his new introduction, Gold saw his novel as a powerful counterpoint to Hitler's
rise to power in pre-World War II Germany. In this new context, a book about
poor Jews was no longer simply an example of "Proletarian Realism" that would
"reflect the struggle of the workers in their fight for the world" (Folsom 205).[6]
Now it served as a counterargument to anti-Semitic beliefs that Jews controlled
banks and international finance.

The 1935 introduction began with a powerful anecdote about the German
translator of his work. Several Brown Shirts broke into her house while she was
busily translating:

> The officer picked up some sheets of her manuscript, and read, "Jews
> Without Money,"
>
>   "Ho, ho, ho!" he roared. "So there are Jews without money!" And
> all the Brown Shirts laughed with him at the marvelous joke. How
> could there be Jews without money, when as every good Nazi knew
> with Hitler, Jews were all international bankers? (Gold, "Introduction,"
> n.p.)

Gold uses the introduction to reply to the Brown Shirts as he did to Dreiser:
"The great mass of Jews in the world today are not millionaire bankers, but pau-
pers and workers. . . . And Jewish bankers are fascists everywhere. Hitler has
received their support, both with money and ideas. . . . Jewish bankers are fascists; Jewish workers are radicals; the historic class division is true among the
Jews as with any other race" (n.p.). Gold repeats the pattern established in his
response to Dreiser and illuminated by his "transcendence" into a socialist consciousness. In *Jews Without Money*, the protagonist "transcends" the cycle of
exploitation and depression in an international movement predicated on the
shared interest of workers.

Prior to the last page, the characters and plot devices in *Jews Without Money* show that the "desire to transcend" into a socialist future (or at least a pan-racial working-class present) simultaneously establishes and transgresses notions of racial and ethnic difference. It is at the moment of transcendence that the youthful, "not-yet-Socialist" Mikey transforms into the socialist narrator of *Jews Without Money*. The avenger in Mikey would never be satisfied with the limited options available: suicide, flight to the West, praying to "the Jewish Messiah," or a life of "drinking and whoring." The childhood play with racist categories constructed an oppositional viewpoint that was able to avenge anti-Semitism and class exploitation in the short term. While Gold ultimately became an eloquent spokesperson for the importance of art to socialism, *Jews Without Money* reveals a different story: racial identities were always present, even if their meanings shifted to fit the contingencies of the moment.[7]

NOTES

1. The interchange between Hapgood and Dreiser resulted from a forum in the *American Spectator* in September 1933.

2. Gilroy described this as one of the pitfalls of utilizing "crude" ideas of racial difference. "The especially crude and reductive notions of culture that form the substance of racial politics today are clearly associated with an older discourse of racial and ethnic difference which is everywhere entangled in the history of the idea of culture in the modern West" (Gilroy 7).

3. For example, Alex Haley's widely quoted anecdote of Malcolm X in an airport: "Waiting for my baggage, we witnessed a touching family reunion scene as part of which several cherubic little children romped and played, exclaiming in another language. 'By tomorrow night, they'll know how to say their first English word—*nigger*,' observed Malcolm X" (Haley 399).

4. As Eric Lott wrote of the minstrel show in *Love and Theft*: "I would define the minstrel show precisely as a case of popular racial ventriloquism, which, because it was spoken in vernacular accents, could never be counted on to stifle undesirable responses. Despite the often hegemonic intentions or beginnings of popular forms, they can occasionally retain subversive dimensions, or for a time be invested with them. That is why the hegemony of what Gramsci termed the historical bloc is never secure, has constantly to be reconquered, and why there is a continual state of play in and over the popular sphere" (Lott 102). Similarly, Gilroy writes: "Even where African-American forms are borrowed and set to work in new locations they have often been deliberately reconstructed in novel patterns that do not respect their originators' proprietary claims or the boundaries of discrete nation states and the supposedly natural political communities they express or simply contain. My point here is that the unashamedly hybrid character of these black Atlantic cultures continually confounds any simplistic (essentialist or anti-

essentialist) understanding of the relationship between racial identity and racial non-identity, between folk cultural authenticity and pop cultural betrayal" (98–99).

5. Robin Kelley argues that white immigrants mimic the powerful in order to "secure a comparatively privileged position within the prevailing system of wage dependency" (Kelley 100).

6. See Mike Gold, "Proletarian Realism" reprinted in Folsom 203–08. Gold argued that "in proletarian literature, there are several laws which seem to be demonstrable. One of them is that all culture is the reflection of a specific class society. Another is, that bourgeois culture is in process of decay, just as bourgeois society is in swift decline. . . . Proletarian literature will reflect the struggle of the workers in their fight for the world" (205). See also "Towards Proletarian Art" (Folsom 62–70).

7. See Morrison's discussion of Willa Cather's *Sapphira and the Slave Girl* (28).

"Smashing Cantatas" and "Looking Glass Pitchers"

The Impossible Location of Proletarian Literature

LAWRENCE HANLEY

Perhaps one of the most infamous slogans to ring out in the "literary class wars" of the early 1930s was the one pronounced by Jack Conroy at the 1935 American Writers' Congress: "We prefer crude vigor to polished banality" (146). It would be easy to write off Conroy's motto as a prime example of the "cultural Know-Nothingism" (Howe 277) of proletarian writers, especially in light of the visceral populism of their chief promoter and cultural broker, Mike Gold. Yet even "Know-Nothingism" is a rhetorical strategy, and Conroy's targets included not just "decadent" bourgeois writers of the kind vilified by Gold in his notorious 1930 review, "Wilder—Prophet of the Genteel Christ," but also politically sympathetic, fellow-traveling writers in attendance at the Writers' Congress. In other words, Conroy's slogan belongs less to a history of American literary innocence, and ignorance, than to a particular conflict on the cultural Left in the early 1930s between two different kinds of cultural capital: one, represented by Conroy and young working-class writers like those he published in *The Anvil*, his magazine of proletarian fiction, that depended on the conversion of subaltern experience into cultural authority; and another cultural capital, represented by defectors from the middle class like John Dos Passos, Granville Hicks, and Kenneth Burke, that secured its cultural authority in the familiar, traditional currencies of education, social networks, and credentialed expertise. The decade of the '30s is unique in American literary history because it witnessed a momentary, but broad and decisive shift in the reigning economies of literary value and cultural capital formation. Proletarian writers in the early '30s, with limited or low-status schooling (at the City College of New York or midwestern state colleges, for instance) and zero social capital, could gain access to the dominant literary system on the basis of authentic working-class experience and its representation. Lacking such credentials of "authenticity," established writers, on the other hand, introduced "commitment" and "ideology" to the critical lexicon as a way to mediate the discrepancies between class position and involvement in left-wing cultural politics.[1]

"Today the bourgeois writer and the vanguard of the proletariat," a fellow-traveling Edmund Wilson wrote of the controversies surrounding proletarian literature in 1933, "can meet on the basis of the classless Marxist culture—which is accessible to both" (44). Indeed, for a brief historical moment, a shared commitment to radical politics joined working-class and established writers together in a "great alliance," as advertisements for the 1935 American Writers' Congress called it. If "proletarian literature" names anything, then, it signifies not so much a stable body of texts, motifs, or writers, but this awkward cultural space, underwritten institutionally and ideologically by the Communist Party, but most fundamentally structured by conflicts about and around the relations between class position, literary production, and cultural capital. Revisionist critics have recently begun to assemble a mass of sophisticated readings of proletarian fiction and poetry, much of it inspired by feminism (Rabinowitz, Coiner), cultural studies (Nelson), and reappraisals of the Communist Party (Foley), but these revisionists have largely avoided the contradictions that plagued "proletarian literature" as a cultural formation. At one level, these contradictory dispositions of cultural capital revolved around the circulation of proletarian writing: what did it mean, as Louis Adamic, for instance, asked in an infamous 1935 Scribner's article, "What the Proletarian Reads," that texts written by and for the working class were read and valued by a middle-class literary establishment? Alternatively, as Douglas Wixson's recent biography of Jack Conroy exhaustively documents, these contradictions involved the social and cultural positions of working-class writers themselves: what was the relationship between the terms "working-class" and "writer" in a system of authorship and value constructed by and for the middle class? Proletarian novels, for example, narrated strikes, political conversions, and bottom dog realities, but they just as insistently and consistently narrated their own ambiguous cultural situations. In my argument, these allegories of class and culture belied the optimism, or "revolutionary romance," often attributed to proletarian fiction; more usually, even when embedded in "revolutionary romances," these allegories narrated the impossible location of working-class literature within the contemporary, bourgeois cultural field.

William Saroyan's short story, "Prelude to an American Symphony," published in the New Masses in October 1934, shortly after the release of his critically acclaimed The Daring Young Man on the Flying Trapeze, provides a succinct illustration of proletarian narrative's persistent cultural self-consciousness. Narrating the consciousness of the working-class O'Hara as he prepares to perform his "American Symphony" for a middle-class audience, Saroyan's story dramatizes its protagonist's passage across social and cultural boundaries and, in turn, neatly allegorizes the ambivalent status of proletarian literature. The main action in "Prelude" is simply O'Hara's insistently repeated declaration of difference from, and hostility to, the audience of "artistic people" gathered to hear his music. "He was a fellow from the street," O'Hara tells himself. "Just one more drink and he'd be ready to let them know he came from the street and didn't care if he did because the street was a damned sight realer than they'd ever be" (14). O'Hara's ambitions and abilities have transported him into alien territory, and his mantra of resentment asserts the boundaries between high and low, inside and outside, spurious and genuine, even as it is the recognition of their permeability that solicits this constant reiteration. Through his anxiety, O'Hara recognizes his anomalous status as a crossover success—of but no longer in the working class and in but not of the middle-class "artistic people" who surround him.

This contact zone between classes complicates the authority and transparency of O'Hara's relations to "the street" because, once he is alienated from his original place, O'Hara's working-class identity becomes simply a matter of signs and signification. "He was from the street," O'Hara says, "and he was proud of it, only he didn't want them to get it wrong" (14). "Getting it wrong" means enjoying O'Hara and his symphony not as direct expressions of working-class experience, but instead as the spectacle, as O'Hara phrases it to himself, of a "God damned monkey" playing classical music. Monstrosity is a familiar metaphor within proletarian literature, and more generally '30s culture, for registering the excessive meaning and indeterminate status of those caught between classes—for instance, the scab, the fellow traveler, and the middle-class documentarians described by Louis Adamic in 1938 as "earnest objective socio-politico-cultural Darwins" conducting field work "in the vast Sargasso Sea that was America" (44).[2] Working-class writers in particular resorted to images of the grotesque and of themselves as "gargoyles"[3] to represent the dislocating effects of their own cultural ambition. Thus in a scene echoing Stephen Deadalus's meditations on the "cracked mirror" of art in *Ulysses*'s opening pages, the autodidactic and autobiographical protagonist of Jack Conroy's proletarian novel, *The Disinherited* (1933), catches his own reflection in the steel cylinders of a factory assembly line: "The glistening mill reflected my body with all the ludicrous distortions of an amusement park mirror. I grimaced, squatted, and thrust my head near. Instantly I was metamorphosed into a snarling ogre with a monstrous head and toothpick legs. I drew my head back, thrust out my chest, and rose to my full height. I became a pin head with a massive bust" (165). The scene that follows illustrates the sources of Larry's monstrous self-image when he woos a fellow worker with the genteel poetry of Arthur Davidson Ficke and then brusquely tries to take sexual advantage of her. "I thought you was different" (173), the woman shouts at Larry. Larry's sexuality makes him the same as his fellow, male workers, even as his cultural literacy marks his difference. This excessive signification makes him monstrous, and Larry's inability to reconcile what *The Disinherited* structures as an opposition between mind and body, reason and desire, writing and labor, middle and working class, surfaces repeatedly in the novel's images of proletarian monsters and grotesques.

In "Prelude," however, the spectacle of O'Hara as a "God damned monkey" points to another problematic feature of cross-class communication. This transgressive event, and not the sound of the "American Symphony," threatens to displace O'Hara's real performance because, as Roland Barthes once noted in *Mythologies*, otherwise disturbing signifiers of social difference can be easily recuperated and naturalized by the bourgeoisie under the sign of the "exotic." O'Hara's hysteria flows from the semiotic dangers inherent in cross-class, or cross-cultural, communication; as known, naturalized codes of interpretation give way to new audiences and contexts, the artist's or writer's power to control the meanings and effects of his performance is constantly threatened by opportunities for misappropriation and misinterpretation. In "Prelude," displacement across class and cultural borders thus creates a familiar "paranoia of minority representation" (Torres-Saillant). As one of the great meditations on this paranoia, Ellison's *Invisible Man*, shows us, for those who move from margins to centers, the problem of visibility—through representation and performance—can be as unnerving and painful as the problem of invisibility. Figures of the reader and scenes of reading and writing thus tend to proliferate in texts by working-class and other minority writers, as a way of meeting these dangers and projecting closure and control onto the instabilities of language and narration as acts of communication. While this self-reflexivity points to a Derridean critique of writing as infinite deferral and displacement of the proper, the literal, the signified, et cetera, it also enacts a particular understanding of the way social difference overdetermines the circulation of cultural meanings and values.

The anxieties unleashed by border crossing in "Prelude to an American Symphony" are more than just reflections on the fate of "selling out" or the fear of being "co-opted," to use an older idiom of border crossing. The self-reflexivity that haunts "Prelude" and proletarian narrative can be seen as a structural effect of the class organization and institution of culture: cultural legitimacy is the product of struggles to consolidate the very hierarchies and distinctions that separate working and middle classes. Thus, as Pierre Bourdieu has written:

> the sacralization of culture and art fulfils a vital function by contributing to the consecration of the social order: to enable educated people to believe in barbarism and persuade the barbarians within the gates of

their own barbarity, all they must need do is to manage to conceal themselves and to conceal the social conditions which render possible not
only culture as a second nature in which society recognizes human
excellence or 'good form' as the 'realization' in a habitus of the aesthetics of the ruling classes, but also the legitimized dominance of a particular definition of culture. ("A Sociological Theory" 236)[4]

As in O'Hara's case, to achieve cultural legitimacy is to gain access to a structure that works ceaselessly—through material apparatuses like education, the
media, libraries, and publishers—to articulate class difference with a "natural
cultural" difference between the "tasteful" and the "barbaric." Thus, in "Prelude," O'Hara's hysterical panic embodies a paradoxical situation: rather than
liberating him, his desperate assertions of a "barbaric" identity conform to and
confirm the "sacralizing" logic outlined by Bourdieu and thus bind him ever
more tightly to the very "art-culture system" (Clifford) he seems to detest.
Though little else unifies them formally or thematically, "proletarian" texts consistently exhibit O'Hara's class-crossing anxieties. These anxieties, in turn,
become the motivation for the allegories of class and culture so common to proletarian narrative. Indeed, the proletarian literary movement's most fundamental contribution to the project of a "working-class literature" lies in its
success at exposing, pace Bourdieu, the "social conditions" that naturalize the
class organization, definition, and imposition of "culture." Thematizing the
class logic of cultural distinction, proletarian narrative characteristically delineates the non-identity of working-class literature, its necessary location on the
other side of every class border.

At a certain point, the cultural formations built around and
within political movements must typically deal with a paradoxical ennunciative
situation: texts that "speak" for and about subaltern constituencies—working-
class, African American, queer—often end up "speaking" to, and claiming
recognition from, hegemonic audiences and institutions. Gayatri Spivak's land-
mark essay, "Can the Subaltern Speak?" is one of the most recent efforts to negotiate this dilemma; others would include work by black British cultural critics,
like Kobena Mercer, Isaac Julien, and Paul Gilroy, on the minority artist's "burden of representation" (Julien and Mercer). For Spivak, this dilemma is structured by the opposition between metropolitan centers and post-colonial
margins; proletarian narrative, on the other hand, characteristically maps the
same ennunciative dilemmas in terms of the relations between bourgeois cultural authority and working-class cultural production. Two proletarian novels
centrally concerned with these dilemmas are Albert Halper's *The Foundry* (1934)
and Thomas Bell's *All Brides Are Beautiful* (1936). Halper and Bell share simi-

lar literary careers: children of immigrant communities and cultures, first-generation college-goers; each enjoyed a measure of success and fame as young, working-class writers in the '30s, only to lose their literary status with the postwar breakup of "laboring culture" and the anti-communist repression of the '50s.[5]

Neither writer has benefited from the new revisionist work on the 1930s, and this neglect attests to the inescapable selectivity of even revisionist critiques of the canon's partial, incomplete status. In their novels, Halper and Bell intentionally adopt decentered, more ethnographic narrative structures and styles. Focusing on a typical year in the life of an electrotyping plant, Halper's novel attempts a kind of "shopfloor" realism. As Bell's title implies, by contrast, his novel's focus on marriage, family, romance, and home life strives for a proletarian "domestic" realism. While their emphasis on the quotidian implies a critique of other proletarian styles, especially those centered on contrasting apocalyptic chronotopes of the strike and the conversion, this emphasis also tends to preclude them from anti-canonical projects that construe a more heroic version of the '30s and, perhaps, of the critic's work. If it's possible to talk of minor writers within a minor literary and cultural tradition, then Halper and Bell are excellent test cases. Refusing to read them as failed candidates for the canon, we might read them as symptoms of both a more general problem (of minority representation) and a more particular history (of proletarian literature's cultural formation in the '30s).

Contrasting the more egalitarian marriage of its main couple, Susan and Peter Cummings, to the more rigid and traditional relationships of their in-laws, the fractious Beasley clan, the domestic realism of Bell's *All Brides Are Beautiful* sets out to elaborate an ideal of the reformed, modernized working-class marriage, one founded, as Peter describes it, on "friendship and comradeliness" (231). Peter sympathizes with the Communist Party; he reads, for instance, the *Daily Worker* and John Strachey's *The Nature of the Capitalist Crisis*, attends *New Masses* benefit dances with Susan, and faithfully marches in the party's annual May Day parade. Yet, Peter's political commitment oscillates throughout the novel between radicalism and resignation, militance and reserve. Though the narrative contrasts Peter's proto-communism with his brother-in-law Hank Beasley's disdain for the party, and radicalism in general, both characters ultimately share the same ambivalent relation to class politics. Having at last found a job, three-quarters of the way through the novel, Peter tells himself that "there was in him no zeal to change the world. All he wanted was to be let alone, to have a home, a little security, a chance to raise a healthy family and do the work he liked" (328). And Hank, despite his suspicion of radical politics, practices a rudimentary ethic of solidarity when he refuses to cross a picket line to take a much-needed job. Peter's political oscillations never achieve dramatic force in the novel; throughout, issues of political commitment and action supply topics for discussion and reflection, but never sources of narrative conflict. In pointed distinction to other proletarian texts, Peter emerges in *All Brides Are Beautiful* as a nonheroic representative of the working classes, a proletarian whose dilemmas strain toward larger significance but never escape the local circumstances of Ogden Avenue in the Bronx.

Against this effort to reproduce the lived textures of working-class experience, the novel uses the contrast between Peter and the Beasleys to draw sharper distinctions around the themes of class, culture, and taste. *All Brides Are Beautiful* introduces these issues in its opening pages when Peter defends his reticence about declaring his artist ambitions: "I just don't want people to get me wrong," he says to Hank in terms that echo Saroyan's "Prelude." "I like to draw but I'm a long way from being a real artist" (15). Peter's ambiguity about being a "real artist" expresses his anxiety about differences—in politics, marital ideals, ambition—that might disturb his working-class identity. But the question of the "real artist" also reflects Peter's nascent understanding of his position within the cultural field of art. The appellation of "real artist" is central to the structure and dynamics of the cultural field because, Bourdieu has argued, cultural authority works by consecrating works and artists. In turn, these consecrating practices invoke "principles of legitimacy" grounded in the "power to say with authority who are authorized to call themselves writers [and artists]" ("Field" 42). As Peter's deprecations imply, the legitimacy of the claim to being a "real artist" depends on recognition by those with authority to make such distinctions. Where, how, and whether a working-class painter (in Peter's case) secures such legitimating recognition is an important narrative problem in *All Brides Are Beautiful*.

Responding to Peter, Hank does seem to "get him wrong." Instead of the charcoal sketches he labors over, Hank suggests that Peter ought to paint "big pitchers with a model in a studio the way they show it in the movies." "It must be all right to be an artist," Hank continues, "though I guess they see so many naked models that after a while there ain't any kick in it for them. Like a doctor. Ain't that a hell of a thing to happen to a man" (16). In Hank's mass-cultured imagination, the "real artist" is legitimated by his sexual license. But if this same license associates him with the middle-class professional, the "real" artist's legitimate interest in the female body desexualizes and demasculinizes him. Equating the detached gaze of the clinical and aesthetic interest in bodies, Hank's common sense tells him that becoming an artist means crossing the border between classes and thus forfeiting a working-class identity. Like Hank, working-class characters in *All Brides Are Beautiful* are "wise" to the ways of art especially when, throughout the novel, they interpret Peter's ambition in terms of financial and sexual self-interest. "I just been telling Andy here about me offering you ten bucks for a pitcher of a naked woman ever since I know you,"

Peter's other, politically connected brother-in-law tells him at one point. "And they talk about starvin' artists" (111). Weaned on mass culture, immersed in the parochialism of everyday life, and guided by an appreciation for use-value, working-class characters (male and female) in Bell's novel distinguish between a "pure" gaze, associated with the middle class, and a "vulgar" taste associated with the working class and based on the "systematic 'reduction' of things of art to the things of life" (Bourdieu, *Distinction* 44). The cultural boundary between classes is thus also class boundary. Like Susan Cummings and Martha Beasley putting jumpers in the fusebox to cheat the power company or like Hank's efforts to earn some extra cash by renting out half his family's apartment, Peter's art is seen in practical and instrumental terms as another way of "getting over" on the system, even if this time it's the art-culture system.

Peter's encounter with the marketplace of bourgeois art and taste ironically confirms this working-class verdict. Susan works in a Manhattan bookstore owned by Franklin Pierce Higgler, "a small, brisk, busy little man—plump, bald, with a babylike face and a set of teeth magnificent in their shining, their perfect, their utter falseness" (48). Higgler's prosthetic appearance foreshadows the play of appearance and reality, refinement and vulgarity, that defines the novel's delineation of bourgeois culture's "real artist." Though he sells the usual bestsellers, greeting cards, and "modern first editions," Higgler's real profits come from his illicit trade in "the acknowledged classics" of erotic literature, illustrated volumes by Cleland, de Sade, Aretino, and "the rest of literature's gamey birds" (49). Higgler first establishes his business when, years before, he buys a private library from a doctor's wife. Arranged in double rows, the book-seller discovers that "in front were medical books of complete respectability; behind, books that were neither medical nor respectable" (51). Like the doctor's library, Higgler's bookstore is a "cultural" front where art and profit meet in sala-cious conspiracy and where the real business of matching demand with supply is carried on behind conventional trappings and a respectable New England demeanor. Bell's portrait of the pornographer may seem a little forced, but his real interest is less in Higgler's hypocrisies and more in anatomizing class taste. The doctor's clinical interest in the body represses a more vulgar and sexual interest that might link working-class and bourgeois subjects. Avoiding this kind of contamination requires the differentiation of legitimate and illegitimate desires and interests in bodies through resort to the "classical," the "genius," and "tradition," in short, the familiar tools deployed in the name of "literariness" to sort and organize the ephemeral from the eternal, the simple from the complex, and the vulgar from the refined. When Higgler decides to publish a private edi-tion of Martial's *Epigrams*, advertised as an account of "THE PURPLE PAGANISM OF ANCIENT ROME," he hires Peter to do the art work that will eroticize, and hence commercialize and modernize this classical text. Higgler's use of Peter's rendering of "several nude figures lounging about the pedestal of Venus, only the lower half of which was visible" (164) on a selectively circulated handbill attracts the attention of the authorities and, eventually, leads to his downfall as a pornographer. Later, when one of Higgler's competitors solicits Peter's skills for an "on-the-level flagellation item" (276) to be titled *The Golden Whip*, Peter angrily rejects the proposition and leaves to march with his metal-workers union in the party's May Day parade.

In the end, working-class and middle-class desires are not so far apart; Higgler's books are not so different from Hank's proposition to Peter that they "go into business drawing pitchers on looking glasses in saloons" (60). In Bell's allegory of class and culture, the middle class distinguishes its similar "barbaric" desires through resort to the mechanisms of taste, but this differentiation also structures the cultural field and its subjects in contrasting ways. The novel's parody of bourgeois cultural capital posits a cultural field organized around the individualized subject for whom reading is a private act and for whom even pornography supplies the grounds for discrimination; eschewing the middle class's guilty pleasure, Hank's "pitchers on looking glasses in saloons" subordinate art to other forms of socializing and encode more public and communal functions and subjects for art.

As a proletarian critical of capitalism and its ruses, Peter's rejection of the illicit, even decadent, market-driven culture of Tomash and Higgler is unsurprising. What seems more surprising is his rejection of working-class culture, especially its communal and public dimensions. For instance, Peter and Susan, along with the Beasleys, attend a St. Patrick's Day dance sponsored by a local political club. The dance features the music of "Patty Dean's Radio Ramblers," an "Irish tenor who bellowed 'When Irish Eyes Are Smiling,'" a Jewish tenor who "wailed 'Eli, Eli,'" and a "child prodigy who sang about love" (109). The scene is dominated by images of the material, libidinal working-class body. Everywhere, Peter sees sweaty, drunken men and women decked out in flashy clothes designed to glamorize and sexualize. In one vivid moment, Peter observes his "strikingly handsome" sister-in-law "in a tight-fitting evening gown of pale green satin—she was like a blare from a trumpet, like a swaggering, noisy actress shouting a song" (106). Bell's description of the dance is one of the decade's finest evocations of urban, working-class entertainment, but Peter is slightly bored and disgusted by the whole event. While others enjoy themselves dancing and drinking, Peter, as the narrator reports, "customarily returned from these affairs stupefied not with alcohol but with noise, bad air, and the conversation" (109). The indiscriminate "multiculturalism" of the dance's entertainment combines with a working-class sensorium of unruly sound, sight, smell, and voice to overwhelm Peter, who is cast in this scene as a beleaguered, bourgeois subject suffocated and repulsed by his immersion in working-class hedonism. Peter's disgust here, coupled with his rejection of Higgler, repeats what Peter Stallybrass and Allon White see as an inaugural scene of literary "authorship." In *The Politics and Poetics of Transgression*, Stallybrass and White analyze the ways in which the institution of a specifically bourgeois notion of authorship involved efforts by writers like Jonson, Dryden, and Wordsworth "to stabilize and dignify an emergent place for authorship at a distance from the aristocracy and the plebians. The insertion of professional authorship between these was a fraught negotiation of a 'middle' space and a complex contestation of traditional dichotomies" (74–75). Seeking to clarify his status as a specifically working-class artist, Peter struggles to locate a "middle" space between working-class and bourgeois conceptions of the artist, art, and the cultural field. This effort to distinguish himself puts Peter, however, in the difficult position of producing an art that discerns no particular audience.

Bell's exposition of Peter's cultural dilemma comments self-reflexively on the fate of his own narrative because his protagonist's ambitions and aesthetic so closely resemble those of the novel *All Brides Are Beautiful*. We never get to see Peter's portfolio, titled "Bronx Drawings," but we do get several thorough accounts of the sensibility that inspires his artistic work. That sensibility expresses a mystical, Whitmanian reverence for the masses in their active, heterogeneous, and quotidian motion. Discussing Peter's ambition and their future on a pedestrian bridge that spans the Harlem River, Peter and Susan turn from Manhattan to view "the Bronx sprawled across the earth, houses and streets and people without end" (239). Peter gestures to this dense zone of working-class life when he describes his notion of art to Susan:

> "Catch and hold," he chanted. His hand opened and lay cupped, as though holding in itself miniatures of the bridge, the scurrying cars, themselves. "Everything: the wind, the click of your heels on the sidewalk, warmth in your mouth, laughter in your throat. No job, the rent due next week, the Bronx waiting to swallow us. A car sounding its horn and right after it—you hear? a locomotive's shriek. There—it's gone already." (244)

Peter's vision is extensional, and the purpose of his art is essentially mnemonic, terms that equally describe Bell's novel. Focusing on family, marriage, and everyday life, the plotless narrative of *All Brides Are Beautiful* mutes intensities of character and action to emphasize the commonplace textures of working-class life. It also scrupulously backgrounds what Roland Barthes would call the "proairetic code" of typical actions and events—the "Strike," the "Political Education of the Worker," "Proletarianization," for instance—that weave themselves through both proletarian narrative and '30s culture at large. Family spats, Susan's and Peter's anxieties about the future, and Peter's political hesitations ripple across this surface, but barely disturb the novel's finely grained sense of daily routine and ritual. Having enjoyed their moment of narrative significance, the novel self-consciously "swallows" Peter and Susan back into the anonymous byways of the Bronx in its final sentence: "Their laughter and voices fading as they went down the dark, quiet street, and around its curve, and the street was empty" (360). Bell's novel counters the lurid tastes of its working-class and middle-class characters with its own romance of everyday life. But having staged its relations to these representations of culture, the novel also describes an impossible situation for its proletarian narrative. Neither working-class nor middle-class culture holds a place for the "real artist." The audience that might value Peter's drawings is emphatically absent from the narrative of *All Brides Are Beautiful*; likewise, there is no room in the novel's allegory of class and culture for a reader who might value the ungarnished narrative of Peter and Susan.

All Brides Are Beautiful thematizes the corruptions of bourgeois culture, a common trope in proletarian narrative, and the "vulgar" dynamics of working-class culture. Creating an art without an audience, Bell's protagonist figures the absence of a known social and cultural space for proletarian literature; the working-class artist lacks access to a cultural field beyond those dominated by either bourgeois market or working-class instrumentality. This is a dilemma treated and resolved with varying degrees of success by Albert Halper in his first two novels, *Union Square* (1933) and *The Foundry* (1934). Both books are "collective novels." In the first, Halper uses multiple plots and their intersection in Union Square to question, explicitly and implicitly, the project of proletarian literature. In his most direct critique, Halper has one of his central characters in *Union Square*, the cynical Jason Wheeler, "at one time one of the most promising poets of the last ten years" (282) but now a "pot-boiler writer for cheap sex-story magazines" (11), visit a poetry reading at "The Kremlin," a Greenwich Village apartment house for bohemian writers and painters turned proletarian artists. Wheeler decries the poetry he hears as "pretty rotten stuff" (284) and excoriates his audience for making bad art out of good politics and forgetting that "the Revolution must be a workers' revolution and not a rising by the intelligentsia" (293). To one budding writer who suffers from "Manhattan communism" (293), Wheeler retorts: "Pardon me, comrade. You are working on the great American proletarian novel, therefore you must be a worker" (290). If Halper points to the uncomfortable avant-gardist structure of "proletarian literature," its uneasy condensing of revolutionary politics with the engine of heterodoxy and innovation that drives the literary system, such embittered fusillades, even from the mouth of a hard-boiled pulp writer, could hardly be expected to win approval from leftist readers in 1933. In the *New Masses*, Mike Gold turned Wheeler's charges back on Halper and declared *Union Square* nothing more than a futile exercise in "stale bohemianism." "It is the book,"

Gold averred, "of one who has no real social passion. The whole novel is a syn-thesis, like a Hollywood movie, or a jazz song" ("Stale Bohemianism" 8).

Gold was right. The "synthetic" structure of Halper's novel is most obvious when it uses a communist rally in Union Square to synchronize the narrative crises of each of its dispersed, multiple plots. As the communists gather noisily in the Square, a guilt-driven barber, Mr. Franconi, quietly commits suicide; an aging divorcee, Mr. Boardman, discovers his young lover's infidelity; an unem-ployed worker named Hank Austin is beaten unconscious by the police; and Leon Fisher, a likeable communist and "photo-retoucher by day, artist by night" (8), has his heart broken by the beautiful Comrade Helen. The artifice of Halper's symphonic climax is compounded by the obviously melodramatic—perhaps "Hollywoodesque"—plots that lead each protagonist to his chosen fate. Some of these moments are directly connected to the rally, others only by coin-cidence or timing. But the rally's catalyzing power, its use as a grand climax of "plotting" itself, foregrounds the power of discourse over story and emphasizes the triumph of novelistic time and order over the arbitrary, contingent space of Union Square.

Halper is, however, more self-conscious about the synthetic features of his "collective" novel than Gold credits him. Against the extravagantly plotted rep-resentation of its main events, *Union Square* contrasts the unplotted existence of characters like Pete, the guy who runs the Crystal Lunchroom, Celia, the daugh-ter of Leon's landlady, James Nicholson, the neighborhood crackpot, and Grandma Vogel and Mr. Feibleman, a pretzel seller and hot chestnut vendor, respectively, who battle for culinary dominance of the Square. These characters are permanent features of the landscape and remain locked in the rhythms of "Time and Tide" constantly invoked by the novel's narrator: "Seasons roll round like huge wagon wheels," the narrator comments early on, "each spoke a month, each revolution a year; the thick fat hubs are solid as fate" (5). As peripheral but consistent objects of narrative attention, Grandma Vogel and Mr. Feibelman ironize the history that streams around them, and underscore the artifice of the narratives that melodramatize characters like Leon, Boardman, Franconi, and the rest. The mode of repetition and ritual that defines these characters resists narrativization; the novel's plots entertain an eccentric relationship to the Square's "urban folk" best exemplified by James Nicholson, who parodies the narrator's "plotful" efforts by scattering printed nonsequiturs ("Eat Today Tomor-row You Die" (27), "Man's Destiny Is War" (46), and "For A United Front" (356), some of Nicholson's cards read) amidst the Square's crowds, and who rewrites the events of *Union Square* as a demented version of the Fall of Rome. Marcus Klein correctly points out that Halper's book manages to "intimate a continuous theme . . . that there is a social actuality out there which is not being appre-hended—not by anybody and especially not by Communist literary people"

(147). More fundamentally, by refusing to mediate or "suture" the gap between the plotful and the banal, *Union Square* refuses the "philosophical topos" (de Certeau 2) of "the everyday" whereby legitimate discourses ground their authority in their ability to speak about and through the "ordinary man."[6] Thematizing the difference between its main protagonists and its minor characters, its melodramatic plots and static setting, between "time" and "tide," *Union Square* enacts the limits of its own narrative and literary power to represent the margins of History, a place where, as Peter Cummings also believes, the diurnal passage of everyday life transpires unmarked.

In *The Foundry*, Halper discards characters like Leon, Boardman, Franconi, and Hank Austin, but he uses the "collective" structure of *Union Square* to recount one year in the daily operations of the Fort Dearborn Electrotype Foundry to more fully explore the problem of representing the "everydayness" of the working-class experience. With more characters and a more even distribution of narrative attention than *Union Square*, the action in *The Foundry* is more diffuse and organized around more mundane conflicts and crises: the battle between shopfloor caricaturist and his boss, the off-stage death of a worker's baby, the problems one older worker has with his "modern," Americanized kids, the election of a union foreman, various on-the-job romances, and the arrival in the foundry of Karl Heitman, the "most radical electrotyper in the city" (133). Class struggle emerges in *The Foundry*'s "shopfloor" realism as a conflict between bosses and workers over job assignments, work rules, and control, a theme that reaches its syndicalist climax with the introduction of a new labor-saving machine, "The Big Smasher," and the foundry workers' covert (ultimately successful) work slowdown. But this episode is almost incidental to a narrative structured around the "time and tide" of passing seasons and communal events like a Fourth of July picnic and a company talent show.

Even though it abandons *Union Square*'s multiple plots and synthesizing crisis to exhaustively chronicle the everyday life of the Dearborn Foundry, similar kinds of narrative disjunction reappear in Halper's second novel. The narrator of *The Foundry* foregrounds the textual relations between reader, fictional subject, and narration through his consistently ironic treatment of the novel's characters. Referring to Kubec, a recently married worker, the narrator declaims: "Ah, what a healthy animal the man was! Look at those arms, that stocky torso" (406). Later, he admonishes his character: "Now Kubec, the molder, it's your own fault, you can't put a sensitive little woman alone in the center of a great prairie with only a skyline to talk to. You know that!" (408). Halper's comic, sometimes condescending voice is certainly a novelty in proletarian fiction. With one eye on his reader and the other on his characters, the narrator insistently parodies the sentimental wellsprings of the most "heroic" representation of the working class. When an older worker shyly presents a rose to a coworker, the narrator quickly forecloses on the bathetic possibilities of such a scene: "[I]t should have been accompanied by music," he comments to the reader, "somewhat on the order of what is being done with so much artistry now at the radio studios" (222). By repeatedly addressing his readers as "good people, kind sirs" (416, 421, 436), Halper's narrator defines his role in the narrative as a kind of self-deprecating ringmaster, or as Joe North complained in his *New Masses* review: "I got the feeling [the narrator] was an interlocuter in some literary minstrel show. The white, superior interlocutor with Bourbon condescension introducing the black-face characters" (24). North's discomfort with Halper's turn at Mr. Bones points to a more general anxiety over the "authenticity" of proletarian narrative, especially the fear that proletarian narrative might simply be, as O'Hara's performance anxiety also implied, a matter of signs and masks, nothing more than a "literary minstrel show" that substituted "classing down" for "blacking up."[7] William Rollins, author of the critically acclaimed, *New Masses*-endorsed proletarian novel, *The Shadow Before* (1934), would admit as much when he explained in 1934 that because of their "middle-class antecedents," he did not consider himself or most other radical writers to be "writers, in the real sense, of proletarian literature." Despite his best efforts to portray working-class life, Rollins admitted that he "could no more hope to express the actual being of the proletariat than I could, were I, say, an ardent Francophile, hope to express what under such circumstances I would probably call the soul of France" (23). Thus, by implication, the "proletarian" characters that dominate his novel are creatures of cross-class ventriloquy, and as the figure of a middle-class scion named Harry Baumann in *The Shadow Before* suggests, of cross-class desire and narrative investment. Likewise, the performance of Halper's narrator raises the specter that all of proletarian literature might be summed up in the business card tacked to an apartment door of "The Kremlin" in *Union Square*: "Eli Dorfman, worker" (281).

In *Union Square*, Halper doesn't satirize workers; he satirizes the cross-class investments of bohemians and various other middle-class characters suffering from what V. F. Calverton called "proletarianitis," an idealization of class difference and its powers of redemption. What North's brilliant epithet exposes and obscures is the way in which Halper's excessive narrator mocks the same structure of identification and disavowal to be found at the heart of minstrelsy (Lott). Using his irony to negotiate solidarity with his readers, the narrator of *The Foundry* signals his own distance from, and above, the novel's working-class characters while simultaneously deflating the literary and political pretensions of "proletarian" narrative by mocking the middle-class reader's desire for class difference. Mediating the gap between middle-class reader and working-class

subject, the narrator defines the work of proletarian literature as entertainment—not the edification or radicalization—of the reader; he transforms *The
Foundry* into a spectacular or theatrical production, a textual metaphor made
explicit by his occasional analogies for the shopfloor: "It roars. From its industrial gusto is born the crash of its smashing cantata. The din is terrific, enough
to give the outsider an earache. The hammers, the roughers, and the saws burst
into swelling discord" (425). Halper's juxtaposition of narrator and narrated
underscores the difference between working-class life and literary representation by "outing" Saroyan's "artistic people" in the text; preemptively marking
and framing the role of the middle-class reader, Halper presents, and simultaneously discounts, one version of the projection and displacement involved in
reading and writing across class borders. In *The Foundry*, he recognizes that proletarian literature is a middle-class phenomenon, one that converts working-
class experience into cultural capital by translating the "earache" of class
difference into more euphonious ideological and textual experience.

But if *The Foundry* stages its representation of the proletariat for consumption by middle-class readers, the novel also imagines a more organic relation
between culture and class. Counterposed to the novel's theatrical narrator is
August Kafka, an aspiring composer and fledgling member of the foundry's
community. When he's commissioned to write and perform a piece for the company's talent show, August synthesizes his modernist musical tastes and his experience of the foundry's pounding rhythm to produce his own "smashing
cantata" titled "The Printing-House Blues." August aims to write a "song of iron
men and iron floors" (412) and the foundrymen collaborate by explaining each
part of the foundry to August because, as they tell him, "in order to write about
machines, you've got to understand them" (399). Still, on the night of the big
performance, things get off to a rocky start. August uses off-key harmonics, sand
rattled in old tomato cans, untuned violin strings, and "prolonged mournful
sounds" (472) to imitate the foundry's various machines. But his modernist pro-
clivities only give his working-class audience an "earache." "No, I don't understand it," Nero, the shop's union chairman, tells his wife, "All I hear is noise"
(473). Yet slowly, as each foundryman recognizes the sound of his own machine
and as "The Printing-House Blues" builds to its final movement, a symphonic
rendering of the whole foundry working together, August's colleagues "for the
first time in their lives" become "fully conscious of the song of their own
machines" (476). "The foundrymen, listening, sat electrified in their seats," the
narrator writes. "Their throats, filled with the dumb thick wonder of their labor,
began to expand, shouting voicelessly" (477). At the close of the performance,
amidst thunderous applause, even Nero finds himself amazed by the transfig-
uring power of August's composition. "Now, I don't propose to know much
about music," he tells his wife, "but there was something to that piece.—No, I

can't put into words just what it was, but there was something—something" (479). Alienated by art, the workers' experience of the foundry is returned to them by "The Printing-House Blues" with new meaning and effect.

It is exactly this intense identification between audience and performance, or reader and text, that is denied—to all readers—by the narrator's performance in *The Foundry*. Constrained by his attention to a class-marked reader and by his role as mediator of social difference, the narrator refuses to duplicate the relations between subject and text that furnish August's performance with such powerful effects. The "something" referred to by Nero turns out to be a rudimentary form of class consciousness; fortified by August's music, the foundrymen return to work after the talent show to finish a rush order while, at the same time, the foundry's owners unsuccessfully cope with the events of October 1929—one suffers a heart attack, another a nervous breakdown, and the last kills himself in the foundry office. With its synthesis of modernist form and class experience, Halper uses "The Printing-House Blues" to theorize one possible function of culture and its texts, a function which includes the production of new subjectivities and, consequently, the fostering of solidarity. By contrast, the novel's narrator sees himself as producing "mere" entertainment. In the difference between August's and the narrator's performance, Halper's novel points to the paradox of proletarian literature: to succeed with one audience of "good people, kind sirs," *The Foundry* cannot conduct the transaction it might establish, like August, with its proletarian subjects. Seeking to fashion its "representative" power on the terrain of bourgeois culture, *The Foundry* thus disavows the very power it grants to "The Printing-House Blues."

In his novels and in short stories like "Scab" and "A Morning with Doc," Halper's fiction throughout the '30s is marked by a consistent, self-conscious attention to the limits of the literary representation of class. Halper's mediating figures, be they narrators or characters, signal a non-identity between discourse and story that is semiotic as well as social: the reader of proletarian fiction never coincides with the characters represented by proletarian fiction. Saroyan's narrator in "Prelude to an American Symphony" lives this difference as an existential crisis; O'Hara's breakdown performs the border between working-class and middle-class experience as a site of alienation, anxiety, and contradiction. Halper splits O'Hara's conflicted enunciative position in two, leaving August Kafka to perform "in the street" and *The Foundry*'s narrator to address the "artistic people" who are the novel's readers. This split, in turn, describes the impossible location of proletarian and working-class literature: if literary value only exists within and for a specifically bourgeois "market for symbolic goods" (Bourdieu), then working-class *literature*, whatever its form or content and despite its polemic or political intentions, must always be alienated from the working class.

This hardly means that working-class writers should stop writing, or that we should stop reading working-class fiction, poetry, autobiography, and the rest. Rather, Halper's and Bell's allegories are important because they point to a way of reading working-class literature outside of a multiculturalism that confuses symbolic with political representation and canon revision with social change. Because it fails to grapple with the social relations of "literature," this kind of multiculturalism celebrates working-class writing, and other minority literatures, without challenging the structures of distinction and exclusion that sustain literariness itself. Contemporary academic multiculturalism tends to collapse the difference between curriculum and institution, assuming that fuller discursive "representation" in the former (through canon revision, revised syllabi, expanded course and program offerings) must somehow imply the fuller "representativeness" of the latter. But, as John Guillory argues, institutions reproduce social distinction by reproducing attitudes toward and ways of dealing with texts, meaning, and knowledge. Central to this "class habitus," defined largely by "the relation to culture inculcated by the school" (41), is the formation and accumulation of cultural capital, an objective defined less by the language of texts than by the linguistic performance of students. Thus, whatever its content, historically the literary curriculum distributes cultural capital and reproduces social distinction by serving as "the pedagogic vehicle for producing the distinction between credentialed and uncredentialed speech" (63). A multiculturalism that ignores the institutional realities of literary representation, that pursues radical pluralism in matters curricular without questioning its social location, runs the risk of becoming, as Hazel Carby forcefully puts it, "totally compatible with — rather than a threat to the rigid frameworks of segregation and ghettoization at work throughout our society" (12). Guillory's analysis of multiculturalism doesn't necessarily forsake the goals of canon revision and fuller cultural representation for some more militant, revolutionary task of dismantling higher education. Rather, it forces multiculturalists to rethink their project through two necessarily linked questions: (minority) representation for whom? greater access to what (curriculum)?

In Halper's and Bell's novels, the very possibility of working-class literature founders on similar questions: "literature" rewards writers with what kinds of alienation from which readers and experiences? Writing "literature" implies what kinds of readers doing what kinds of things to a writer's narratives? In short, what are the social relations involved in the circuits of cultural capital, where writing becomes "literature"? Working-class literature, whether written by, for, or about the working class, is almost always writing driven to distraction by anxieties about its own legitimacy and value. Thus, for instance, we need to read beneath the smoother, more ideologically glossed surfaces of proletarian literature for the disjunctures, ambivalences, and confusions that characterize allegories of culture and class like Halper's and Bell's. More importantly, perhaps, the often acknowledged fragmentary, incoherent, dissonant textualities of working-class writing—from Jack London to Anzia Yezierska to Luis Rodriguez— need to be read less as emblems of literary defect or the surplus of raw expressiveness than as diagrams of impossible locations and ambiguous situations. Animated by the desire for cultural legitimacy and recognition even as it acknowledges the exclusionary social economies of this legitimacy, working-class literature continually finds itself, like Saroyan's O'Hara, split down the middle and stuck in between. If we listen closely enough to this "Printing-House Blues," we might hear a vamp on our own dilemmas of cultural representation and social difference.

NOTES

1. For one representative moment in this conflict, see the series of exchanges between Horace Gregory, Meridel le Sueur, and Edwin Seaver in *New Masses*: Gregory, "One Writer's Position"; Seaver, "Another Writer's Position"; Le Sueur, "The Fetish of Being Outside"; Seaver, "Ceaser or Nothing." The role that "ideology" plays as a strategy for interpollating intellectuals into revolutionary class politics has been noted by Perry Anderson in *Considerations on Western Marxism* and more polemically by Ellen Meiskins Wood in *The Retreat from Class*. Wood argues that the contemporary post-Marxist "autonomization" of politics and ideology, their increasing detachment from class experience and social structure, assigns the job of social change to "right-minded people" and, in particular, invites intellectuals "to act as the revolutionary consciousness of the people, to put themselves in the place of intrinsic class impulses and interests as the guiding light of popular struggles" (23).

2. For the scab as grotesque, see, for instance, Halper's "Scab!", but also the black strikebreaker in Conroy's *The Disinherited* who stumbles late one night to the Donovan family's door, having been beaten by striking miners: "One eye closed. The other glisten[ing] chalky white. His lips were battered" (60). On the fellow traveler as grotesque, see, for instance, Joe Freeman's "Introduction" to *Proletarian Literature in the United States*, esp. pp. 19–28. For the "grotesque" intersections of class, politics, and gender in narratives by women writers of the '30s, see Paula Rabinowitz's "Grotesque Creatures: The Female as Intellectual Subject" in *Labor and Desire*.

3. In *Permanence and Change* (1935), Kenneth Burke describes periods of ideological confusion and crisis as "the realm of gargoyles" (69). The "gargoyle," for Burke, provides an instance of the "grotesque," a form whose powers of symbolic dissociation and transgression (or "perspective by incongruity") "tend [toward the] revolutionary" (112) because the grotesque "violate[s] one order of classification" (112) by rewriting or transcoding it into another. Thus, Burke applauds the "gargoyle element in Marx's formula of class-consciousness" because it represents "a new perspective that realigns something so profoundly ethical as our categories of ethical allegiance" (113). In Burke's

scheme, gargoyles and the grotesque are figures of transition and change; their monstrosity exemplifies and enacts the passage from one social and symbolic order to another. In *Permanence and Change*, Burke explicitly presents this passage as a transition from capitalism to communism.

4. Elsewhere, Bourdieu has written that the "dominate class"[sic] intervene in struggles over cultural legitimacy "only as a passive reference point, a foil. The nature against which culture is here constructed is nothing other than what is 'popular,' 'low,' 'vulgar,' 'common'." Further, he argues the cross-class border crosser in search of cultural legitimacy "must pay for his accession to everything which defines truly humane humans by a change of nature, a 'social promotion' experienced as an ontological promotion, a process of 'civilization,' a leap from nature to culture, from the animal to the human; but having internalized the class struggle, which is at the very heart of culture, he is condemned to shame, horror, even hatred of the old Adam, his language, his body and his tastes, and of everything he was bound to, his roots, his family, his peers, sometimes even his mother tongue, from which he is now separated by a frontier more absolute than any taboo" (*Distinction* 251). In fact, Caliban's relations to his or her past are much more ambivalent than this. Nostalgia, sentiment, idealization are as common as shame and horror. See, for instance, Richard Hoggart's *Uses of Literacy* (1957).

5. The phrase "laboring culture" condenses Michael Denning's "laboring of American culture," his useful term for the social-democratic, Popular Front cultural formation of the later '30s and '40s. See Denning. For Halper's career and life, see his memoir, *Good-bye, Union Square* (1970) and Hart (1980). For background on Bell, see Demarest, "Afterword" (1991).

6. Within scientific and philosophical discourse, de Certeau argues, invocations of "the ordinary" provide "theory with a secure place" (3) because they allow intellectuals to generalize particular knowledges and ground these knowledges in the authority of "everyday" experience. Thus, as de Certeau notes of Freud: "the ordinary man renders a service to Freud's discourse, that of figuring in it as a principle of totalization and as a principle of plausibility" (4). Critiquing the "cleavage" between expert and "everyone" that "organizes modernity" (6), de Certeau, in his own efforts to make popular practices legible, refuses to identify with or idealize "everydayness." "It is a matter," he writes, "of restoring historicity to the movement which leads analytical procedures back to their frontiers, to the point where they are changed, indeed disturbed, by their ironic and mad banality that speaks in 'Everyman' in the sixteenth century and that has returned in the final stages of Freud's knowledge" (5).

7. The fear of, and contempt for, faking it played a key role in debates within the '30s Left that are often conceived of as involving political or ideological differences. Mike Gold's most important manifesto of proletarian literature, for instance, was hardly concerned with ideology or doctrinal politics. Instead, Gold's "Proletarian Realism" sought to define an "authentic" proletarian literature against the slumming, sensationalist representations offered by bourgeois and working-class writers (like Jim Tully).

Marching! Marching! and the Idea of the Proletarian Novel

JON-CHRISTIAN SUGGS

In 1923, *Survey Graphic*, an illustrated American magazine that reached a general readership, devoted its March issue to aspects of life in the Soviet Union. Among the twenty or so articles and sketches was Soviet Commissar of Education A. V. Lunacharsky's essay "Proletarian Culture." Short on concrete examples or even titles of works in any genre, the essay set out some issues surrounding the idea of a proletarian culture. Among these were the development of culturally particular forms while engaged in violent class struggle, the low level of education and experience with cultural production among the proletariat in general, the lack of resources, technical and economic, and the resident power of bourgeois culture.

These problems notwithstanding, Lunacharsky felt certain that a vital proletarian culture would emerge not only in the Soviet Union but among working classes everywhere: "In Europe, and very likely, in America, the proletarian masses have already begun the work through their thinkers who have either come from the proletariat or have been drawn to it by its growing political power and the hopes that wreathe its banner" (61). Not every observer of the cultural moment was as sanguine, however. An editorial in the same issue began: "One of the Russian translators in New York asked to help with the Russian articles in this issue point blank refused to translate Lunacharsky's manuscript. 'Proletarian Culture,' he exclaimed, 'why there can be no such thing! Then why should I take the trouble to read about it?'" ("Editorial" 63).

A decade or so later, in June of 1934, *New Masses*, a magazine which had not even existed when *Survey Graphic*'s translator scoffed at the idea of proletarian culture, announced "a prize of $750 for the best novel on an American proletarian theme submitted before April 1, 1935" (7). Such a novel was found and announced to the world in the 10 September 1935 issue. It was titled *Marching! Marching!* and it had been written not by an intellectual recruited from the industrial proletariat but by an ex-Stanford university student, Clara Weatherwax, living in the hills outside Berkeley, California, with her husband. Nevertheless, Lunacharsky's assumptions that proletarian cultural production in literature and the arts would be "little inclined toward individualism," would "reflect the majesty of the collectivist pan-psychic ideal," would "pulsate with anger directed against [the] enemy, sorrow for his victims, contempt for the crumbling world, passionate love for the world in birth throes, an austere and brotherly cult of his heroes" and "[b]y shifting the center of gravity from 'I' to 'we,'" would "rise above the problem of the grave which torments the bourgeois and the intellectual," were borne out in the novel that was selected (Lunacharsky 62). Ironically, *Marching! Marching!* garnered no respect from either the broader world of literature or within the more closely held world of proletarian arts and letters despite the prize; and indeed, within a year, the very idea of an American proletarian literary culture had been, for all intents and purposes, abandoned to the dustbin of literary history.

We know now that such was not the literal fate of proletarian fiction, but the "program" for such fiction was dismantled by 1937. A look back at Weatherwax's novel and at some assumptions about the mix of literature, class struggle, and the "reader" will help us appreciate the complexity of the pursuit of that program while it was in play.

Probably no other literature poses such a knot of theoretical and practical problems for the relationships among writers, critics, and readers than does proletarian fiction. Left novelists in general wanted to produce fictions that, when read by the working and middle classes, enhanced that audience's understanding of and the probability of its enlistment in the contradictions of American working-class experience. This "enlistment" meant not only an imaginative sympathy for those caught in such contradictions but an identically intense commitment to a class-based political understanding of the origins of those contradictions as well as a concomitant commitment to a political, even revolutionary, solution to the problems generated by them. How then was one to write a long narrative that would meet the political and artistic demands of such a charge and at the same time be attractive to two classes of readers among whose shared characteristics was, one might say, an aversion to serious literary art? Was there a set of conventions, a format, a practice that would produce texts that gripped a literarily unsophisticated audience *and* instructed it? And the problem could grow more complex if one broadened its scope by seeking to influence the intellectual reader of any class.

Marx and Engels, whose affections for the works of antiquity, for those of Shakespeare and Balzac, are well documented, had not anticipated the "highbrow, low-brow" cultural distinction of the twentieth century when they suggested that less tendentiousness and more irony, less didacticism and more character development, were necessary for the revolutionary art with which they would be aesthetically comfortable. By the 1930s, however, the same technological advances that had revolutionized the relationships between labor and capital had significantly altered the interplay between artists and their audiences. Forms of mass production and distribution made art cheaper and more plentiful. They also made art more varied. Not all of it was considered art by all of its potential consumers.

The problem became particularly sticky for those who wanted to use art as a weapon in the class struggle. Which, they wondered, of the array of weapons spread before them, would carry the day? In 1935, a Soviet commentator noted:

> I must admit . . . that I have not always the patience to read our revolutionary literature. I cannot read it and I do not understand it; I am not a specialist. But insofar as I know the masses, the workers and their psychology, I must say: no, this will not meet with much approval from the workers. The worker looks at these books and sees that they contain no figures, no examples to emulate. A revolutionary writer is not one who merely repeats: Long live the Revolution! (Josephson 300)

Similarly, proletarian fiction written in the United States failed to capture the public imagination. The brave, even complex, figures and their strikes and meetings drawn by "writers on the Left" in books from small presses printed in even smaller lots had little of the appeal of American popular culture. In midsummer of 1934, Wallace Phelps (William Phillips) and Philip Rahv considered the problems of meeting this kind of literary challenge:

> The very existence of two main types of revolutionary writing, the more intellectual and the more popular, shows that there is a division in our audience in terms of background and class composition. Workers who have had no literary education prefer the poetry of Don West to that of S. Funaroff, whereas intellectuals reverse this choice. The proletarian writer should realize that he is functioning through his medium within the vanguard of the movement as a whole. As such, his task is to work out a sensibility and a set of symbols *unifying* the responses and experiences of his total audience. Insofar as this cannot be done overnight, his innovations must be constantly checked by the responses of his main audience, the working class, even while he strives to raise the cultural level of the masses. (250)

What, then, was the cultural level of the masses in America in the 1930s? What did they read? If we were to look to book sales for evidence, we would not find one "proletarian" novel in the list of best or even "better" sellers, with the possible exception in 1939 of John Steinbeck's *Grapes of Wrath*. (The caveat is not about sales figures but whether Steinbeck had written a proletarian novel at all.) Between 1929 and 1940, in general, Americans read romances and mysteries, and looked for big books, historical novels epic in range and filled with many strong typical characters in support of one or two romantically conceived central figures. The data on which these observations were made was available from publishing and sales records reported in various trade publications. The statistical definition of a "bestseller" in the standard study (Mott) was sales equivalent to one percent of the population of the continental United States.

So, for instance, in 1792, John Trumball's mock epic poem *M'Fingal* was a best seller with a total of at least 25,000 copies sold (Mott 304). These titles were among best sellers between 1930 and 1939 with sales of at least 1,200,000: Pearl Buck, *The Good Earth*; Ellery Queen, *The Dutch Shoe Mystery*; Hervey Allen, *Anthony Adverse*; Margaret Mitchell, *Gone with the Wind* (313–14). Mystery novels appear on the 1930–1939 lists as ten of nineteen titles. The two novels listed as best sellers for 1934, the year Clara Weatherwax began work on her response to the *New Masses* contest call, were murder mysteries by Earle Stanley Gardner. Sales figures for "proletarian" novels in 1934 are hard to come by, but in a letter from January 1935, an editor at Knopf is quoted as giving the following figures at a John Reed Club symposium on publishing:

> Dale Curran, The House on the Street—800; James T. Farrell, Calico Shoes—800; Henry Hart, The Great One—800; Edward Dahlberg, Those Who Perish—1000; William Rollins, Jr., The Shadow Before—1200; Jo[sephine] Herbst, The Executioner Waits—1600; Langston Hughes, [The] Ways of White Folks—1800; Grace Lumpkin, To Make My Bread—2000; J.T. Farrell, Young Manhood of Studs Lonigan—2000. (Snow 1935)

One source of information on publishing and readership was Pen & Hammer (later the National Research League), the research arm of the Communist Party USA. Pen & Hammer did surveys, conducted studies, and wrote position papers on matters of physical and social science, including cultural production and consumption as phenomena. In 1932, Leonard Gross, a Pen & Hammer member in New York, reported on a 1931 study of American reading preferences.

These topics were listed as in the "upper four deciles" of interest by men and women who worked in factories:

> scientists
> laws and legislation

prices and living costs
personal success
successful marriage
modern civilization
adult education
personal hygiene
parents relationship to children
interesting people
public health
prevention and treatment of disease
the nature of human nature
personal qualities analyzed
college and higher education
interesting places in the U.S.

These topics, on the other hand, were relegated to the "lowest four deciles" by the same three groups of male and female factory workers:

authors
criticism of government policies
foreign politics
the money market
advertising
marketing
developments in farming
engineering
courts and justice
superstitions and beliefs
the reporter and the press
the family car
political organizations
marine life
theories about society and social progress

These topics were chosen, Gross reports, from a list of 115 items (which he does not include in its entirety, referring to the published study instead). He concludes that "[t]he generalization that emerges is one of the two that emerge in all psychological studies of this sort—the principle of human limitations. People want to know a little more about what they already know (or perhaps some extreme novelty or salutary thing). Such facts are of course no argument for extreme vulgarization because any extreme vulgarization would be short-sighted" (Gross 181–82).

Gross is arguing that whatever the desires of the proletariat for that which
they already know in the form they already know it, it would be a mistake to try
to capture their readership by pandering to this characteristic in the extreme. It
is the "what" and "why" that are missing in his remarks. What would constitute
such pandering and why would it be short-sighted? What would be lost to the
immediate effect of gaining their attention? Was it solely that such vulgarization would neglect the duty, remarked later as we have seen by Phelps and Rahv,
to raise the cultural level of the masses while being informed by their desires?
To fill in the gaps, we can look at another study conducted by Pen & Hammer
in 1934, this one on the content and form of fiction in the two major formats of
American magazine publishing, the "pulps" and the "shinies."[1]

The pulps and the shinies were differentiated by the paper on which they
were printed. Taken together, they were the major source of non-newspaper
print information available to the working class. Pen & Hammer wanted to
know what was in them:

> Efforts to account for the ideological weakness of the American work-
> ing class cannot disregard the influence of the popular American mag-
> azines. Analysis of the number, character, and circulation of the "pulps"
> and "shinies" . . . shows that proletarian writers and critics face a seri-
> ous political problem in undertaking to offset and destroy the ideologi-
> cal influence of these publications. The development of a powerful
> mass literature expressing proletarian—not bourgeois—ideology is the
> most effective weapon; we have its beginnings today in a host of maga-
> zines which have mushroomed over night, and in a growing shelf of pro-
> letarian novels. Also needed, but still lacking, is a critical literature,
> written for the masses rather than solely for the writers and critics, expos-
> ing the class character of the popular magazines. ("Pulps" 219)

And they were popular. Of the ninety magazines in both categories, nine (the
pulp *True Story Magazine* and shinies *American Weekly, Saturday Evening Post,
Woman's Home Companion, Liberty, Collier's Weekly, American, Hearst's International Cosmopolitan*, and *Home*) had distributed paid circulations of over one
million each. The paid circulation of the ninety taken together was over thirty-
five million a week, fortnight, or month. Left magazines, some independent,
such as *Contempo, Anvil, Left*, and *Dynamo*, and others with institutional ties to
the organized Left, such as John Reed Club magazines *Partisan Review, Left
Front, New Force*, and *Partisan*, reached a much more limited audience. The
larger, older *New Masses*, the leftist magazine of culture most closely associated
with the CPUSA and the recipient of the benefit of its national network of book-
stores and subscription appeals based on national party membership lists, had a
circulation in 1934 of only 23,000 (Snow, "Carbon" 264). *Anvil*, one of the most

respected of the purely literary proletarian magazines, had a circulation per issue (paid subscriptions plus newsstand sales) of four to five thousand.

For their analysis of the impact of popular magazine fiction, Pen & Hammer identified four fiction categories that appeared regularly in the sixty-four pulps owned by the five major pulp publishers: love and romance; detective and mystery; western and adventure (including sports); and war and flying. Each of these had its own criteria, for the most part built on principles of escape and romance, adventurous escapades, or the swift resolution of criminal cases. Love stories for the pulp *Dream World*, for example, were to "carry real illusion . . . pretty romances, charming love stories, free from horrors and tragedy." Usually these were stories of "modern everyday people, in which things happen that the average girl would like to (have) happen to herself." Others were more "true" to experience, featuring stories of love winning out over great odds; but "stark realism" was to be avoided. This is not to say that, like many popular films of the period, pulp magazine fiction suggested the audience identify its interests with the idle but good-hearted rich by putting them at the center of their fictions. Pen & Hammer notes with some urgency "the fact that writers are, in general, instructed to choose their characters from the working class; identification of reader with characters thus is made easier for the worker and an enervating ideology is most effectively forced upon him" ("Pulps" 220).

Pen & Hammer's critique of magazines in the other three categories was basically of one piece, that the implicit "lessons" of detective, adventure, and war stories were those that reinforced the fundamental interests of the capitalist class on a larger scale. They argued that just as war stories reinforced a war hysteria useful to capitalist imperialism, and adventure stories featured xenophobia, nationalism, and racial stereotyping that kept the international working class divided,

> [s]ignificant from a proletarian point of view are the implicit demand [in detective magazines] for glorification of the police, detective and private operatives, those strike-breaking enemies of the working class, and the editor's instruction that stories shall deal with "the conflict of right and wrong intentions," i.e., with intentions right or wrong from the capitalist point of view; implicitly this involves cloaking the responsibility of the capitalist class for so-called "wrong" intentions, cloaking the class nature of crime and punishment, and emphasizing instinct and biology, not the institutions around us as the source of crime. ("Pulps" 220)

As for the shinies, whose circulation per title was higher than those of the pulps and whose total circulation accounted for considerably more than half of the total in the study, Pen & Hammer had one major observation to make:

The ideology of the shinies is rabidly nationalistic and capitalistic. For example, the editor of *American Magazine* advises contributors: "Material is strictly American, that is, its fiction must be American in characterization and environment; its articles must be about prominent American citizens, also its sketches." By "prominent American citizens" is meant, of course, leading financiers, industrialists, politicians, et al.; those through whom two great capitalist myths can be exploited—the myth of equal and unlimited opportunity for all, and the myth of the inevitability of financial success for all (no matter how "humble") who have energy, courage and "inborn" ability. ("Pulps" 221)

In fact, it is this massive purveyance of capitalist mythology that seemed the most insurmountable problem for proletarian art to counter. It was not only that leftist outlets reached too few readers, but also that the machinery of popular cultural production was geared to represent what proletarian novelists and critics of the 1930s never quite grasped, that Americans identify at least one class level *above* their actual class position. Socioeconomic movement in that direction is, after all, the most commercially viable form of the American dream. Only in the most displaced manner, usually by posing a hypothetical and somewhat ratiocinated question, can you get working Americans to identify with their own class or one below it.

Part of the problem can be understood as the ideological conflict between individualism and class solidarity translated into the tasks of both characterization and plot construction. In the "strike" story, for example, a fairly common form of proletarian fiction, the movement is always away from the individual or even the biological family as the locus of value formation and realization to class affinity. When a character first exhibits courage or compassion, it is usually in response to some conflict involving his or her family and the world of work, e.g., a decision must be made about taking a more hazardous but better paying new or second job to make ends meet, or a menacing foreman or manager must be somehow confronted about work rules and conditions or even personal relationships (but even these "personal" issues must be seen as being generated from capitalism's over-investment in class interest or privilege). Ultimately, the affiant ties pose seemingly irresolvable contradictions: how can the worker define and maintain his own class interests when the clearest medium available to him, the labor strike, may cause even greater hardship to his family? In order for the strike to occur, an act with both material and symbolic value, his loyalty must be transferred from family to class. Usually this transfer is foreshadowed by scenes wherein the comradeship of labor is made momentarily manifest by personal sacrifice in times of physical danger, when a worker risks his life for a comrade who is not a member of his own family. Later, this existential commitment at the moment of physical risk is transformed or is, in recollection, understood to be transformative, into a conscious commitment to a more programmatic risk-taking, to social and political action on behalf of *all* one's comrades regardless of immediate or long-term personal cost.

In mainstream popular culture, only the isolate hero is capable of altruistic behavior; the masses of men and women are fear-ridden and unpredictable; personal acts of bravery among them remain idiosyncratic and never foreshadow political or social acts or commitments. They are explained in the stories as atypical and not derived from class affinity but idealistically motivated by love or some other culturally defined emotional tie to another individual—such as guilt or fear—and are arrived at only under conditions of extreme stress. Whereas the proletarian version of altruism—class interest and solidarity—occurs where action is subordinate to thought, the popular fiction with which its art competed posits the base of human relationships among the masses as instinctive stimulus response. There, acts of sacrifice never transcend the limits of self and family or, in the case of detective, adventure, sports, and war fiction, some other identification with a non-class-based organization of individual experience. The oppositional structure framing the hero and the masses is common in American culture, high and low, which generally records an American flight from rather than toward collective experience. The most reflective portrayals in American literature of attitudes toward collective identity and action are those in which the individual moves from the center, away from the collective consciousness of the community, to the fringes of his or her social or psychological world, or beyond those fringes. There, at least in popular mass fiction, he or she finds self-realization and ultimate meaning.

It ought to be observable that however widespread has been the belief in the inevitable upward social mobility of the individual in American society, the chart of that progress has been irregular and the points on its graph maldistributed. Nevertheless, even at the depth of the Great Depression of the 1930s, the expectation of vertical expansion, the American pride in flexibility for survival, remained strong enough and so widely held that there was no real serious social upheaval, although at moments it appeared as though the limits would be tested. Despite the evidence of a general commitment to the myth of the American experience, proletarian fiction tended to insist that its protagonists, and by implication its readers, could embrace and even pursue the reverse order of experience. The mimesis of class affinity in proletarian fiction was always premised, or was said to be premised, on the historical inevitability of the triumph of the working class and its interests. All virtue was shown to reside in the working class in those fictions, either implicitly when general alienation was overcome or explicitly revealed in the characters of the newly radicalized workers. Attempts were even made to portray the necessity of middle-class identification with the goals of the working class by suggesting that economic conditions under capitalism disenfranchised the middle and lower middle classes to such an extent that they shared common goals with the working class.

The failure of proletarian narrative to attract an audience of either workers or middle-class wage earners had little to do with the validity or invalidity of its arguments. There is a nuance to America's myth of upward mobility that needed to be understood by the literary Left that seemed to have escaped it, including the members of Pen & Hammer. While proletarian fiction could and did extol the virtues of the working class, the American myth of class requires that one not only exhibit those qualities but retain them while freeing oneself from the constraints of class identity. Americans would prefer to have the qualities of the common man and the wealth of the capitalist, the capacity for honorable work and the authority to compel it from others. Put another way, the American wants to have "made good" without having lost the common touch, moderate appetites, his common sense. To possess these latter qualities as a member of the working class is not the trick, in the popular mythology of the first three quarters of this century; the trick is to retain those qualities while rising *out of* the working class. The focus of this aspect of the myth, as in popular culture but not in proletarian fiction, is on an exceptional individualism with a core of loosely class-defined qualities. This is, I think, a manifestation of the democratic center of the myth, the oxymoronic definition of American-ness as the mass experience of exceptionality. Garrison Keillor gets it right with the gentle irony of his civic creed for mythic Lake Wobegone: "Where all the men are strong, all the women are good-looking, and all the children are above average."

The important omission in Pen & Hammer's analysis of popular magazine fiction is any attention to formal questions. The survey of types of fiction was almost entirely focused on content with some brief consideration of genre. It would seem that the contrary was the case in the awarding of the 1935 John Day-*New Masses* novel contest prize. The original call for submissions said nothing about formal criteria. After lauding the progress of proletarian literature in recent years and declaring its intention of fostering even more creativity in the field of fiction, *New Masses* went on to propose rather ordinary contest rules about submissions and blind entries and deadlines and then simply required that, "All novels submitted must deal with the American proletariat" ("Announcing" 7).

In the subsequent gloss of the rules, the editors of the magazine went on to explain: "Any novel dealing with any section of the American working class may be submitted in this contest. For the purposes of the contest it is not sufficient that the novel be written from the point of view of the proletariat; it must actually be concerned with the proletariat" (7). At first glance, this requirement seems to suggest that *New Masses* had taken a position on one of the thornier questions in proletarian literary theory. The insistence that the novel "be concerned with the proletariat" would, if read strictly, exclude novels sympathetic to workers' issues from even the most revolutionary positions if those novels were not about workers and would specifically exclude novels of middle-class life in which protagonists awoke to their natural class affinities with the workers. What was given with the left hand, however, was somewhat taken away by the right:

> The term proletariat, however, is defined in its broadest sense, to include, for example, the poorer farmers, the unemployed, and even the lower fringes of the petty bourgeoisie as well as industrial workers. The characters, moreover, need not all be drawn from the working class so long as the book is primarily concerned with working-class life. (7)[2]

Whatever the novel was to be about, there seemed little to be said about how it was to be written. The editors suggested only that the judges (a *New Masses* editor, a *Daily Worker* former editor, a national officer of the John Reed Clubs, and two representatives from the John Day Company, co-sponsors of the contest and guarantors for the publication of the winner) would "try to consider all relevant factors." Those factors, as the announcement gave them, were the author's "purpose" and how well he achieved it, the degree to which characters were representative and convincing, the "significance of the theme by their understanding of the present situation and temper of the American proletariat," and the author's "conception and aim" (7). While the issues of "conception and aim" might be formal ones, how they were to differ from "purpose" was not clear. The editors were, however, concerned about one aspect of form; they worried that entries from workers who were not professional writers might "be handicapped in certain obvious respects." To offset this disadvantage, they declared that "[the worker's] firsthand knowledge of his theme can give his work an authenticity that the observer rarely achieves, and this is a quality that the judges will value highly when they have to make their final decision" (7).

Fifteen months later, after an extension of the deadline prompted by the unsuitability of the first round of submissions, the winner of the contest was announced in the 10 September 1935 issue of *New Masses*.[3] The announcement was only a part of the "Reader's Report" given to the *New Masses* audience by Alan Calmer, one of the judges of the contest. Calmer went to some pains to describe the range of responses to the contest call and to comment on how and why some entries failed to pass the scrutiny of the panel. By the time the extended deadline expired, "more than ninety" manuscripts had arrived. More

than thirty of these were by women. None of the entrants were established proletarian novelists; in fact, Calmer estimated that "with the exception of five or
six writers who have published a fugitive piece or two in the left-wing press, all
of the contributors were unpublished authors" (325).

The lack of literary experience on the part of some 95 percent of the entrants
caused the judges no little trouble. Despite the intention to privilege the
authenticity of worker experience in otherwise untutored manuscripts dealing
with working-class concerns, it was just that authenticity that was too often lacking. Although Calmer noted that more than half of the submissions were
"explicitly Communist" and all but about a dozen were proletarian in outlook,
the actual range of subject matter and plot was strangely wide. There were western novels in the Zane Grey mode, temperance novels, novels of high finance
and exposés of capitalist corruption, utopian novels in the manner of Edward
Bellamy's *Looking Backward*, Hollywood-style romances, a melodrama, and a
religious fantasy in which Christ helps defeat American fascism. Some borrowed the characteristic storylines of what Calmer called the "smoothies," those
popular slick magazines Pen & Hammer had called "shinies":

> One dealt with most phases of the life of modern youth: sports, bumming
> around, love, looking for a job, etc. The second [about a poor farmer who
> becomes a Communist and his son who follows in his footsteps] was full
> of psychological clashes of individuals in personal relationship rather
> than social. . . . The subject matter and treatment of these two books were
> similar to the type of stuff that the largest section of the American audi-
> ence is accustomed to reading at the present time. (325)

Calmer and his colleagues also had trouble with manuscripts in which the
ordinary problems of how to tell a story were solved in less than an artistically
satisfying way. As Calmer noted, most of the manuscripts, even those with
authentic backgrounds in working-class experience, were unpublishable for the
same reasons that most manuscripts were unpublishable. One of these was the
influence of popular narrative forms, particularly movies, specifically the tendency to "twist realistic material into stock formulas" and to employ the worst
of popular Hollywood's melodramatic touches, such as coincidence and last-
minute escapes or reprieves: "Stories in the contest centering around [sic] a
machine shop, a textile factory, a coal mine, displayed nearly every phoney [sic]
characteristic of the American talkies" (324).

As the saying goes, the contestants couldn't win for losing, as Calmer saw
it. When they weren't using every plot cliché in the Hollywood handbook, they
were erring on the other side by failing to fictionalize at all, or enough, their
working-class experience. These writers devoted pages of loving energy to the

description of work but almost none to a context in which this description advanced a story. Almost all failed to "churn a mass of experience into literary form" (324). However, those who did try for some literary effect failed too. Calling most of these efforts farcical in consequence, Calmer weighed in against their "'literarious' drivel," "florid descriptive passages," "stilted dialogue and clichés" that added up to "hopelessly archaic," "fifth-rate corruption[s] of Victorian and pre-Victorian sensibilities" (324). Their great failing was their seeming ignorance "of all developments in modern fiction from Henry James on" (324). All of them needed serious exposure to Hemingway, Faulkner, Joyce, and Proust—to modern literary form. The absence of any knowledge of modernism's influence on narrative practice contributed to what Calmer considered the gravest problem with proletarian fiction as a system of representation, the inability to convey the ideological content of the struggle through any means other than the set speech or oration, usually at the least likely moment in the story. Calmer agreed that "speeches and arguments are a genuine part of literary experience; but it is also a fact that they are not the ordinary materials of recent literature" and left-wing writers needed to know how to make the principles of the class struggle rise from the action rather than from the slogan.

It was the opinion of Calmer and the rest of the judges that Clara Weatherwax's manuscript avoided these problems. In fact, it seems clear, if not explicit, from Calmer's published report that part of the appeal of her novel was its attempt to fashion a "proletarian" narrative modernism whose practices would carry both action and argument while privileging the fundamental assumptions of the communist Left about individual versus collective consciousness. These virtues placed *Marching! Marching!* ahead of its close competitor, Martin Russak's *A Weaver's Son*. Russak's manuscript had been received before Weatherwax's and until hers appeared was considered to be the obvious choice for the prize. The son of labor organizers in the needles trade, Russak had written a fairly well constructed "American" version of a late nineteenth-century European realist novel of the need for social reform. As Calmer put it, not unsympathetically, "Although [Russak's manuscript] was full of effective writing and human characters, it seemed to lack an intimate feeling for the overtones of recent fiction; in places its style was a little dated. But it is a competent first novel and will be published" (326).[4]

Weatherwax's manuscript was chosen, it seems, as much for the possibility that its experimentation with modernist techniques would advance the formal growth of the proletarian novel as for its story and its ideology. In fact, the setting for the story was not a new one. There had already been two proletarian novels centered on the same place and event. The place was Aberdeen, Washington; the event was an attempt at a general strike among lumber and marine industry workers; the previous novels were Louis Coleman's *Lumber* (1931) and Robert Cantwell's *Land of Plenty* (1934).

Of the two earlier works, Cantwell's was the more highly regarded, for its authenticity of tone and for its innovative narrative construction—a series of over-lapping chapters, each from a different character's point of view. The issue at hand in each of the novels was the representation of a specific moment in the American version of class struggle, labor unrest. The failure, or refusal, of the leaders of the American Federation of Labor (AFL) to adequately represent the interests of industrial laborers in Fordist and Taylorized American factories had stimulated American workers as never before to think of themselves as members of a common class. The major effect of that recognition was to open the possibility of a national organized industrial labor movement. Although that possibility culminated late in the 1930s with the formation of the Congress of Industrial Organizations (CIO), earlier efforts had been made to organize this class-based energy.

Three dominant and competing voices in the argument over the shape of industrial unionism were those of the Industrial Workers of the World (IWW), the various socialist parties, and the Communist Party of the United States of America (CPUSA). The three positions converge in the American northwest late in the 1920s. The IWW had been active in the state, particularly in its logging and wood-processing industries, since the opening of the century, however. Seeking to place the control of every productive facility in the hands of the workers and to abolish the wage system that enabled owners to exploit workers, the IWW met with immediate and powerful resistance not only from capital in its forms of ownership and management but from civic and patriotic groups whose interests were identified with the owning class. Clashes between the IWW and American Legion-led attackers in Everett and Centralia, Washington, left scores dead in 1916 and 1920. In each case, IWW leaders were arrested but no charges were filed against American Legion mob leaders or members.

Marching! Marching! attempts to represent the resolution of sectarian positions into a single class-based industrial consciousness at the point of crisis in the struggle for unionization in the lumber mills and veneer plants of an unnamed town very much like Clara Weatherwax's native Aberdeen, Washington.[5] While the historical moment is literally a fiction, the novel is based on the economic and labor history of the region and certainly reflects the tensions in and around Aberdeen in 1934 when the novel was being composed. What Weatherwax understood was that a composite moment that fictionalized historical forces would allow her the literary freedom to argue as she liked about the meaning of class identity and experience. Years later, Philip Rahv wrote complaining that no one in the proletarian camp understood the proper relationship between history and fiction. He overlooked Weatherwax in this case:

"What really happened in the nineteen thirties is that due to certain events the public aspect of experience appeared more meaningful than its private aspects, and literature responded accordingly. But the subject of political art is *history*, which stands in the same relation to experience as fiction to biography; and just as surely as failure to generalize the biographical element thwarts the aspirant to fiction, so the ambition of the literary left to create a political art was thwarted by its failure to lift experience to the level of history. (. . . A political art would succeed in lifting experience to the level of history if its perception of life—any life—were organized around a perspective relating the artist's sense of the *society* of the dead to his sense of the *society* of the living and the as yet unborn.)" (368–69)

By the time Rahv wrote the passage cited, 1940, he had already moved considerably far from the extreme leftist positions of his early years in the long-defunct Rebel Poets and his editorship of *Partisan Review* when it was the periodical voice of the New York City John Reed Club and not yet an independent showcase for social democratic modernism. In those earlier days he had presided over a discussion of the proletarian novel in the pages of *PR*, one contribution to which was Edwin Berry Burgum's comment that "at the present [1935] moment in American history the proletarian is synonymous with the revolutionary novel: i.e., the revolutionary novel is the proletarian novel considered from its political rather than its social or its aesthetic aspect" (303). That political aspect in fiction, for Burgum, was not derived from anything as metaphysical as Rahv's sense of the societies of the dead and the as yet unborn, but from the simple formula of the influence of dialectical materialism from the point of view of the class-conscious proletariat brought to bear on the relations of production at a specific historical moment. The consequence, Burgum was confident, would be a literature that was neither escapist as written under the influence of idealistic philosophy nor despondent as written under the influence of pragmatism. Burgum argued that

> Insofar as the bourgeois novel is concerned with the proletariat, it is pessimistic; insofar as the proletarian novel is concerned with the bourgeoisie, it is pessimistic; but though the bourgeois novel may be pessimistic about the bourgeoisie, the proletarian novel is never pessimistic about the class-conscious proletariat. This is by reason of the fact that both by observation of American life and by Marxist theory the proletariat is defined as class-conscious when it acts in the belief that only its conscious cooperation is necessary to promote the immediate direction of history toward the dictatorship of the proletariat. (303)

It is in his last phrase that Burgum anticipates Weatherwax's dilemma as a
novelist. How was she to depict the conscious cooperation of the proletariat with
the project of history without falling into the sloganeering and speechifying that
marred so many attempts at that same task? Her answer was to create an unconscious collectivity-as-mind that she could both shape and mine. By eschewing a
single and singular protagonist whose destiny would of necessity shape her narrative and by refusing to privilege a single narrative voice, Weatherwax left open
the ground of narration to the collective voices and destinies of the class on which
she would focus. To prevent such a collectivity from being an inchoate welter of
voices, Weatherwax used a nominal third-person omniscient narrator. That is,
when an identifiable character is not talking or thinking, the story is moved along
by a minimally intrusive voice that simply reports but never reflects, and it never
reports what a character thinks or feels. That information is provided by Weatherwax's adaptation of the stream-of-consciousness technique.

By omitting a privileged center, she gives equal voice to every character and
that voice is both public and private, reflecting in action, not in narratorial intervention, multiple public and private sensibilities. By the acts of speaking and
thinking, the individual characters move the narrative collectively, haltingly at
first and ever more efficiently as their class-consciousness gains residency in
their unconscious valuation of their and others' lives. The story moves not by
disclosures about what happened to Joe-the-hero and what he thinks about that.
Weatherwax's task is to help us understand how the historical moment is the
product of the collective material consciousness of the people, revealed to us
through their individual and then collective unconscious.

To establish a collective unconscious, she works inductively with us, piling
up episode after episode of individual response, response presented to us absent
the barriers between internal and external vocalization. Weatherwax simply
drops all traditional punctuation and syntactical markers when she moves from
interior voice to exterior and relies solely on the visual clue of a change from
roman to italic font, holding to lower case as often as she can:

> *All these years* she thought swiftly, understanding, with the paper
> clenched in her fist *All these years and they just now decided to put him
> away* already running inside to grab her coat and beat it to find Matt
> and talk this over—find out who put them up to it *That'd tell us more
> than anything we ever got out of Silly's crazy gab* tearing out of the house,
> leaving the grubby peaked hat where it had been, tossed when they
> hauled Silly away, drooling moaning towards it. (153–54)

In effect, most of the book is speech or thought. There is very little exposition of any traditional kind that does not come from those two sources. Once,

tellingly, Weatherwax falls back on the expository function of the narrator's voice. At a strike rally, Steve, a college friend of one of the organizers, plays "revolutionary" music on the piano. But it is not the *Internationale* or "Down with Fascist Terror" or even "I Dreamed I Saw Joe Hill" that he plays. Weatherwax gives over the job of describing the pianist's appearance at his instrument and the physicality of his playing to a traditional narrative turn; what we see is what the voice tells us the workers see, a tall, hawkish, intense young man who hunches over the keyboard, his too-short coat sleeves making his hands seem huge. Then he falls on the keys and attacks them, even playing with his forearms. A fist. And then when he was finished, from his "easy height" smiling gently at the workers. She has told us what they see, but what they have heard is reported only through their private and public voices:

> *The intervals don't sound right* Granny thought uneasily *but he's doing it on purpose.* . . .
>
> "The best I ever heard!" "It's like a battlefield!" "Seems like all us longshoremen marching!" . . .
>
> *I don't like it I don't like it but I want to hear it again. It says something. It says something wonderful.* . . . (196–97)

The intended effect of Steve's playing points up the contradiction between this kind of political art and its purpose. The contradiction is that while it is the "conscious cooperation" of men and women with history that is to be imitated, the mode of imitation, "art," often leads us to *feel* its validity rather than know it in any syllogistic way. Thus, when Pete introduces Steve and says, "This music fits our times. It's revolutionary. You never heard anything like it before. It's what you get out of it that counts. It's how it makes you feel" (196), he is claiming for Steve's art a function that his own organizing activity cannot exercise. Throughout the novel it is the unassailable logic of the moral right of men and women to the products of their labor that is supposed to carry the day. Consequently, the intrusion of "art" into the novel's own imitation of the development of working-class consciousness needs to be tamed, or at least subordinated to the discipline of the movement.

Characters try very hard not to lose sight of the logically apprehendable validity of their political position. Matt begins with a lengthy analysis of why the workers are right: "We all know that a capitalist society is built and maintained for the profit system. But it's so full of contradictions that it's doomed from the start. Look: . . . " (204). His speech ends in a call for a strike and the meeting rises "(Stamping whistling, pandemonium. 'Jeez! That's the stuff!' 'Matt sure makes it plain!' 'Damned right we'll pull this strike!')" (206) but subsides into order for the reading of the resolutions of the meeting: a policy of strike struggle, industrial unionism based on class struggle, solidarity and sympathy strikes as necessary weapons, against company unions, for the right to form unions, to strike and to picket, for AFL members to belong to any political party they like, for a struggle against fascism at home and abroad and in their city and factories, freedom for anti-fascist fighters, against all syndicalism laws and frame-ups. These positions, read, debated, understood, are the political will of a class-conscious proletariat. It is this action, this bringing into being an agenda for change, that is their permanent common consciousness. The revolutionary emotions that were roused in them by Steve's atonal attack on the western European symphonic poem have subsided and have been replaced by the careful march of charge and resolution.[6]

There are sixteen chapters in this novel and the first fifteen are guided, however minimally but surely, by the third-person omniscient sensibility I have noted. As Weatherwax has her characters slip in and out of first private, then public, then private voice again and again, the inherent identity of their common private and public selves becomes visible, however, and by the last chapter she drops the third-person voice and allows the collective identity of the working class to emerge in complete control of the text. When we get to the last chapter we see that Weatherwax has been gradually easing "herself" off stage so that at the moment of crisis, we will see that it arrives not by accident or by her desire but as the expressed will of a working class "consciously cooperative" with history. Like the state under communism, the author has withered away and has been replaced by the people:

> It's day. For hours we've been coming together, eager to start. . . . Everyone laughs and talks. We look forward and back at our strength and numbers. A feeling of live power ripples through us like electricity, feeding and renewing itself on the charged air around us, full as it is of the sounds we are making, of the sweaty smell of our own flesh in movement, and of the oil, fish, wood, pulp, gasoline, factory smells of our working clothes. . . . Not much talking now. Even the kids step strong like men. . . . "They've called out the militia!" . . . *Our boys wouldn't gas and shoot their own fathers and mothers and brothers and sisters.* . . . There are machine guns. . . . A few of us gasp, flinching the way horses do from the menace of snakes, but we don't stop or slow. . . . *Jeez! Bayonets! Machine guns! They got gas masks in those bags around their necks.* . . . *Come over to our side. Why should you kill us? We are your brothers.* . . . Then suddenly Annie turns and waves a signal to our marshals. Each lifts a hand for a moment while a word is spoken rank to rank. The signalling hands go down in unison and we're all singing:

>   Hold the fort for we are coming;
>   Workingmen be strong! . . . (253–56)

No one liked her novel unequivocally, or even very much, it seems. The reviews, except for the obligatory but half-hearted praise in *New Masses*, managed in some cases to find her innovations interesting or her authenticity compelling or the coming-to-consciousness of the workers moving, but for the most part she was dismissed as minimally skilled or uncontrolled. Today, an argument can be made, I think, that Clara Weatherwax addressed almost every problem of the proletarian novel as it was understood in the early 1930s. And one could argue that she provided answers for most of them. She certainly met the call for the contest she entered, and then some. Her formal adaptations, though not pyrotechnical in their application or even in their impact, seem designed to meet the very real political tasks she set out to confront. In her novel, form follows the function of the artifact. And ironically, given that her efforts came at what at first seemed the high point of the period of proletarian culture in the United States but soon was revealed as the moment at which most of the institutions that had nurtured it abandoned it, Weatherwax fulfilled the assumptions made in 1923 by Lunacharsky. Her novel was "little inclined toward individualism;" did "reflect the majesty of the collectivist pan-psychic ideal" and even gave some shape for once to that peculiar notion of the pan-psychic; did "pulsate with anger directed against [the] enemy;" expressed "sorrow for [the] victims, contempt for the crumbling world, passionate love for the world in birth throes;" gave faces to "an austere and brotherly cult of . . . heroes;" and "[b]y shifting the center of gravity from 'I' to 'we,'" rose "above the problem of the grave which torments the bourgeois and the intellectual" and posited an ennobled and realizable future for the American working class conscious of its destiny.

It seems equally clear, if not ironic, that she tried to answer the demands of two audiences, a literarily literate middle class and a working class whose tastes and paradigms were already shaped by the mass production of disposable culture. She was less successful with the second than it would seem she thought. There is too much, even in her working class characters' honest speech, of the topics workers wanted to avoid and too little of the things they wanted to know. All of those ersatz "movie" novels Alan Calmer rejected had something of the right idea about what workers, not the class-conscious proletariat, would read. It looks like almost everyone, even Clara Weatherwax, forgot that the class-conscious proletariat didn't need convincing. They needed celebrations of their role in history, what Soviet critics sometimes called "revolutionary romanticism," not speeches and arguments. Perhaps there should have been two working-class literatures from the Left, one a revolutionary romanticism for the already committed and another, a Marxianized version of good melodrama, a comedy of capitalist contradictions with clever "tricky servants" outwitting those "blocking humor" capitalists all in the name of removing the alienation between the worker and his labor or his destiny or his girlfriend as his class destiny. Somehow I think Charlie Chaplin in the 1920s and Lina Wertmuller in the 1970s had it right. History is comedy; it moves teleologically toward the integration of experience with destiny. But then, Marx said that, too.

Clara Weatherwax had a glimpse of the answer. She wasn't able to avoid preaching to the choir, but she did know that the movement of history was with the masses toward the future. The hope in the marchers' collective voice was that they would arrive to save the day, that the militia were their brothers, and that the sheer logic of that relationship, the fraternity of working men and women, would reshape the world. In representing the processes through which that hope is shaped and manifested in action, Clara Weatherwax wrote a literarily innovative, politically revolutionary, formally satisfying comic novel of working-class consciousness.

NOTES

1. In 1933, Pen & Hammer conducted an experiment in collecting data on aesthetic preferences by creating a poetry questionnaire involving responses by fifty City College of New York students to four poems, two "revolutionary" poems (one good and one bad), and two "bourgeois" poems (one good, one bad). In a follow-up study the questions were put to seventy New York University students, the assumption being that the City College students were quite left-oriented because of their proletarian origins and the NYU students, all middle class, would provide control data for the experiment. It is not clear what was learned from this exercise ("Arts" 179; "Life" 179, 182; "Upper" 182).

2. A month before the contest call, Edwin Seaver had written in *Partisan Review* of the proletarian novel: "It is not necessarily a novel written by a worker, about workers or for workers. . . . [I]t is possible for an author of middleclass origin to write a novel about petty-bourgeois characters which will appeal primarily to readers of the same class, and yet such a work can come within the classification, Proletarian Novel. Thus Albert Halper's *The Foundry*, although altogether about workers, does not seem to us a genuine proletarian novel, while Josephine Herbst's *The Executioner Waits*, which deals primarily with middleclass folks, most certainly does" (5).

3. In a letter to the postmaster of New York requesting the extension, from 1 April 1935, to 1 July 1935, the president of the John Day Company argued: "For some reason, only a few manuscripts have been submitted, and those received thus far have been of such low quality that it would be impossible to award a prize to any one of them as it would expose the author, the *New Masses*, and other contestants to ridicule in the literary world" (Suggs, "Introduction" xxxiii).

4. In fact, it was never published, but a chapter did appear later in *New Masses*.

5. Weatherwax's family had been owner-managers of lumber mills around the turn of the century. Her grandfather had been among the capitalists who donated money for railroad ties so that a spur of the Northern Pacific could be laid to Aberdeen in 1895.

6. It is interesting to speculate how far Weatherwax and her husband had resolved this tension. Gerald Strang was an avant-garde composer, a pioneer in twelve-tone composition and in electronic music. After his wife's novel won the prize, they used the money to move to southern California and Strang became first a graduate assistant and then arranger for Arnold Schoenberg. After her untimely death he stayed on at Long Beach State and became a professor of music there. I suppose the portrayal of Steve and his music owes something to Strang or his circle. Steve's music and performance may in fact be based on the compositional and performance style of Henry Cowell, a high-modernist composer-theorist with ties to the Left through the New School for Social Research and a loose association with the Composers' Collective, a section of the CPUSA-backed Workers Music League. Strang and Cowell were friends and Cowell visited the Strang-Weatherwax household while the novel was being written. His performative style was much as Weatherwax depicts in the novel.

Time, Transmission, Autonomy

What Praxis Means in the Novels
of Kenneth Fearing

DAVID JENEMANN AND
ANDREW KNIGHTON

"All that is required is imagination and political good faith."
—Kenneth Fearing, *Clark Gifford's Body*

*"Telling a story means having something special to say, and
that is precisely what is prevented by the administered world, by
standardization and eternal sameness."*
—Theodor W. Adorno, "The Position of the Narrator
in the Contemporary Novel"

Today, with the exception of *The Big Clock*, each of Kenneth
Fearing's novels is out of print, out of sight, and largely out of memory. Among
his contemporaries, even those who putatively shared his political views, Fearing's novels were dismissed as inconsequential. "To shift abruptly to secular matters," writes one reviewer, *"The Big Clock* by Kenneth Fearing is a well-done
book, though not, to my mind, worth doing" (Hardwick 587). The scant academic discourse currently devoted to Fearing concentrates almost exclusively on his
poetry, and save for those few anthologized poems, Fearing has been excised
from U.S. literary history. At one time, however, Fearing was perhaps the most
important left-wing poet. Allen Guttmann credits his first book, *Angel Arms*,
with inaugurating the genre of proletarian poetry (252),[1] and Alan Wald claims
that his death is the symbolic end of the Old Left (9).[2] But even those scholars
most attuned to the evolution of the literary Left who would give Fearing his
due as a poet seem congenitally averse to granting him any credit as a novelist.
Most recently, Rita Barnard, in her book *The Great Depression and the Culture
of Abundance*, condemns Fearing to be remembered almost exclusively as a poet,
dividing her book neatly in two: the novels of Nathanael West are counterposed

to Fearing's poetry. For his part, Wald describes Fearing's novelistic output in terms of economic necessity as "an enforced new career as the author of thrillers and mysteries" (226). Indeed, the overall impression one gleans of Fearing as a novelist is that his work has been dismissed as apolitical pulp.

Yet it may be Fearing's overlooked thrillers that most clearly reveal his intervention into questions political, cultural, and ethical. Despite their heft and "proletarian" credentials, Fearing's poetry volumes are confined by the formal limits of his man-on-the-street style and the impressionistic nature of poetry itself. On the other hand, by confronting the demands of realist narrative, Fearing's novels invite a sustained consideration of the form's political implications as well as its limits. With his relentless use of multiple narrators, condensed and expanding timelines, and excerpts of simulated mass media publications uncomfortably shoehorned into the body of the text, Fearing conceals behind the seeming simplicity of pulp a challenge to literary norms and the structures of bourgeois experience.

Diagnosing the conformity, bureaucracy, and dehumanization of modern experience, Fearing's novels reflect an uneasiness at the bad faith that results when one persists in trying to tell an individual's story at the same time that mass technologies threaten to render the very notion of "individualism" increasingly problematic. In recognizing this paradox, Fearing anticipates Theodor W. Adorno's observations regarding the narrator's tenuous position in postwar fiction:

> Apart from any message with ideological content, the narrator's implicit claim that the course of the world is still essentially one of individuation, that the individual with his impulses and his feelings is still the equal of fate, that the inner person is still directly capable of something, is ideological in itself; the cheap biographical literature that one finds everywhere is a byproduct of the disintegration of the novel form itself. (Adorno, "Position of the Narrator" 31)

In her study of Kenneth Fearing's poetry, Rita Barnard makes use of Adorno as a lens through which one can assess Fearing's appropriation of mass culture and his suspicions regarding the atrophying subject. While these concerns saturate Fearing's novels—and beg a fair reconsideration—Barnard's analysis of the cultural industrial aspects of both Fearing and Adorno falls short of illuminating the extent to which both writers treat mass-mediated modernity as part of a larger ontological question.

Just as it has been a disservice to Fearing to underestimate his contributions as a novelist, it is similarly unproductive to label him as a "proletarian" or "leftist" author without further probing those terms. Such a characterization would surely come as a surprise to those who supposedly knew Fearing best: "He didn't believe in politics," his son once wrote in a letter, "he believed in poetry" (Bruce

Fearing, Qtd. in Santora 318). Either a "proletarian" poet or a poet without politics: whether dismissing his politics or taking them for granted, most critical evaluations fail to apprehend Fearing's more radical notion of what praxis means: it is this that makes his position unrecognizable according to the dusty dialectics and sagging syntheses of much leftist "politics."

In contrast, we propose that Fearing's novels suggest a new object for political praxis. As opposed to those of his contemporaries, Fearing's works illustrate how it was that "traditional" Marxisms, misidentifying the culprit in modernity's world-historical caper, painstakingly pursued that perpetrator into a number of theoretico-political deadends. Recent theoretical reassessments of Marx's *Grundrisse*, a text thought to be more self-reflexive than Marx's earlier works and more directly political than the canonical *Capital*, have aided in revealing a crime that has been committed by capitalism under our noses all along.[3] It is in the spirit of these reassessments that we appeal to the *Grundrisse* as a means of theorizing the specific social powers with which Fearing struggled.

The *Grundrisse*'s value is to foreground the social relations proper to capitalism in all their varied antagonisms, to depict a capitalism that is not merely embodied by the ruthless few, but is rather a pervasive web of systemic command underpinning all activity as it is constituted in modern society. Here Marx most directly theorizes a capitalism that imprisons free time no less than it does work time, free thought no less than the affirming groupthink of the ideological combines. In tune with this refined model of capital's social forms, Fearing's politics are something more than a celebration of the illusory exteriority long romanticized by adherents to notions of leisure, "culture," and the proletariat. Fearing instead posits the dissolution of those "outsides" to capital—questioning whether they have, in modernity, ever existed at all.

Fearing's novels are shot through with this implicit skepticism; in novels such as *Clark Gifford's Body, The Loneliest Girl in the World,* and *The Big Clock,* his doubts about the modern condition take the form of a sustained meditation on electronic transmission, abstract temporality, and political autonomy. Ultimately, by situating his narratives within the confines of what the Frankfurt School derided as the "culture industry"—and by often taking that industry itself as his theme—Fearing's novels dispute the independence of political action. His works suggest that no object, event, or idea—however heroic—escapes the taint of the market: "All time and all space in every medium is merchandise, so expensive and so profitable in the great treasure hunt of the day that not a moment, not a line can be wasted on matters irrelevant to communications as a flourishing commerce (Fearing, "Reading, Writing, and the Rackets" xix).

Given the inescapability of the market and its proliferating technological seductions, Fearing and his characters confront the imperative of fashioning a new praxis responsive and endogenous to the modern, mass-mediated milieu. The novels—often quite explicitly, as in the case of *Clark Gifford's Body*—serve as imaginary testing grounds for such praxis, as a forum for experimentation with a new age, and as a means of launching a new politics:

> "I think I'll go into politics," he said, finally.
>
> I said, "How can you? You know you're a socialist, and socialists never get elected."
>
> He laughed at that so hard we nearly had to stop dancing.
>
> "Not that kind of politics," he said. "Something else. This is a strange age we are coming into." (267)

Transmission

Fearing intercedes at a historical moment when the form of the novel was to prove increasingly inadequate to the demands it traditionally shouldered. In the years surrounding World War II, the realist novel rapidly lost touch with reality. Not only did the atomization of subjects make it difficult, as Adorno indicates, to tell individual stories that weren't mockeries of the notion of individuality itself, but in addition the mediation of material phenomena through prose suffered in comparison to the allegedly unmediated presentations of radio, television, and the cinema. To think the changes wrought on the narrative fictions of the mid-twentieth century, one must consider not only the evacuated subjectivity assumed to be the precondition of postmodernity but also the electronic transmissions that make this change all but inevitable.[4]

The hard-boiled fictions of the 1930s and 1940s perfectly illustrate the winnowing of the atomized narrative subject into a figure suffering from a type of bipolar disorder.[5] With no access to reality—either of the nostalgic interior or mediated exterior varieties—the classic noir hero is reduced to irrational violence directed not at objective conditions but at those people closest to him. Coupled with this irrationality is an utter lack of emotional content in narrative descriptions. Reactions to events, should they materialize at all, sneak up on the characters after the fact:

> "All of a sudden, I found out I was crying too." (Cain, *The Postman Always Rings Twice* 30)
>
> "The siren started to scream and at first he thought he was making the noise himself." (West, *The Day of the Locust* 185)
>
> "I don't know when I decided to kill Phyllis." (Cain, *Double Indemnity* 85)

Further, the conversations between characters sap their interactions of any affect. Connections are distilled to the smallest admissible linguistic link. Sentences are chipped off from their speakers, offering no clue to their subjective origins, betraying no interior at all.[6] Only the briefest consents or negations are admissible and then in the form of direct repetition. Sex is violent and animalistic, isolating the characters precisely at the point of consummating a union. "Bite Me! Bite Me!" Cora commands Frank in *The Postman Always Rings Twice*, and he complies, carrying her upstairs while she bleeds. In *The Day of the Locust*, Faye Greener's come-hither look is no promise of happiness but one of death: "Her invitation wasn't to pleasure, but to struggle, hard and sharp, closer to murder than to love. If you threw yourself on her, it would be like throwing yourself from the parapet of a skyscraper, you would do it with a scream" (West 68).

For his part, Fearing deals with the mutilation of the traditional narrative subject as a direct consequence of the rise of mass-media transmissions and, in so doing, effects a critique of transmission itself. Combatting the spurious individualism that pervades the bourgeois narrative from Defoe forward—as well as undermining the "narrowing of the soul" Georg Lukács attributes to the novel—Fearing distributes his narrative tasks among a variety of incommensurable viewpoints. The effect is comparable to channel-surfing on the television or twisting the radio dial. His first novel, *The Hospital*, for example, diffuses one half-hour at a New York hospital among twenty-eight different narrators arrayed from the operating table to the boiler room. In *Clark Gifford's Body*, Fearing thwarts the desire for closure by rapidly shifting among thirty narrative voices across a sixty-year time frame. His refusal to give credence to any one narrator, often falsely promising that, as in a newspaper or magazine, their tales will be "Continued on Page 58," draws our attention to the loose ends of history and the objects for which it purports to speak.

While our jaded postmodern eyes may view such techniques as old hat, what these novels successfully convey is a cacophony of transmitted voices, whose dissonant chorus renders a univocal subject position untenable. Fearing's nearest ancestor in this regard is Dos Passos; but whereas the "Newsreel" and "Camera Eye" sections of the *U.S.A.* trilogy threaten the overthrow of a unified subjective position still held tenaciously by Dos Passos's characters, in Fearing, the individual's battle against the culture industry has already been decisively lost. To some extent, Fearing's scattershot technique parallels the expansive offerings of consumer culture, whose multiplicity of alternatives is little more than an increasingly sophisticated and pernicious means of entrapment. Exemplary of this problematic is the poem "Radio Blues," where, despite the endlessly escalating radio volume, the proliferating sonic sludge spewing from the speakers can never completely account for the range of a subject's desires. "Is that just right to match the feeling that you want?" the poem queries, forcing the reader to conclude that, despite the infinite augmentation of the radio's offerings, they are never "just right" (62).[7]

In comparison to *Clark Gifford*'s thirty voices or the radio's promise of infinite variety, *The Loneliest Girl in the World*, with its seven narrators, seems relatively conservative, until one takes into account that one of the novel's most compelling voices is that of an inanimate recording device named Mikki. Not only does Mikki engage in "spontaneous" arguments with household guests—his automation matched and surpassed by the predictable responses of his supposedly human interlocutors—he also contains within his wire transcriptions "everything fine ever reproduced in sound." The fact that "some of it is absolutely unique, not known to be recorded anywhere else on earth," privileges Mikki over the majority of human beings he encounters, who are an assembly of clichés and banalities (30–31). Mikki is the ultimate narrative voice; his very uniqueness is the limit of the elusive individuality that haunts the novel form's nostalgic memory.[8] "Some juke-box," one character marvels, echoing an earlier Fearing poem that pointedly asks, "What can you do that a juke-box can't, and do it ten times better than you?" ("King Juke" 25). But Mikki does not simply exhaust the word. He functions, at his most fantastic, as a repository for all information, of every kind, everywhere.

> Now, we saw not only a continental network offering instantaneous information to anyone, on any subject, but also a general repository for all the data a businessman might need in the daily conduct of his affairs. His correspondence, his estimates, inventories, invoices, receipts, bills paid and due, all memoranda, everything he now committed to paper and placed in his cumbersome and bulky individual files, not recoverable a good part of the time, could go on deposit with us, on tape or on wire, quickly available at all times. (171)

The entirety of information, professional and private, is contained on the wires of Mikki's electronic brain, administered by an information technology company, and distributed instantly. The beneficiary is the world of global business that conserves resources, expands information capital, and conquers time in the process. Everyone's information is personalized at the same time that it becomes available to all. Here we have the appeal of the psychological novel writ large upon the world of international capital: the information dispensed by the inwardly directed narrator claims to account for all human experience. Fearing's Mikki conjures, in 1951, a culture-industrial dream not far removed from the contemporary reality offered by Dell and Microsoft, a box that uniformly provides for each individual need, no matter how diverse, from the same source. The infinitely expansive—yet oppressively inadequate—programming of "Radio Blues" finds its ultimate realization in Mikki.

While it is worth lauding Fearing's prescience with regard to the form taken by Mikki's information innovations, his is nevertheless a cautionary vision. Not only do Mikki's transmissions indulge the ruse of "pseudo-individuality," outlined by Adorno and Horkheimer in *The Culture Industry* and elsewhere,[9] but the false promise of both Fearing's Mikki and the globally networked present is that the disseminated information somehow provides increasingly unfettered access to reality. Instead, what Mikki provides is an excuse for excess, coupled with the spurious belief that being exhaustive is equivalent to being right and to being unique. Thus, the rakish son of Mikki's inventor can brag about the multiple versions of a song compiled in Mikki's memory: "And do you know how many recordings I have of the *Saint Louis Blues*, alone? Twenty-eight, Jim. Every single one of them with a different feature, of course. Distinctive" (92).

The very breadth of his collection makes it difficult to argue that any one of these versions constitutes the reality of the *Saint Louis Blues*—if anything, one is tempted to further sympathize with Adorno's arguments regarding the damage done to autonomous artworks in the process of their transmission. In "The Radio Symphony," he laments the capitulation of Beethoven's Fifth Symphony to the technical constraints of its broadcast, turning a critical ear toward everything from the disappearing second violins to the radio "hear-stripe" (the sound of the mechanism itself). Taking the first movement as an example, Adorno argues that the "creation *ex nihilo*, as it were, which is so highly significant in Beethoven" is undermined by the flattening performed by the radio. "As soon as it is reduced to the medium range between piano and forte," Adorno claims, "the Beethoven symphony is deprived of the secret of origin as well as the might of unveiling." The dialectical relation that powers the Fifth, "which makes out of the Nothing of the first bars virtually the Everything of the total movement . . . is missed before it has been actually started" (122–23). That which gives the Fifth its power and guarantees its autonomy is made impotent and unpalatable when every sound is blended into sonic goulash. Adorno thus proposes a theory of the symphony in which the mode of its reproduction is integral to the social appreciation of its form, and ultimately he concludes that the music bearing the name "The Fifth Symphony" is, when played over the radio, really no symphony at all.

Lest one think of this strictly as the cultural elitism of an "expert" listener, one should note that Adorno is consistent in his argument across the range of technological media, elsewhere expanding his critique to television and film, and noting how their narrative structures abuse the novel in the same way that the radio mutilates the symphony.[10] Intricately constructed characters are condensed into "mechanical simplifications;" stereotypes interact with stereotypes at only the most superficial level, as television broadcasts undermine the splendor of the bourgeois novel, depriving the viewer of even the illusory inner freedom once promised the reader (Adorno, "How to Look at Television" 148).

Adorno outlines the political implications of this degradation in his "Social Critique of Radio Music," arguing that in a commodity society subtended by the profit motive, "human needs are satisfied only incidentally." The ostensibly unique, subjective aspects of the autonomous artwork—the "ethereal and the sublime"—congeal into objects, "trade marks." Radio broadcasts achieve "the ideal of Aunt Jemima ready-mix for pancakes extended to the field of music," and as music on the radio becomes culinary, an object of lip-smacking consumption, "the listener suspends all intellectual activity . . . and is content with consuming and evaluating its gustatory qualities." Charles Vaughn's collection of twenty-eight versions of the *Saint Louis Blues* reduces each to an interchangeable piece of aesthetic currency in a pile of hoarded musical wealth—or better, a musical flavor, larded as if "the music that tasted best were also the best possible music" (Adorno, "Social Critique" 210–11).

The "Social Critique" intervenes at the point where the ideological effects of the radio transmission and the complementary mystification of social antagonisms are intertwined. "Music under present radio auspices serves to keep listeners from criticizing social realities; in short, it has a soporific effect upon social consciousness" (212). This is the ideological effect of atomized listening, and it has real implications for any sort of socially responsible aesthetics, for, like the first bars of the Fifth Symphony, the social knowledge conveyed by transmission is a ringing clarion reaffirming our own well-determined beliefs and attitudes. In Fearing's estimation, the institutional structures of the musical and the political are of a piece, as "this [media] industry is not merely one more among many; it is the central nervous system that actuates, or paralyzes, a whole society" ("Reading, Writing and the Rackets" xix). This system functions by perpetuating the illusion that the multiple voices spewing forth from radios, televisions, newspapers, and global information networks have transparent access to the truth of artworks, individuals, or historical events. For Fearing, the seeming self-evidence of these broadcasts makes them suspect: "It seemed that the more accurately messages were sent," Ellen Vaughn muses in *The Loneliest Girl in the World*, "the more skillfully one sought to misunderstand, conceal, or obliterate them. While poor signals set up an impulse to be restored and received, in a perpetual instability of flight and pursuit between two poles" (186).

Yet Fearing's novels are populated by characters who are too willing to believe that the smooth, clean transmissions of the culture industry guarantee authenticity. *Clark Gifford's Body*, for example, evokes both Welles's infamous *War of the Worlds* broadcast as well as the raid on a German radio station that served as a flimsy pretense for Germany to attack Poland in World War II.[11] In

Gifford, a band of revolutionaries and engineers organize the takeover of strate-
gically located radio transmitters and convince the populace that an armed
revolt is being waged against an authoritarian regime. However, the force of
these amateur broadcasts is nothing compared to the might of the institutional
culture machinery that drowns out the guerillas in a wave of newspaper reports,
press releases, counterbroadcasts, and clever propaganda.

Though the critical engagement with the tools of mass media is what drives
Adorno's and Fearing's most heated prose, that concern is embedded in a
broader critique of realism and the spurious ontology it promises. As we have
seen, Adorno contends that the realist novel increasingly reveals itself as ideological, and that the author who indulges in a realist aesthetic furthers the deceit
that things are as they say they are. "He would be guilty of a lie," Adorno claims,
"the lie of delivering himself over to the world with a love that presupposes that
the world is meaningful; and he would end up with insufferable kitsch" ("Position of the Narrator" 30).

Adorno's confrontation with realism is congruent with his attack on Hei-
deggerian ontology, to the extent that both take the concept of "transmission"
to be central.[12] The notion that things are what they say they are, that Being tau-
tologically defines itself, is the target of the most potent assaults in *Negative
Dialectics*; Adorno sarcastically suggests that in Heidegger's fantasy of *Dasein's*
Being, "Transmission is transmitted by what it transmits" (99). In order to prove
Being's authenticity, Heidegger must stage the same ruse that culture-industrial
broadcasts and Mikki's conversations enact—namely that events and individuals exist anterior to the network of social domination, and that the mediation of
transmission does not in any way alter or mutilate that existence. The result is,
as Adorno insists, a kind of "nonobjective objectivity" that embodies the inade-
quacy of not only ontology but also realism: "If the novel wants to remain true
to its realistic heritage and tell things how things really are," Adorno claims, "it
must abandon a realism that aids the facade in its work of camouflage by reproducing it" ("Position of the Narrator" 30).[13]

Fearing's destruction of the uniform novelistic voice serves simultaneously
to illustrate the exhaustive proliferation of mass media broadcasts and to challenge the presumption that these transmissions somehow provide their audiences with an unmediated link to reality. Not only are the narrators
contradictory—and therefore occasionally unreliable—so too, and especially,
are purportedly accurate electronic transmissions. Even Mikki's catalogue of
recordings leaves itself open to dramatic interpretation, its supposedly objective
data a patchwork of possibilities. Thus, Ellen Vaughn is capable of reorganiz-
ing Mikki's clues into a coherent narrative time frame that can either absolve
her father and brother of wrongdoing or convict them. Her attorney, recognizing the slipperiness of Mikki's electronic evidence and willing to concede that

juridical truth has no ontological grounds, advises her to simply believe what she wants to believe. This open-ended historicism affords Ellen the willful ignorance and belief in her own noncomplicity that typifies the historical sensibility of the modern subject. Through narrative techniques generally described as postmodern (montage, pastiche), Fearing condemns a postmodern subjectivity that would treat history as arbitrary, contingent, and thereby meaningless.

In an overblown conclusion, Ellen literally takes a gun to history, decimating Mikki's wires, and thereby severing all ties to the objective conditions that led to her predicament. Freed, if only in her own mind, from the constraints of history, she can rewrite the story to fit the predominant logic of her own needs, the legal system, and the press. This gesture, appearing at first as Ellen's liberation from the legacy of her father and the control of the machine, reverses itself to become part of the same old story. After destroying Mikki, she decides to take a job in communications and to pursue a traditional romance. Rather than shattering history into its myriad contradictory moments, Ellen "triumphs" by reinscribing the authority of the realist narrative and progressive, chronological time. Mikki may be gone, yet the novel ends with the historicist insistence that "[t]he fresh wire of the present flows magically on, different, shining, always unknown" (237).

Temporality

Ellen's high-rise sanctuary is suggestively known as "The Roof," and throughout the text it is explicitly counterposed to the laboratory and the office; it nevertheless remains the scene of not only Mikki's transmissions but also economic competition. As a result, the time that Ellen spends there, far from being a retreat, can be productive of value, history, and her own lonely subjectivity. Her plight makes clear enough that resistance to dominant social forces can hardly take the form of a hermit-like reclusiveness. The very conception of a private sphere—a realm of freedom antithetical to the realm of necessity—becomes increasingly untenable, as the propagation of ideology no longer stops at the door of the worksite.

Here and elsewhere, Fearing's characterizations of modern life stress the importance of free time to this process of political and economic command. His conception of market hegemony spares no time whatsoever—all must become productive, and this holds true as much for radio listeners and cinemagoers as it does for suits and lackeys. And it is precisely the most private modes which, in postmodernity—the society of the spectacle, the culture of consumption—become the primary arena of capitalist value creation. Adorno concurs here, suggesting that the enterprise once thought of as "leisure," a now almost archaic concept designating a certain autonomy and self-determination of activity, has been supplanted by its reified counterpart: "free time." The unique character of "free time" is that it remains intractably "shackled to its opposite," no longer outside of the productive machinery (Adorno, "Free Time" 162).

Free time is, according to Adorno, subjected to two different mutilations; it either follows after the model of the workplace (regimented recreational activities, time-demarcated TV guides, et cetera) or else it must be consigned to the realm of the unproductive. Either way, the end result is the same. In the time that by definition should elude the punchclock mentality of the workday, there is reinforced only the primacy of the workday. "[T]he prevalent ethos is suspicious of anything which is miscellaneous, or heterogeneous, of anything which has not clearly and unambiguously been assigned to its place. The rigorous bifurcation of life enjoins the same reification, which has now almost completely subjugated free time" ("Free Time" 164). The well-worn formulas of time expenditure afforded the late-capitalist consumer—especially indulgence in mass-mediated culture industrial enticements—strangle the potentially productive character of his or her "free" activity.

Time is lived abstractly as the succession of discrete instants elapsing in quantifiable units. Activity is gauged not by its qualitative, particular character, or in light of its specific utility, but rather by its abstract measure. Marx unfolds his labor theory of value out of this condition, and dramatically asserts in the *Grundrisse* that "all economy ultimately reduces itself" to the "economy of time" (173). Moishe Postone thus defines advanced capitalism by way of its increasingly regulated abstraction of time, arguing that under capitalism, time confronts activity as something external to it, instead of following from human events. Rituals, natural cycles, and variable rhythms give way to the structures of the clock-driven workday.

Because the capitalist mode of production is grounded upon this historically specific conception of time, thinkers such as Adorno and Postone, as well as Antonio Negri and Giorgio Agamben, have identified time as an indispensable strategic terrain upon which capital's tendential expansion occurs—and toward which opposition to capital must be directed. As Agamben forcefully notes, "The vulgar representation of time as a precise and homogeneous continuum has thus diluted the Marxist concept of history: it has become the hidden breach through which ideology has crept into the citadel of historical materialism" (91). That vulgar understanding of bourgeois time—alien from human activity and demanding conformity to its intervals—is the topic around which Fearing constructs his novel *The Big Clock*.

That time will be featured as the theme of this thrill ride is as evident from the title as it is from Fearing's central consideration of the subject at the novel's outset. The word—"Time"—blasts from the page, a paragraph by itself, with no need for a predicate, much less an orienting topic sentence (15). The word triggers a crescendo of musings that swell in the mind of white-collar journeyman George Stroud—he ponders, moment to moment, the intricacy of time's mechanism, its traps and pitfalls, its illusions, its inescapability. We have been indirectly prepared for these ruminations by Fearing's insistent characterization of Stroud as no stranger to time's exigencies. His resumé, prior to taking up with Janoth Enterprises (the publishing house whose chief is guilty of the murder that Stroud is called upon to investigate—and in which he himself is also incriminated[14]) reads as a veritable apprenticeship in managing instants and interpreting their value. Whether as a racetrack detective, an all-night broadcaster, or a timekeeper on a construction gang, he is consistently thrust into service at the hands of time and abides by its sovereignty in even the most minute matters: "I got a quick shave, and after that I had a quicker breakfast, and then a split-second drink" (41). Moreover, the workday expands to consume his entire existence; even the fling that incriminates him is circumscribed by the office, since the woman with whom he happens to sleep (thereby precipitating the convolutions of the narrative) is none other than the boss's mistress.

Stroud ponders time precisely in its abstractness; the big clock that haunts him is undeterred by any questions of quality or individuality; it establishes a time immanent to itself and alien to the human subjects it governs. "In short, the big clock was running as usual . . . Sometimes the hands of the clock actually raced, and at other times they hardly moved at all. But that made no difference to the big clock. The hands could move backward, and the time it told would be right just the same." And that relentless abstract time, the ominous ticking of which echoes across the social field, is that "to which one automatically adjusts his entire life. . . ." (5–6).

That the big clock mandates a specifically dehumanized time becomes apparent—"one runs like a mouse up the old, slow pendulum of the big clock, time" (15)—just as it does that this time is fundamentally bound up with the creation of monetary value. Marx, in the *Grundrisse*'s "Chapter on Money," suggests that:

> The individual carries his social power, as well as his bond with society, in his pocket. Activity, regardless of its individual manifestation, and the product of activity, regardless of its particular make-up, are always *exchange value*, and exchange value is a generality, in which all individuality and peculiarity are negated and extinguished. (157)

This sentiment is echoed by Stroud's colleague Roy Cordette, who innocently indicates, concerning a St. Paul bank heist, that money and time boil down to the same thing, to the extent that they both serve as abstract and exchangeable measures of equivalence. "'Figures again,' [Roy] delicately judged. 'What is the difference whether it is a half million, half a thousand, or just half a dollar? Three years, three months, or three minutes?'" (23).

When measurable time provides a medium for the smooth exchange of activity's value, production for need recedes in favor of production for exchange.[15] As Marx famously claims, "the social connection between persons is transformed into a social relation between things; personal capacity into objective wealth" (*Grundrisse* 157). That very interchangeability is precisely the formal means by which *The Big Clock* succeeds as a thriller, as anyone who traces a path backward from its arbitrary conclusion will discern. This conclusion is by no means an organic eventuality; a different culprit could easily have been indicted simply by means of an investigator rearranging or de-emphasizing some of the assembled, equivalent events. Thus for large parts of the text, those on Stroud's staff undertaking the investigation are unsure whether the criminal they pursue is a murderer or a player in a high-level business conspiracy—the implication of guilt shared alternately by Stroud and Janoth effectuates a dissolve through which their transgressions seem to become indistinguishable. As Stroud literally races against the clock to devise a means of escape, it becomes clear that the big clock's verdict is indifferent to the concrete reality of its subjects' guilt, and that indifference is what ensures the satisfaction of the page-turning suspense buff who reads the novel. In the same way that the big clock transforms all historical events into a network of interchangeable equivalences, Fearing reveals that many of the central metaphors of the thriller genre—guilt and innocence, clues and evidence, crime and the investigation—each lead to the inevitable conclusion that time will inexorably subsume and destroy all contingencies, anomalies, and possibilities of escape.

At the same time that Stroud's efforts to evade the command of the big clock occupy his mind, his very position in the publishing industry puts him at the service of that command. The very titles of Janoth Enterprises's journalistic products read as indices of the encroachment of mass-reproduced opinion through time (consider *The Actuary, Frequency,* and *Plastic Tomorrow*) and into the most reputedly personal of zones (*Homeways, Personalities, Fashions,* and *The Sexes*). "What we decided in this room, more than a million of our fellow-citizens would read three months from now, and what they read they would accept as final. They might not know they were doing so, they might even briefly dispute our decisions, but still they would follow the reasoning we presented, remember the phrases, the tone of authority, and in the end their crystallized judgements would be ours" (27). Behind this evident swagger, though, materializes a compelling moment of self-reflection on the bad faith essential to Stroud's survival as a servant of the culture industry: "Where our own logic came from, of course, was still another matter. The moving impulse simply arrived, and we, on the face that the giant clock turned to the public, merely registered the correct hour of the standard time" (27).

What begins here as a rather vulgar recapitulation of classical Marxist ideology theory—a conception of top-down power harnessed by those with access to the means of dissemination and influence—concludes much more subtly. The big clock, as the mechanism whereby unequal exchange is regulated, demands not only carefully crafted ideological concepts, but rather an entire mode of existence, governed by a time so thoroughly naturalized as to appear as a kind of ethereal energy, a logic of obscure or concealed origins. Its determining impulse is motivated not by subjective intention, but rather through a complicated machinery as alien and intangible as it is pervasive. Thus in many of Fearing's novels the deaths of the characters who most explicitly embody social power—Earl Janoth, Adrian Vaughn, Clark Gifford, Steve Crozart, et cetera—hardly impede the continued exercise of that power.

Fearing's understanding of capitalist time thus shifts the focus of social command away from the discrete space of production (where traditional Marxism has most consistently pursued its ramifications) and toward the sphere of reproduction. In this he anticipates the later investigations of Antonio Negri, for whom the dictates of capitalist production have spread beyond the enclosure of the factory across the social terrain. Production of commodities, to this line of thinking, is supplanted by more intangible forms of production—the intellectualized processes of subject-formation in a world where immaterial production of knowledge, skills, and character traits becomes the wellspring of capitalist value. The production of subjects, whose identities fluctuate along with consumer trends and career shifts, becomes capital's greatest concern precisely because, in a world characterized by virtually instantaneous transmission, this kind of production proves the most efficient of all. Overcoming the spatial distantiation of production and consumption additionally becomes the most crucial challenge to a globalizing capitalist market. Since, as Marx reminds us, the time that it takes capital to circulate from place to place can only be a negative determination of value—circulation time never produces value, it only impedes value production—reduction of the time of transmission is the goal of capital. Extended spaces are made manageable by the mastery and reduction of time.

The quickened pace of modern production is clearly facilitated by the modern media, where instantaneous transmission of consumer heuristics collapses the chasm between production and consumption—Mikki's dream becomes reality. The process becomes nearly immediate, though its further abbreviation remains capital's primary aim, as Marx notes: "[Circulation time's] abbreviation . . . [means] in part the *creation* of a continuous, and hence an ever more extensive market; and in part, the development of *economic* relations, development of forms of capital, by means of which it *artificially* abbreviates the circulation time. (*All forms of credit.*)" (*Grundrisse* 542). Marx's parenthetical allusion to credit is taken to its extreme in Fearing's vision of a Janoth Enterprises endeavor known as "Funded Individuals," in which subjects are reduced to the status of an investment whose backers then capitalize on the success of their creations:

> In theory, Funded Individuals was something big. The substance of it was the capitalization of gifted people in their younger years for an amount sufficient to rear them under controlled conditions, educate them, and then provide for substantial investment in some profitable enterprise through which the original indebtedness would be repaid. The original loan, floated as ordinary stocks or bonds, also paid life-insurance premiums guaranteeing the full amount of the issue, and a normal yearly dividend. (18–19)

The Funded Individuals initiative is met by the staff of Janoth Enterprises with a sort of suspicious awe, as if to reflect in their ambivalence the dialectical condition by which the staggering promise of human civilization's advancement is simultaneously human civilization's greatest bane. The magazine feature introducing Funded Individuals ("Crimeless Tomorrow: Research Shows Why. Finance Shows How") argues for the utopian qualities of this system, in which the temporal cultivation of human potential is predicated upon eradicating transgressions against market power. Yet there is something unnerving about such a transparent structure of command: This "revolutionary vision in the field of social security" is a radical transformation that in fact merely masks the perpetuation and intensification of the same system. Fearing condemns Funded Individuals for its empty promise of change—its "revolution without a revolution"—ideologically deployed to hide the fact that its amortization of all human effort according to the big clock's temporal dictates comes only at the expense of the political potentials of the present: "We are accustomed to thinking that crime will cease only in some far-off Utopia. But the conditions for abolishing it are at hand—right now" (29).

Though *The Big Clock* practically begs to be the cornerstone of Fearing's contribution to a rethinking of modern time, a similar preoccupation forms the backbone of virtually all of Fearing's novels. Significantly, he pays specific attention to the implications of this for art and artists in *Dagger of the Mind*. Another crime thriller, the novel is set at Demarest Hall, a kind of summer camp established to allow invited artists to pursue their projects in a setting free of the most pernicious demands of work and the everyday world. Demarest Hall architecturally and symbolically separates art from the objective reality of material need, by implication constructing the aesthetic as a sphere resistant to market forces external to production. This conception is contemptuously affirmed by a police agent visiting after the first of the novel's murders: "None of these artists ever did a lick of work in their whole lives" (93). That idea is, however, belied by the policeman's interlocutor, who in his counterargument complicates the idea of aesthetic unproductivity: "You have to take my word for it that these cluckaroos are not ladies and gentlemen of leisure. They work, and hard. Damn hard. And you must take my word for it that, although they may be screwballs on the surface, underneath all of that, there's a real reason, a perfectly sensible reason, for every crazy move they make" (93).

From the very first sentences of *Dagger of the Mind*, it becomes clear that while these artists may avoid the drudgery of the conventional workaday world, they cannot escape the determining structures of time. As if the novel itself has to abide by the punchclock, it opens with Christopher Bartel, an amateurish painter of cheaply sentimental canvases, ruing the strict breakfast schedule of the hall. Once underway, the novel's depiction of Bartel's holiday unfailingly portrays the way time interferes with his existence, often through the recurring motif of his lazy alcoholism. His frequent tippling—which one might moralistically dismiss as sheer unrecuperable unproductivity—is temporally regulated with a rigor that is virtually Taylorist. To wit:

> Let's have a drink. I don't think I'll do any more with this for a time. It's four o'clock. (39)
> It was about noon when I decided to quit work, for the time being, on the new canvas. (19)
> I tried to figure out whether I was ahead or behind in my usual drinking schedule. (43)

Ultimately, it will prove to be precisely this link between time and alcoholism that unravels the mystery, for when Bartel's drinking becomes truly excessive—reaching blackout proportions—he can no longer hew to time's dictates. At the conclusion, Bartel admits his guilt in the three Demarest Hall murders (though, as in *The Big Clock*, any number of other culprits are plausible enough), but since each of the murders occurs during an alcohol-induced stupor, he only retroactively recalls his fragmentary hours, never with the certainty to respond to questions about where he was at such-and-such a time. The inability to account for his whereabouts—especially to himself—frees him from suspicion until late in the book.

Of course, Christopher Bartel, George Stroud, and those others in Fearing's novels who stage resistances to abstract time ultimately fail and are brought back under its command by force or contingency. The minutes Bartel must count at the end are those ticking away prior to his execution, and the novel's conclusion finally eradicates not only the protagonist but also the notion that art can stand outside of time and the demands of the market. The only recourse the novel offers is a choice between the execution chamber or the abjection of the drunken blackout. For those nostalgic for the affirming interior of the subject or the purported independence of aesthetic production, these are the sole, debased avenues of escape that remain. Fearing reveals them to be one and the same.

Autonomy

Clearly, part of the conclusion that Fearing draws in his novels is that art is incapable of taking an opposing stance against the society that makes it possible. The interpenetration of the culture industry with the new deployments of productive free time prohibit the artist or activist from voicing their opposition from a space outside of reification and the logic of capital. As the case of Christopher Bartel illustrates, art's claim to exteriority from capital is predicated on a nostalgic retreat into the interiority of the subject. However, that escape can at the same time never be anything other than the negation of that subject. Fearing's works illustrate this conundrum by depicting the market's immanent and immediate saturation. As Negri would argue, no critique can take place from a vantage point above the market. Rather, "we are in that world made of money. Money represents the form of social relations; it represents, sanctions, and organizes them" (*Marx Beyond Marx* 23).

Fearing doesn't need Negri to tell him this. He need do little more than cursorily glance at the advertisements in *Time* magazine as he's tracking down reviews of his books. In the same month that *Dead Reckoning* is published, he would find that the machinery of transmission, oblivious or perhaps even callously indifferent to its content, barely masks the contradictions it disseminates. Among these are the conflicts Rita Barnard discerns in her work on Fearing's poetry, including the proscriptions made regarding the acceptable deployment of disposable income and disposable time, as readers are exhorted to buy while admonished to spend frugally.[16] Thus, in the 27 January 1941 issue of *Time* magazine, a Carrier air conditioner advertisement does not merely extol the virtues of air-conditioned comfort but also highlights the potential profit businesses may reap from investing in central air. The focal image of the advertisement is a caricature of traditionally dressed, pony-tailed Chinese men—the stereotypical "Coolie" reinforces the functional qualities of Carrier's product—and the copy under their impossibly happy faces, replete with wispy beards, promises:

Ships and Shoes and Better Chop Suey
You don't have to be Chinese to appreciate the extra taste and freshness
Carrier Air Conditioning imparts to Chop Suey. Carrier low tempera-
ture equipment keeps ingredients fresh the year 'round. Carrier Control helps make many products better at lower cost. (71)

But Carrier goes beyond making the products themselves better, it makes the
consumers better too. The air conditioner does more than merely provide a
respite from the heat; it is an integral component in the joy of buying and selling things.

> *It's a Pleasure* to shop in an air conditioned store . . . to work there . . .
> to own one. For the Carrier Self-contained Weathermaker which fits air
> conditioning to store requirements as a shoe is fitted to your foot, keeps
> cost down, clerks cheerful and customers in a buying mood. (71)[17]

However, in the following month's *Time*, which includes the review of Fearing's
Collected Poems, an advertisement for the *Saturday Evening Post* warns about
the dangers of putting people in a mood to spend:

> *This American gave $250,000.*
> *This American's fund grew to $2,500,000.*
> *This American gave $750,000.*
> WHOSE MILLIONS BACK COMMUNISM IN THE U.S.?
> This week's Saturday Evening Post names the names of "American"
> business men, manufacturers, playboys, misguided wealthy widows,
> government employees, and clergymen who have supported commu-
> nist and other, left-wing propaganda to the tune of more than
> $3,000,000. Here's the story of some home-bred fortunes that went in
> for hand-biting. On Page 9 of the Post—now on sale. *Read MUDDLED
> MILLIONS by BENJAMIN STOLBERG.* (February 17, 1941)

Despite the provocative language, which promises to "name the names" years
before HUAC gave that term its cultural cachet, what is fascinating about this
advertisement is its indictment of profligacy. While the Carrier advertisement and
hundreds of others extol the virtues of a "spend, spend, spend" mentality, the *Saturday Evening Post* clearly states that certain spending is "misguided" or "mud-
dled," and it is no surprise whatsoever what sort of spending draws scorn: fiscal
support for communism. "Left-wing propaganda" that separates wealthy widows
from their pensions is reprehensible, a violation of common sense, but "capitalist propaganda" in the form of advertisements that laud the spending of income
on everything from shoes to chop suey makes perfect sense. This is the logic of

reification at its most refined, for so successfully have the pages of *Time* articulated for the readers what type of objects we ourselves are that from week to week, issue to issue, page to page, we are unable to grasp the contradictions inherent in the messages transmitted to us. As upstanding citizens, we should spend our hard-earned wages. As upstanding citizens, we would be foolish to spend our hard-earned wages. It is up to *Time* magazine and its advertisers to define for us what "upstanding citizens" are from moment to moment, just as Janoth Enterprises, in *The Big Clock*, is successful in the main because it accurately anticipates the "needs" of its readers by creating their needs for them and, as a result, creating the readers themselves.

In a world characterized by rationalized time and mass-mediated transmissions, the production of subjects is simultaneously the most pressing economic and ontological question. The standpoint from which critique may operate should not be taken for granted, and the only possible critique is that which proceeds immanently. It is therefore not surprising that in the review for *The Hospital*, Fearing foregrounds precisely the constructedness of his own subject position, bragging, "Hell, I've been a character in some good novels" ("Feverish" 52)—in so saying, he refuses the transcendence of authorship, agency, and activism. It may be that, given the complicity borne by an author whose mastery of transmission necessarily implicates him in the bad faith of aesthetic reproduction, retreat into the pages of a novel may be the only politically legitimate recourse. Fearing's refusal to use his novels as a means of communicating explicit political content is itself an intervention. This tactic is more responsive to the realities of capital's sedimentation into all realms of existence than is either the rickety individualism of the avant-garde artist or the romanticized proletariat of "revolutionary" literature.[18] Amidst the maelstrom of conflicting pitches that bombard media subjects in all times and places, Fearing's aversion to outright participation may bring his novels closer to political truth.

In this, Fearing aspires to that condition which Adorno would call autonomy. Adorno's insistence that the autonomous artwork need neither be productive nor participate in an overt political challenge to the status quo is a vital element of *Aesthetic Theory*: "What is social in art is its immanent movement against society," Adorno suggests, "not its manifest opinions." The notion that a text should be useful *for* something effects a reversal that reduces the artwork to a means rather than an end in itself. "By crystallizing in itself as something unique to itself, rather than complying with existing social norms and qualifying as something 'socially useful,' [the artwork] criticizes society by merely existing, for which puritans of all stripes condemn it" (226–27). This is essentially the same critique leveled at Brecht and Sartre in the essay "Commitment," where Adorno inveighs against the arrogance of modern subjects who, convinced of their agency in a time of objective powerlessness, force art to do that which by definition it should not. Because of their rage for aesthetic agency, politically committed artists are accessories to that coercion against which they believe they stand.

In his "U.S. Writers in War," Fearing the essayist echoes this sentiment by insisting on the autonomy of the writer in the face of overwhelming political pressure. Noting that simply by publishing poetry one earns the status of a "public enemy" (Qtd. in Santora, 320), Fearing pursues through his very obstinacy a radical autonomy. Branded as he is by the demand for transmission and the cruel realities of the market, the originality of his refusal lies not in denying that taint but by giving it narrative form as that which cannot be escaped, no matter the strength of the individual, the heroism of the gesture, the appeal of the movement.

> All things considered it would be simpler, I suggest, for the individual writer to forget about himself as a moulder of public opinion. Writers are, collectively, moulders of opinion—but collectively, writers do not represent any unique viewpoint in the national life; collectively, they represent the same variety of views held by the general population. And I have never heard of a lone literary crusader who seized the stream of history and started it moving in an opposite direction. It will be enough if the writer refuses to lend himself to the more prodigious lies that mushroom in times like these. ("U.S. Writers in War" 322)[19]

As elsewhere, Fearing's position provokes a reconceptualization of politics adequate to the historical moment in which the ontological productivity of temporality and transmission has revealed the bad faith and shared futility of both strident political commitment and attempted escape. The apparent lack of outright political commitment in Fearing's novels, which may have earned them their obsolescence in the eyes of his contemporaries, might be better understood as his strategy for eluding some of the oppositional Left's pitfalls. Instead of pursuing a romanticized exterior to the system, Fearing demonstrates the necessity of a novel politics from inside, a praxis relieved of not only the burdens of individualism but also the sanctity of the righteous exile: an engaged refusal.

NOTES

1. Note how Fearing's writing takes on the status of a world-historical event: "[P]role-tarian poetry as an American literary movement of permanent importance began in 1929, with the publication of Kenneth Fearing's first book, and ended—to assign an arbitrary date—in 1939, with the start of World War II. A political event, the Seventh Congress, of the Communist International quite appropriately divides the period into two parts."

2. In a combination of bildungsroman and hagiography, Wald likewise rhetorically establishes Fearing as a world-historical individual, while at the same time granting him political credentials that he may or may not have claimed for himself: "The death of Fearing, the premier poet of the communist cultural movement who turned maverick mystery writer, thirty-two years after the stock market crash of 1929, occurred at perhaps the nadir in the history of left-wing poetry. . . . Fearing, whose sensibilities were formed during the 1920s and who reached maturity in the 1930s, who lived on as a lonely left-wing fighter on the cultural front in the 1940s and 1950s, and who anticipated New Left cultural and political attitudes in his Kafkaesque view of modern bureaucracy and neo-Luddite themes, died on the eve of the emergence of the New Left" (*Exiles from a Future Time* 9).

3. Noteworthy among these reassessments are Moishe Postone's *Time, Labor, and Social Domination* and Antonio Negri's *Marx Beyond Marx: Lessons on the* Grundrisse; it is to the former that the concept of "traditional" Marxisms is indebted. Negri especially lauds the *Grundrisse* as the key to rethinking central Marxist concepts and categories — value, money, time — with greater immediacy and militancy than is afforded by traditional readings of *Capital*.

4. On that evacuation, see particularly the "Dedication" to Adorno's *Minima Moralia* (15–18) and Fredric Jameson's *Postmodernism: Or, the Cultural Logic of Late Capitalism*.

5. In his analysis of interwar German cinema as an evolution toward fascism, Siegfried Kracauer points to the confession of the child killer in *M* as an example of this split. The killer, cornered by gangsters and tailed by the cops, reveals that his crimes are the inevitable result of his failure to contain this duality.

> "I am always forced to move along the streets, and always someone is behind me. It is I. I sometimes feel I am myself behind me, and yet I cannot escape. . . . I want to run away—I must run away. The specters are always pursuing me— unless I do it. And afterwards, standing before a poster, I read what I have done. Have I done this? But I don't know anything about it. I loathe it—I must—loathe it—must—I can no longer . . . " (221)

6. Chandler's Philip Marlowe might be the desperate dialectical flipside to this rule, straying into a Baroque consciousness (and language) that reflects back on the utter vacuum that surrounds him. Whereas Cain's characters evoke the true emptiness of reified consciousness, Chandler's solitary hero expresses a crucial aspect of enlightenment subjectivity: there is only one interior—and it's mine.

7. As Rita Barnard has argued, this condition effects the co-optation of one of Marxism's great utopian promises—the amelioration of scarcity—by the forces of industrial culture. But the political implications of this appropriation are perhaps most memorably explained by Adorno and Horkheimer, who assert that "something is provided for all so that none may escape."

8. Moreover, Mikki represents the potential to embody every story, every novel, even as those forms become obsolete, displaced by "Audiobooks." Fearing envisions, in one of the final projects developed by Mikki's inventor (years before the business commuter could obliterate the post-industrial landscape by concentrating on the latest Clancy

techno-thriller) a world where the wire audio-brain of Mikki would contain every novel in a space one-tenth its original, material size. The perceived customer of this development is not, as most of the characters of *Loneliest Girl* presume, the disabled. Rather, Audiobooks has its real potential in alleviating the strain of the businessman. "Now in the case of this Audiobooks development, for instance. I said I understood it was for the blind. Oliver, I remember now, did not put it quite like that. The market appeal of books on wire, according to him was to relieve the eyes of the enormous load put on them in business and professional life" (*Loneliest Girl in the World* 121–22).

9. For example, James Agee's critique of popular music, "Pseudo-Folk," anticipates the language of *Dialectic of Enlightenment* even while Horkheimer and Adorno are discovering the most pernicious aspects of American mass culture.

10. Specifically, Adorno repeats this critique about the mutilation of symphonic music in *Composing for the Films*. In movies, as on the radio, the broad band of sonic resources is reduced to an underwhelming middle ground. "The different degrees of strength are leveled and blurred to a general mezzoforte," Adorno insists. And here he draws specific attention to the fact that, "incidentally, this practice is quite analogous to the habits of the mixer in radio broadcasting" (18).

11. For an account of Alfred Helmut Naujock's Nuremberg affidavit, see Shirer's *The Rise and Fall of the Third Reich* (693).

12. In *Negative Dialectics*, *Vermittlung* is translated as "transmission." The word, however, more commonly indicates the concept of "mediation" or "communication." However, we have chosen to retain "transmission" as it conveys both the ontological and the technological aspects of the word.

13. Further, with regard to ontology's sham realism:

> Heidegger's realism turns a somersault: his aim is to philosophize formlessly, so to speak, purely on the ground of things, with the result that things evaporate for him. Weary of the subjective jail of cognition, he becomes convinced that what is transcendent to subjectivity is immediate for subjectivity, without being conceptually stained by subjectivity . . . Since the transmissions of our subjectivity cannot be thought out of the world, we want to return to stages of consciousness that lie before the reflection upon subjectivity and transmission. This effort fails. (79)

14. It should be mentioned that this publishing juggernaut is loosely based on Henry Booth Luce's *Time* magazine.

15. Fearing elsewhere suggests the near elimination of the former in favor of the latter:

> Previously I had grasped, battled, connived, and schemed for a share of the immense power and wealth always at stake in that small but mythological cosmos, usually winning far more than my share, but always accepting the results of the last gamble and preparing my play for the next gamble as though the actual power and the literal profits were only a fraction of the bigger meaning behind the whole quest . . . The money itself, like the authority with which I could operate, and the prestige that could or could not be demonstrated in daily use — these tokens had finally become the whole object of the work at hand. The entire meaning of the operations that engaged me had shriveled now to the exact

size of those tokens. There were no goals larger than they were, and there were, in fact, no other goals. (*The Crozart Story* 11–12)

16. In addition to the puritanical self-renunciation that characterizes responses to the Depression, Barnard also outlines the way in which the years following the crash witnessed the consolidation of the modern American consumer society. "[I]n the twenties and thirties . . . the characteristic institutions and habits of consumer culture—the motion picture, the radio, the automobile, the weekly photo news magazine, installment buying, the five day work week, suburban living, and the self-service supermarket—assumed the central position they still occupy in American life" (16).

17. As if the egalitarian spirit of air conditioning possessed the power to truly make all men equal in the modern age, even the "Coolie" can experience the refined joys of being a businessman. Inversely, the burdens of abstract time have the same leveling effect. "The awfulness of Monday morning is the world's great common denominator. To the millionaire and the coolie it is the same, because there can be nothing worse" (*The Big Clock* 83).

18. This is the perhaps spurious binary between modernism and realism outlined by Georg Lukács in later works such as *Realism in Our Time*. The shared flaw of each of these positions is that they assume the possibility of a transcendent standpoint, outside of capitalist relations, from which critique could unfold.

19. Witness here, once again, the language that would come to be called Adornian, yet which is clearly common currency in the years preceding *Dialectic of Enlightenment*: " . . . it is both the privilege and the duty of the writer who calls himself creative to view with suspicion, in these years of war, the claims of the Ministry of Information, and the demands of the *pseudo-patriot* (322, our italics).

⚠️ Works Cited

Adamic, Louis. *My America*. New York: Harper and Brothers, 1938.

———. "What the Proletariat Reads." *Saturday Review of Literature* 1 December 1934: 321–22.

Adorno, Theodor W. *Aesthetic Theory*. Trans. Robert Hullot-Kentor. Minneapolis: University of Minnesota Press, 1997.

———. "Commitment." *Notes to Literature, Volume 2*. Trans. Shierry Weber Nicholsen. New York: Columbia University Press, 1992. 76–94.

———. *Composing for the Films*. Atlantic Highlands, NJ: Athlone Press, 1994.

———. "Extorted Reconcilliation: On Georg Lukács' *Realism in Our Time*." *Notes to Literature, Volume 1*. Trans. Shierry Weber Nicholsen. New York: Columbia University Press, 1991. 216–40.

———. "Free Time." *The Culture Industry: Selected Essays on Mass Culture*. Ed. J. M. Bernstein. London: Routledge, 1991. 162–70.

———. "How to Look at Television." *The Culture Industry: Selected Essays on Mass Culture*. Ed. J. M. Bernstein. London: Routledge, 1991. 136–53.

———. *Minima Moralia*. Trans. E. F. N. Jephcott. London: Verso, 1974.

———. *Negative Dialectics*. Trans. E. B. Ashton. New York: Continuum, 1973.

———. "The Position of the Narrator in the Contemporary Novel." *Notes to Literature, Volume 1*. Trans. Shierry Weber Nicholsen. New York: Columbia University Press, 1991. 30–36.

———. "The Radio Symphony." *Radio Research 1941*. Eds. Paul Lazarsfeld and Frank N. Stanton. New York: Duell, Sloan and Pearce, 1941. 110–39.

———. "A Social Critique of Radio Music." *Kenyon Review* 7.2 (Spring 1945): 208–17.

Agamben, Giorgio. "Time and History: Critique of the Instant and the Continuum." *Infancy and History: Essays on the Destruction of Experience*. Trans. Liz Heron. New York: Verso, 1993. 89–105.

Agee, James. "The American Roadside." September 1934. *James Agee: Selected Journal-ism.* Ed. Paul Ashdown. Knoxville: University of Tennessee Press, 1985. 42–62.

———. "Pseudo-Folk." *Partisan Review* 11.2. (Spring 1944): 219–23.

Agee, James and Walker Evans. *Let Us Now Praise Famous Men.* 1941. Boston: Houghton Mifflin, 1969.

Alaimo, Stacy. *Undomesticated Ground: Recasting Nature as Feminist Space.* Ithaca: Cornell University Press, 2000.

Anderson, Perry. *Considerations on Western Marxism.* New York: Verso, 1979.

Anderson, Quentin. "The Emergence of Modernism." *The Columbia Literary History of the United States.* Ed. Emory Elliot. New York: Columbia University Press, 1988. 695–714.

"Announcing Prize Novel Contest." *New Masses* 11 (5 June 1934): 7.

"The Arts." *Pen & Hammer Bulletin* 1.1 (1935): n.p. In Suggs, *American Proletarian Culture.* 179.

Baker, Christina Looper. *In a Generous Spirit: A First-Person Biography of Myra Page.* Chicago: University of Illinois Press, 1996.

Barnard, Rita. *The Great Depression and the Culture of Abundance: Kenneth Fearing, Nathanael West and Mass Culture in the 1930s.* Cambridge: Cambridge University Press, 1995.

Barthes, Roland. *S/Z.* Trans. Richard Miller. New York: Hill and Wang, 1974.

Bataille, Georges. "The Notion of Expenditure." *Visions of Excess: Selected Writings, 1927–1939.* Minneapolis: University of Minnesota Press, 1985. 116–29.

Bell, Thomas. *All Brides Are Beautiful.* Boston: Little Brown, 1936.

Benjamin, Walter. "A Berlin Chronicle." *Reflections.* Ed. Peter Demetz. Trans. Edmund Jephcott. New York: Schocken Books, 1978. 3–60.

———. "On Some Motifs in Baudelaire." *Illuminations.* Ed. Hannah Arendt. Trans. Harry Zohn. New York: Schocken Books, 1968. 155–200.

———. "Paris, Capital of the Nineteenth Century." *Reflections.* Ed. Peter Demetz. Trans. Edmund Jephcott. New York: Schocken Books, 1978. 146–62.

———. "Theses on the Philosophy of History." *Illuminations.* Ed. Hannah Arendt. Trans. Harry Zohn. New York: Schocken Books, 1968. 253–64.

Benson, Susan Porter. *Counter Cultures: Saleswomen, Managers, and Customers in American Department Stores, 1890–1940.* Urbana: University of Illinois Press, 1986.

Bevilacqua, Winifred Farrant. *Josephine Herbst.* Boston: Twayne, 1985.

Bird, Caroline. *The Invisible Scar.* New York: David McKay, 1966.

Bloom, James. *Left Letters: The Culture Wars of Mike Gold and Joseph Freeman.* New York: Columbia University Press, 1992.

Bourdieu, Pierre. *Distinction: A Social Critique of the Judgement of Taste.* Cambridge, MA: Harvard University Press, 1984.

———. "The Field of Cultural Production." In Bourdieu, *The Field of Cultural Production.* 29–73.

———. *The Field of Cultural Production.* Ed. Randal Johnson. New York: Columbia University Press, 1993.

———. "The Market for Symbolic Goods." *The Rules of Art: Genesis and Structure of the Literary Field.* Trans. Susan Emanuel. Palo Alto, CA: Stanford University Press, 1995.

———. "Outline of a Sociological Theory of Art Perception." In Bourdieu, *The Field of Cultural Production.* 215–37.

Bowers, William L. *The Country Life Movement in America, 1900–1920.* Port Washington, NY: Kennikat, 1974.

Browder, Laura. *Rousing the Nation: Radical Culture in Depression America.* Amherst: University of Massachusetts Press, 1998.

Buck-Morss, Susan. *The Dialectics of Seeing: Walter Benjamin and the Arcades Project.* Cambridge: Massachusetts Institute of Technology Press, 1989.

Burgum, Edwin Berry. "Discussion." *Partisan Review* 2 (April–May 1935): 8–11. In Suggs, *American Proletarian Culture.* 302–04.

Burke, Kenneth. *Permanence and Change: An Anatomy of Purpose.* 1935. Berkeley, CA: University of California Press, 1984.

Cain, James M. *Double Indemnity.* New York: Vintage, 1936.

———. *Mildred Pierce.* 1941. New York: Vintage Books, 1989.

———. *The Postman Always Rings Twice.* New York: Vintage, 1934.

———. *Three Novels by James M. Cain.* Cleveland: World Publishing, 1946.

Calmer, Alan. "Reader's Report." *New Masses* 16 (10 September 1935): 23–25. In Suggs, *American Proletarian Culture.* 323–26.

Calverton, V. F. "Proletarianitis." *Saturday Review of Literature* (9 January 1937): 3–4, 14–15.

Carby, Hazel. "The Multicultural Wars." *Radical History Review* 54 (Fall 1992): 7–20.

Casey, Janet Galligani. *Dos Passos and the Ideology of the Feminine.* New York: Cambridge University Press, 1998.

Clifford, James. *The Predicament of Culture.* Cambridge: Harvard University Press, 1988.

Cohen, Jeffrey Jerome. "Monster Culture (Seven Theses)." *Monster Theory: Reading Culture.* Ed. Jeffrey Jerome Cohen. Minneapolis: University of Minnesota Press, 1996. 3–25.

Coiner, Constance. *Better Red: The Writing and Resistance of Tillie Olsen and Meridel Le Sueur.* New York: Oxford University Press, 1995.

Conroy, Jack. *The Disinherited.* 1933. New York: Hill and Wang, 1963.

———. *The Disinherited: A Novel of the 1930s.* 1934. Columbia: University of Missouri Press, 1991.

———. "The Worker as Writer." *American Writers Congress.* Eds. Granville Hicks, et al. New York: International Publishers, 1935.

Cook, Pam. "Duplicity in Mildred Pierce." *Women in Film Noir.* Ed. E. Ann Kaplan. London: British Film Institute, 1980. 68–82.

Cook, Sylvia Jenkins. *From Tobacco Road to Route 66: The Southern Poor White in Fiction.* Chapel Hill: University of North Carolina Press, 1976.

Cowley, Malcolm. *Exile's Return: A Literary Odyssey of the 1920's.* New York: Viking, 1956.

Dawahare, Anthony David. "American Proletarian Modernism and the Problem of Modernity in the Thirties: Meridel Le Sueur, Tillie Olsen, and Langston Hughes." Diss. University of California, Irvine, 1994.

Dawson, Cara Byars. "Josephine Johnson and Her Kirkwood Family." *Kirkwood Histori-cal Review* 7.4 (December 1968): 50–59.

de Certeau, Michel. *The Practice of Everyday Life*. Trans. Steven Rendall. Berkeley, CA: University of California Press, 1984.

Deloria, Philip J. *Playing Indian*. New Haven: Yale University Press, 1998.

Demarest, David P. "Afterword." *Out of This Furnace*, by Thomas Bell. Pittsburgh, PA: University of Pittsburgh Press, 1991. 415–24.

Denning, Michael. *The Cultural Front: The Laboring of American Culture in the Twen-tieth Century*. London: Verso, 1997.

Dickstein, Morris. "Depression Culture: The Dream of Mobility." In Mullen and Linkon, *Radical Revisions*. 225–41.

Di Donato, Pietro. *Christ in Concrete*. 1939. New York: Penguin Books, 1993.

Dimock, Wai Chee. "Class, Gender, and a History of Metonymy." *Rethinking Class: Lit-erary Studies and Social Formations*. Eds. Wai Chee Dimock and Michael Gilmore. New York: Columbia University Press, 1994. 57–104.

Dingley, Robert. "Eating America: The Consuming Passion of James M. Cain." *Journal of Popular Culture* 33.3 (1999): 63–77.

Dos Passos, John. *The Big Money*. 1936. New York: Houghton Mifflin, 1969.

Eagleton, Terry. "Capitalism, Modernism, and Postmodernism." *Against the Grain: Col-lected Essays*. London: Verso, 1986. 131–47.

"Editorial." *Survey Graphic* 2.6 (March 1923): 736. In Suggs, *American Proletarian* Cul-ture. 63–64.

Eisler, Hanns and Theodor W. Adorno. *Composing for the Films*. Atlantic Highlands, NJ: Athlone Press, 1994.

Eysteinsson, Astradur. *The Concept of Modernism*. Ithaca, NY: Cornell University Press, 1990.

Fadiman, Clifton. "Mr. Cain and Mother Love." *New Yorker* 17 (27 September 1941): 63.

Farrell, James T. "Cain's Movietone Realism." *Literature and Morality*. New York: Van-guard Press, 1947. 79–89.

Faulkner, Mara. *Protest and Possibility in the Writing of Tillie Olsen*. Charlottesville, VA: University of Virginia Press, 1993.

Fearing, Kenneth. *The Big Clock*. New York: Harper and Row, 1946.

———. *Clark Gifford's Body*. New York: Random House, 1942.

———. *The Crozart Story*. New York: Doubleday, 1960.

———. *Dagger of the Mind*. New York: Ballantine Books, 1941.

———. *The Hospital*. New York: Random House, 1939.

———. "King Juke." *Afternoon of a Pawnbroker and Other Poems*. New York: Harcourt, Brace, 1943.

———. *The Loneliest Girl in the World*. New York: Harcourt, Brace, 1951.

———. "Radio Blues." *New and Selected Poems*. Bloomington: Indiana University Press, 1956. 62.

———. "Reading, Writing, and the Rackets." *New and Selected Poems*. Bloomington: Indiana University Press, 1956. ix–xxiv.

——. "U.S. Writers in War." *Poetry: A Magazine of Verse* 56.6. (September 1940): 318–23.

Fearon, Peter. *The Origins and Nature of the Great Slump, 1929–1932.* Atlantic Highlands, N.J.: Humanities, 1979.

"Feverish." *Time* 34.10 (4 September 1939): 52.

Fine, David M. "James M. Cain and the Los Angeles Novel." *American Studies* 20.1 (1979): 25–34.

Fink, Deborah. *Agrarian Women: Wives and Mothers in Rural Nebraska, 1880–1940.* Chapel Hill, NC: University of North Carolina Press, 1992.

Fitzpatrick, Ellen. "Caroline F. Ware and the Cultural Approach to History." *American Quarterly* 43.2 (1991): 173–98.

Foley, Barbara. "Introduction." *Moscow Yankee*, by Myra Page. Chicago: University of Illinois Press, 1995. vii–xxviii.

——. *Radical Representations: Politics and Form in U.S. Proletarian Fiction, 1929–1941.* Durham, NC: Duke University Press, 1993.

Folsom, Michael, ed. *Mike Gold: A Literary Anthology.* New York: International Publishers, 1972.

Foster, Hal. "Prosthetic Gods." *Modernism/Modernity* 4.2 (1997): 5–38.

Fox, Stephen. *Blood and Power: Organized Crime in Twentieth-Century America.* New York: Penguin, 1989.

Frankenberg, Ruth. *White Women, Race Matters: The Social Construction of Whiteness.* Minneapolis: University of Minnesota Press, 1993.

Freeman, Joseph. "Introduction." In Hicks, *Proletarian Literature in the United States.* 9–28.

Gerstle, Gary. *Working-Class Americanism: The Politics of Labor in a Textile City, 1914–1960.* Cambridge: Cambridge University Press, 1989.

Gilroy, Paul. *The Black Atlantic: Modernity and Double Consciousness.* Cambridge: Harvard University Press, 1993.

Gold, Michael. "Go Left, Young Writers!" January 1929. In Folsom, *Mike Gold: A Literary Anthology.* 186–89.

——. "The Gun is Loaded, Dreiser." *New Masses* (17 May 1935).

——. "Introduction." 1935. In Gold, *Jews without Money*, n.p.

——. *Jews without Money.* 1930. New York: Carrol & Graf, 1984.

——. "Proletarian Realism." In Folsom, *Mike Gold: A Literary Anthology.* 62–70.

——. "Stale Bohemianism." *New Masses* 8.9 (April 1933): 29–30.

——. "Wilder: Prophet of the Genteel Christ." *New Republic* 22 (October 1930): 266–67.

Goodman, Charlotte Margolis. "Afterword." *Weeds*, by Edith Summers Kelley. 1923. New York: Feminist Press, 1996.

Gregory, Horace. "One Writer's Position." *New Masses* 15.7 (12 February 1935): 20–21.

Gross, Leonard. "Memorandum to Robert Dunn." In Suggs, *American Proletarian Culture.* 180–81.

Grosz, Elizabeth. *Volatile Bodies: Toward a Corporeal Feminism.* Bloomington: Indiana University Press, 1994.

Guillory, John. *Cultural Capital: The Problem of Literary Canon Formation*. Chicago: University of Chicago Press, 1993.

Gutkin, Irina. "The Legacy of the Symbolist Utopia: From Futurism to Socialist Realism." *Creating Life: The Aesthetic Utopia of Russian Modernism*. Eds. Irina Paperno and Joan Delaney Grossman. Stanford: Stanford University Press, 1994. 167–96.

Guttman, Allen. "The Brief, Embattled Course of Proletarian Poetry." *Proletarian Writers of the Thirties*. Ed. David Madden. Carbondale, IL: Southern Illinois University Press, 1968. 252–69.

Hagood, Margaret Jaman. *Mothers of the South: Portraiture of the White Tenant Farm Woman*. Chapel Hill, NC: University of North Carolina Press, 1939. Rpt. Arno, 1972.

Haley, Alex. "Epilogue." *The Autobiography of Malcolm X*. New York: Ballantine, 1964.

Halper, Albert. *The Foundry*. New York: Viking, 1934.

——. *Good-bye Union Square: A Writer's Memoir of the Thirties*. Chicago: Quadrangle Books, 1970.

——. "A Morning with Doc." *New Masses* 11.7 (15 May 1934): 14–16.

——. "Scab!" In Hicks, *Proletarian Literature in the United States*. 84–91.

——. *Union Square*. New York: Viking Press, 1933.

Hapgood, Hutchins. "Is Dreiser Anti-Semitic?" *The Nation* (17 April 1935): 436.

Hapke, Laura. *Daughters of the Great Depression: Women, Work, and Fiction in the American 1930s*. Athens: University of Georgia Press, 1995.

Hardwick, Elizabeth. "Fiction Chronicles." *Partisan Review* 13.5 (November-December 1946): 583–87.

Hart, John Edward. *Albert Halper*. Boston: Twayne, 1980.

Harvey, David. *Spaces of Hope*. Berkeley: University of California Press, 2000.

Herbst, Josephine. "Counterblast." *Nation* 132 (11 March 1931): 275–76.

——. *Money for Love*. New York: Coward-McCann, 1929.

——. *Rope of Gold*. New Brunswick, NJ: Feminist Press, 1984.

Hicks, Granville, et al., eds. *Proletarian Literature in the United States*. New York: International Publishers, 1935.

Hoffman, Nancy. "Afterword." *Now in November*, by Josephine Johnson. 1934. New York: Feminist Press, 1991.

Hoggart, Richard. *The Uses of Literacy*. London: Chatto and Windus, 1957.

"The Home-maker's Compass." *Progressive Farmer* (26 February 1910): 183.

Hoopes, Roy. *Cain: The Biography of James M. Cain*. 2nd ed. Carbondale: Southern Illinois University Press, 1987.

Horkheimer, Max and Theodor W. Adorno. *Dialectic of Enlightenment*. Trans. John Cumming. New York: Continuum, 1982.

Howe, Irving and Lewis Coser. *The American Communist Party: A Critical History, 1919–1952*. Boston: Beacon, 1957.

Howells, W. D. "Editor's Easy Chair." *Harper's* 127 (July 1913): 310–13.

Hubler, Angela. "Josephine Herbst's *The Starched Blue Sky of Spain and Other Memoirs*: Literary History 'In the Wide Margin of the Century.'" *Papers on Language and Literature* 33 (Winter 1997): 71–98.

"Hungry for Life." Rev. of *This Is My Body*, by Margery Latimer. *New York Times Book Review* (2 March 1930): 9.

Huyssen, Andreas. "Mass Culture as Woman: Modernism's Other." *Studies in Entertainment: Critical Approaches to Mass Culture*. Ed. Tania Modleski. Bloomington: Indiana University Press, 1986. 188–207.

I'll Take My Stand: The South and the Agrarian Tradition, by Twelve Southerners. New York: Harper & Brothers, 1930.

Irr, Caren. *The Suburb of Dissent: Cultural Politics in the United States and Canada during the 1930s*. Durham: Duke University Press, 1998.

"Is It a Joke To You?" *The Farmer's Wife* 35.3 (March 1932): 2.

Jameson, Fredric. *The Political Unconscious*. Ithaca: Cornell University Press, 1981.

———. *Postmodernism: Or, the Cultural Logic of Late Capitalism*. Durham: Duke University Press, 1991.

———. "Reflections in Conclusion." *Aesthetics and Politics*, by Ernst Bloch, et al. New York: Verso, 1977. 196–213.

Jardine, Alice A. *Gynesis: Configurations of Woman and Modernity*. Ithaca: Cornell University Press, 1985.

Johnson, Edgar. "Three Proletarian Novels." *Kenyon Review* 2 (Spring 1940): 245–47.

Johnson, Josephine. "Cotton Share Croppers Facing 'War.'" *East St. Louis Journal* (5 July 1936): 1–2.

———. *Now in November*. 1934. New York: Feminist Press, 1991.

———. Papers. Special Collections, Washington University, St. Louis, Missouri.

Josephson, Matthew. "For a Literary United Front." *New Masses* 15 (30 April 1935): 22–23. In Suggs, *American Proletarian Culture*. 297–300.

Julien, Isaac and Kobena Mercer. "De Margin and De Centre." *Stuart Hall: Critical Dialogues in Cultural Studies*. Eds. David Morley and Kuan-Hsing Chen. New York: Routledge, 1996. 450–64.

Jurca, Catherine. *White Diaspora: The Suburb and the Twentieth-Century American Novel*. Princeton, NJ: Princeton University Press, 2001.

Karanikas, Alexander. *Tillers of a Myth: Southern Agrarians as Social and Literary Critics*. Madison: University of Wisconsin Press, 1966.

Kelley, Edith Summers. Papers. Special Collections Research Center, Morris Library, Southern Illinois University at Carbondale.

———. *Weeds*. 1923. New York: Feminist Press, 1996.

Kelley, Robin D. G. "'We Are Not What We Seem': Rethinking Black Working-Class Opposition in the Jim Crow South." *Journal of American History* 80.1 (June 1993): 75–112.

Klein, Marcus. *Foreigners: The Making of American Literature, 1900 -1940*. Chicago: University of Chicago Press, 1981.

Kocks, Dorothee. *Dream a Little: Land and Social Justice in Modern America*. Berkeley: University of California Press, 2000.

Kolodny, Annette. *The Lay of the Land: Metaphor as Expression and History in American Life and Letters*. Chapel Hill: University of North Carolina Press, 1975.

Kracauer, Siegfried. *From Caligari to Hitler: A Psychological History of the German Film.* Princeton, NJ: Princeton University Press, 1947.

Kramer, Hilton. "Who Was Josephine Herbst?" *The New Criterion* 3 (September 1984): 1–14.

Langer, Elinor. "Afterword." *Rope of Gold*, by Josephine Herbst. 431–49.

——. *Josephine Herbst: The Story She Could Never Tell.* New York: Warner, 1983.

——. Rev. of *Double Lives: Spies and Writers in the Secret Soviet War of Ideas*, by Stephen Koch. *Nation* 258 (30 May 1994): 752–60.

Latimer, Margery. *This Is My Body.* New York: Cape and Smith, 1930.

Lauter, Paul. "American Proletarianism." *The Columbia History of the American Novel.* Ed. Emory Elliot. New York: Columbia University Press, 1991. 331–56.

LaValley, Albert J. "Introduction: A Troublesome Property to Script." *Mildred Pierce.* Ed. Albert J. LaValley. Wisconsin/Warner Brothers Screenplay Series. Madison: Wisconsin Center for Film and Theater Research, University of Wisconsin Press, 1980. 9–53.

Le Sueur, Meridel. "Annunciation." *Ripening: Selected Work.* Ed. Elaine Hedges. New York: Feminist Press, 1990. 124–32.

——. "The Fetish of Being Outside." *New Masses* 15.9 (26 February 1935): 22–23.

——. "I Was Marching." 1934. *Ripening.* Old Westbury, NY: Feminist Press, 1982.

Libretti, Tim. "'What a Dirty Way of Getting Clean': The Grotesque in Proletarian Literature." *Literature and the Grotesque.* Ed. Michael J. Meyer. Amsterdam and Atlanta, GA: Rodopi, 1995. 171–90.

"Life and Poetry." *Pen & Hammer Bulletin* 1.6 (1933): n.p. In Suggs, *American Proletarian Culture.* 179, 182.

Lord, Russell. "Foreword. Treasures at Home," by Liberty Hyde Bailey. *The Farmer's Wife* (June 1932): 7.

Lott, Eric. *Love and Theft: Blackface Minstrelsy and the American Working Class.* New York: Oxford University Press, 1993.

Loughridge, Nancy. "Afterword: The Life." *Guardian Angel and Other Stories*, by Margery Latimer. New York: Feminist Press, 1984. 215–29.

Lukács, Georg. "'Tendency' or Partisanship?" *Essays on Realism.* Ed. Rodney Livingstone. Trans. David Fernbach. Cambridge, MA: Massachusetts Institute of Technology, 1980. 33–44.

Lunacharsky, A.V. "Proletarian Culture." *Survey Graphic* 2 (6 March 1923): 691–93. In Suggs, *American Proletarian Culture.* 60–63.

MacDougall, Ranald, et al. *Mildred Pierce.* Wisconsin/Warner Bros. Screenplay Series. Madison: Published for the Wisconsin Center for Film and Theater Research by the University of Wisconsin Press, 1980.

Madden, David. *James M. Cain.* New York: Twayne, 1970.

Marling, William. *The American Roman Noir: Hammett, Cain, and Chandler.* Athens: University of Georgia Press, 1995.

Marsh, Fred T. "Rope of Gold." *New York Times* (5 March 1939): 6.

Marx, Karl. *Capital: A Critique of Political Economy. Volume 1.* New York: Penguin, 1990.

——. *The Economic and Philosophic Manuscripts of 1844.* Ed. Dirk K. Struik. Trans. Martin Milligan. New York: International Publishers, 1964.

——. *Grundrisse*. Trans. Martin Nicolaus. New York: Penguin, 1973.

Marx, Leo. *The Machine in the Garden: Technology and the Pastoral Ideal in America*. London: Oxford University Press, 1964.

McCann, Sean. *Gumshoe America: Hard-Boiled Crime Fiction and the Rise and Fall of New Deal Liberalism*. Durham, N.C.: Duke University Press, 2000.

Miller, Tyrus. Rev. of *Modernisms: A Literary Guide*, by Peter Nicholls. *Modernism/ Modernity* 4.1 (1997): 175–78.

Moore, Nicole. "'Me Operation': Abortion and Class in Australian Women's Novels, 1920–1950." *Hecate: An Interdisciplinary Journal of Women's Liberation* 22 (1996): 27–46.

Morrison, Toni. *Playing in the Dark: Whiteness and the Literary Imagination*. New York: Vintage, 1993.

Mott, Frank Luther. *Golden Multitudes: The Story of Best Sellers in the United States*. New York: Macmillan, 1947.

Mullen, Bill, and Sherry Lee Linkon, eds. *Radical Revisions: Rereading 1930s Culture*. Urbana: University of Illinois Press, 1996.

Murphy, James. *The Proletarian Moment: The Controversy over Leftism in Literature*. Urbana: University of Illinois Press, 1991.

Needleman, Rae. "Tipping as a Factor in Wages." *Monthly Labor Review* 45 (1937): 1303.

Negri, Antonio. *Marx Beyond Marx: Lessons on the* Grundrisse. Trans. Harry Cleaver, Michael Ryan, Maurizio Viano. Ed. Jim Fleming. New York: Autonomedia, 1991.

Nekola, Charlotte and Paula Rabinowitz, eds. *Writing Red: An Anthology of American Women Writers, 1930–1940*. New York: Feminist Press, 1987.

Nelson, Cary. *Repression and Recovery: Modern American Poetry and the Politics of Cultural Memory, 1910–1945*. Madison: University of Wisconsin Press, 1989.

Nicholls, Peter. *Modernisms: A Literary Guide*. Berkeley: University of California Press, 1995.

North, Joseph. "Still on the Sidelines." *New Masses* 12.13 (25 September 1934): 24–25.

Oates, Joyce C. "Man under Sentence of Death: The Novels of James M. Cain." *Tough Guy Writers of the Thirties*. Ed. David Madden. Carbondale: Southern Illinois University Press, 1968. 110–28.

Olsen, Tillie. "I Stand Here Ironing." *Tell Me a Riddle*. New York: Delacorte, 1961. 1–12.

——. *Yonnondio: From the Thirties*. 1974. New York: Delta Books, 1989.

Orsi, Robert. *The Madonna of 115th Street*. New Haven: Yale University Press, 1985.

——. "The Religious Boundaries of an Inbetween People: Street Feste and the Problem of the Dark-Skinned Other in Italian Harlem." *American Quarterly* 44.3 (September 1992): 313–47.

Page, Myra. *Gathering Storm: A Story of the Black Belt*. New York: International Publishers, 1932.

——. *Moscow Yankee*. 1935. Chicago: University of Illinois Press, 1995.

Parkes, Adam. "'Literature and Instruments for Abortion': 'Nausicaa' and the *Little Review* Trial." *James Joyce Quarterly* 34 (1997): 283–301.

PBS "American Experience" series. www.pbs.org/wgbh/amex/dustbowl/peopleevents/ pandeAMEX05.html.

Phelps, Wallace (William Phillips) and Philip Rahv. "Problems and Perspectives in Revolutionary Literature." *Partisan Review* 1 (June–July 1934): 3–10. In Suggs, *American Proletarian Culture*. 246–51.

Pitts, Rebecca. "The Trexler Trilogy." *The New Republic* 98 (22 March 1939): 202.

Porter, Katherine Anne. "Bohemian Futility." Rev. of *Money for Love*, by Josephine Herbst. *New Masses* 5 (November 1929): 17–18.

Postone, Moishe. *Time, Labor, and Social Domination*. Cambridge: Cambridge University Press, 1996.

Prell, Riv-Ellen. *Fighting to Become Americans: Jews, Gender and the Anxiety of Assimilation*. Boston: Beacon Press, 1999.

"Prof. Buchan Praises Pulitzer Prize Work of a Former Pupil." *St. Louis Globe-Democrat* (8 May 1935): n.p.

"The Pulps and Shinies." *Pen & Hammer Bulletin* 2 (5 April 1934): 117–18. In Suggs, *American Proletarian Culture*. 219–21.

Rabinowitz, Paula. *Labor and Desire: Women's Revolutionary Fiction in Depression America*. Chapel Hill: University of North Carolina Press, 1992.

Radway, Janice A. *Reading the Romance: Women, Patriarchy, and Popular Literature*. Chapel Hill: University of North Carolina Press, 1984.

Rahv, Philip. "The Cult of Experience in American Writing." 1940. In *Literature in America: An Anthology of Literary Criticism*. Ed. Philip Rahv. Cleveland: World, 1957. 358–72.

———. "A Variety of Fiction." *Partisan Review* 6 (1939): 108–12.

Rakosi, Carl. *The Collected Prose of Carl Rakosi*. Orono, ME: National Poetry Foundation, 1983.

Ransom, John Crowe. "Reconstructed but Unregenerate." In *I'll Take My Stand: The South and the Southern Tradition*. 1–27.

Rascoe, Burton. Rev. of *Now in November*, by Josephine Johnson. *Books* (23 September 1934): 3.

Rauch, Angelika. "The *Trauerspiel* of the Prostituted Body, or Woman as Allegory of Modernity." *Cultural Critique* (Fall 1988): 77–88.

Report of the Commission on Country Life. 1909. New York: Sturgis and Walton, 1911.

Rev. of *Mildred Pierce*, by James M. Cain. *The Nation* 153 (25 October 1941): 409.

Rev. of *Rope of Gold*, by Josephine Herbst. *New Yorker* 15 (4 March 1939): 70.

Rideout, Walter B. "Forgotten Images of the Thirties: Josephine Herbst." *The Literary Review* 27 (Fall 1983): 28–36.

———. *The Radical Novel in the United States, 1900–1954: Some Interrelations of Literature and Society*. New York: Columbia University Press, 1956.

Roberts, Nora Ruth. "Radical Women Writers of the Thirties and the New Feminist Response." *Left Curve* 17 (1993): 85–93.

———. *Three Radical Women Writers: Class and Gender in Meridel Le Sueur, Tillie Olsen, and Josephine Herbst*. New York: Garland, 1996.

Roemer, Michael. *Telling Stories: Postmodernism and the Invalidation of Traditional Narrative*. Lanham, MD: Rowman & Littlefield, 1995.

Rogin, Michael. "Making America Home: Racial Masquerade and Ethnic Assimilation in the Transition to Talking Pictures." *Journal of American History* 79.3 (December 1992): 1050–077.

Rollins, William, Jr. "What Is a Proletarian Writer?" *New Masses* 14.5 (29 January 1935): 22–23.

Rubin, Rachel. *Jewish Gangsters of Modern Literature*. Urbana: University of Illinois Press, 2000.

Ryley, Robert M. "Introduction." *Kenneth Fearing: Complete Poems*. Orono, ME: National Poetry Foundation, 1994.

Santora, Patricia B. "The Life of Kenneth Flexner Fearing (1902–1961)." *College Language Association Journal* 32.3 (March 1989): 309–22.

Saroyan, William. "Prelude to an American Symphony." *New Masses* 13.4 (23 October 1934): 14–15.

Scarry, Elaine. *The Body in Pain*. Oxford: Oxford University Press, 1985.

Schoening, Mark. "T. S. Eliot Meets Mike Gold: Modernism and Radicalism in Depression-Era American Literature." *Modernism/Modernity* 3 (1996): 51–68.

Seaver, Edwin. "Another Writer's Position." *New Masses* 15.8 (19 February 1935): 21–22.

———. "Ceaser or Nothing." *New Masses* 15.10 (2 March 1925): 21.

———. "What is a Proletarian Novel? Notes Toward a Definition." *Partisan Review* 2 (April–May 1935): 5–8.

Segrave, Kerry. *Tipping: An American Social History of Gratuities*. Jefferson, N.C.: McFarland, 1998.

Shaffer, Robert. "Women and the Communist Party, U.S.A., 1930–1940." *Socialist Review* 45 (May–June 1979): 73–118.

Shirer, William. *The Rise and Fall of the Third Reich*. New York: Fawcett Crest, 1950.

Showalter, Elaine. *Sister's Choice: Tradition and Change in American Women's Writing*. Oxford: Clarendon, 1991.

Sinclair, Upton. *The Jungle*. New York: Doubleday, Page, 1906.

Slesinger, Tess. *The Unpossessed*. 1934. New York: Feminist Press, 1984.

Smith, Henry Nash. *Virgin Land: The American West as Symbol and Myth*. Cambridge, MA: Harvard University Press, 1950.

Snow, Walter. Carbon Copy to Jack Conroy of Letter to Marvin Sanford (13 December 1934). In Suggs, *American Proletarian Culture*. 264–68.

———. Letter to Jack Conroy (27 January 1935). Jack Conroy Collection. Newberry Library, Chicago, Illinois.

Speckhard, Anne C. and Vincent M. Rue. "Postabortion Syndrome: An Emerging Public Health Concern." *Journal of Social Issues* 48 (1992): 95–120.

Spivak, Gayatri. "Can the Subaltern Speak?" *Marxism and the Interpretation of Culture*. Eds. Cary Nelson and Lawrence Grossberg. Urbana, IL: University of Illinois Press, 1988.

Stallybrass, Peter and Allon White. *The Politics and Poetics of Transgression*. Ithaca: Cornell University Press, 1986.

Steinbeck, John. *The Grapes of Wrath*. New York: Viking, 1939.

Stong, Phil. "Review of *Mildred Pierce*." *Saturday Review* 24 (4 October 1941): 13.

Stott, William. *Documentary Expression and Thirties America*. New York: Oxford University Press, 1973.

Stubbs, Katherine. "Mechanizing the Female: Discourse and Control in the Industrial Economy." *differences* 7.3 (1995): 141–64.

Suggs, Jon-Christian. *American Proletarian Culture: The Twenties and the Thirties, Volume 11*. Dictionary of Literary Biography Documentary Series. Detroit: Gale, 1993.

Suggs, [Jon-]Christian. "Introduction." *Marching! Marching!*, by Clara Weatherwax. 1935. Detroit: Manly, 1990. iii–xliv.

Teal, Laurie. "The Hollow Women: Modernism, the Prostitute, and Commodity Aesthetics." *differences* 7.3 (1995): 80–108.

Time 37.7 (17 February 1941).

Time 37.4 (27 January 1941).

Tisdall, Caroline and Angelo Bozzolla. *Futurism*. London: Thames and Hudson, 1977.

Tomlinson, Charles. "Objectivists: Zukofsky and Oppen, A Memoir." *Paideuma* 7 (Winter 1978): 429–45.

Torres-Saillant, Silvio. Personal Conversation with Lawrence Hanley. CUNY Dominican Studies Institute, New York, NY. (17 June 2001).

Trumbo, Dalton. *Johnny Got His Gun*. 1939. New York: Bantam Books, 1989.

"Upper Class Leftism." *Pen & Hammer Bulletin* 1.10 (1933): n.p. In Suggs, *American Proletarian Culture*. 182.

Van Doren, Dorothy. "Toward a Better America." *The Nation* 148 (4 March 1939): 272.

Van Gelder, Robert. "Sensation Bath." *New York Times Book Review* (5 October 1941): 7, 32.

Von Huene-Greenberg, Dorothee. "A *MELUS* Interview: Pietro di Donato." *MELUS* 14, nos. 3–4 (Fall–Winter 1987): 33–52.

Wald, Alan. *Exiles from a Future Time: The Forging of the Mid-Twentieth-Century Literary Left*. Chapel Hill: University of North Carolina Press, 2002.

———. "The 1930s Left in U.S. Literature Reconsidered." *Radical Revisions: Rereading 1930s Culture*. Eds. Bill Mullen and Sherry Lee Linkon. 13–28.

Walker, Janet. "Feminist Critical Practice: Female Discourse in *Mildred Pierce*." *Film Reader* 5 (1982): 164–71.

Walker, Melissa. *All We Knew Was to Farm: Rural Women in the Upcountry South, 1919–1941*. Baltimore, MD: Johns Hopkins University Press, 2000.

Wallace, Dan. Editorial. *The Farmer's Wife* 22.12 (May 1920): n.p.

Walton, E. H. Rev. of *Now in November*, by Josephine Johnson. *New York Times* (16 September 1934): 6.

Ware, Caroline. *The Cultural Approach to History*. New York: Columbia University Press, 1940.

West, Nathanael. *The Day of the Locust*. New York: New Directions, 1933.

Whalen-Bridge, John. *Political Fiction and the American Self*. Urbana: University of Illinois Press, 1998.

Williams, Linda. "Feminist Film Theory: Mildred Pierce and the Second World War." *Female Spectators: Looking at Film and Television*. Ed. E. Deidre Pribram. London: Verso, 1988. 12–30.

Wilson, Christopher. "'Unlimn'd They Disappear': Recollecting *Yonnondio: From the Thirties*." *The Power of Culture*. Eds. Richard Fox and T. J. Jackson Lears. Chicago: University of Chicago Press, 1993. 39–63.

Wilson, Christopher P. *White Collar Fictions: Class and Social Representation in American Literature, 1885–1925*. Athens: University of Georgia Press, 1992.

Wilson, Edmund. "Art, the Proletariat and Marx." *The New Republic* LXXVI (23 August 1933): 41–45.

———. "The Boys in the Back Room: James M. Cain and John O' Hara." *New Republic* 103 (11 November 1940): 665–66.

Wilson, Elizabeth. *The Sphinx in the City: Urban Life, the Control of Disorder, and Women*. Berkeley: University of California Press, 1991.

Wilt, Judith. *Abortion, Choice, and Contemporary Fiction: The Armageddon of the Maternal Instinct*. Chicago: University of Chicago Press, 1990.

Wixson, Douglas. *Worker-Writer in America: Jack Conroy and the Tradition of Midwestern Literary Radicalism, 1898–1990*. Urbana: University of Illinois Press, 1994.

Wood, Ellen Meiskins. *The Retreat from Class*. New York: Verso, 1986.

Yaeger, Patricia. *Dirt and Desire: Reconstructing Southern Women's Writing, 1930–1990*. Chicago: University of Chicago Press, 2000.

Radical Novels of the Depression Era

A Selected Bibliography

Algren, Nelson. *Somebody in Boots*. 1935. New York: Thunder's Mouth Press, 1987.

Anderson, Edward. *Hungry Men*. 1935. Norman: U of Oklahoma P, 1993.

Appel, Benjamin. *Brain Guy*. 1934. Rpt. as *The Enforcer*. New York: Belmont/Tower, 1972.

——. *Dark Stain*. New York: Dial, 1943.

——. *Power-house*. New York: E. P. Dutton, 1939.

Attaway, William. *Blood on the Forge*. 1941. New York: Monthly Review, 1987.

Bell, Thomas. *All Brides Are Beautiful*. Boston: Little Brown, 1936.

——. *Out of This Furnace*. 1941. U of Pittsburgh P, 1991.

Bontemps, Arna. *Black Thunder*. 1936. Boston: Beacon, 1992.

Brody, Catharine. *Cash Item*. New York: Longmans, Green, 1933.

——. *Nobody Starves*. New York: Longmans, Green, 1932.

Burke, Fielding [Olive Tilford Dargan]. *Call Home the Heart*. 1932. Old Westbury, CT: Feminist P, 1983.

——. *A Stone Came Rolling*. New York: Longmans, Green, 1935.

Cain, James M. *Mildred Pierce*. 1941. New York: Vintage Books, 1989.

Cantwell, Robert. *The Land of Plenty*. 1934. Carbondale: Southern Illinois UP, 1971.

Conroy, Jack. *The Disinherited*. 1933. Columbia, MO: U of Missouri P, 1991.

——. *A World to Win*. 1935. Urbana: U of Illinois P, 2000.

Cunningham, William. *The Green Corn Rebellion*. New York: Vanguard, 1935.

Dahlberg, Edward. *Bottom Dogs*. 1929. New York: AMS P, 1976.

Di Donato, Pietro. *Christ in Concrete*. 1939. New York: Penguin Books, 1993.

Dos Passos, John. *The Big Money*. 1936. Boston: Houghton Mifflin, 2000.

——. *The 42nd Parallel*. 1930. Boston: Houghton, Mifflin, 2000.

——. *Nineteen Nineteen*. 1932. Boston: Houghton Mifflin, 2000.

Endore, Guy. *Babouk*. 1934. New York: Monthly Review, 1991.

Farrell, James T. *Studs Lonigan, A Trilogy* [*Young Lonigan*; *The Young Manhood of Studs Lonigan*; *Judgment Day*]. 1932. New York: Penguin, 2001.

Fearing, Kenneth. *Clark Gifford's Body*. New York: Random House, 1942.

Fuchs, Daniel. *Summer in Williamsburg*. 1934. New York: Carroll & Graf, 1983.

Gilfillan, Lauren. *I Went to Pit College*. 1934. New York: AMS P, 1977.

Gold, Mike [Michael]. *Jews Without Money*. 1930. New York; Carroll & Graf, 1996.

Halper, Albert. *The Foundry*. New York: Viking, 1934.

———. *Union Square*. 1933. Detroit: Omnigraphics, 1990.

Herbst, Josephine. *The Executioner Waits*. 1934. New York: Warner, 1985.

———. *Pity is Not Enough*. 1933. Urbana: U of Illinois P, 1998.

———. *Rope of Gold*. 1939. New Brunswick, NJ: Feminist P, 1984.

Johnson, Josephine. *Jordanstown*. 1937. New York: AMS P, 1976.

———. *Now in November*. 1934. New York: Feminist P, 1991.

Kelley, Edith Summers. *Weeds*. 1923. New York: Feminist P, 1996.

Kromer, Tom. *Waiting for Nothing*. 1935. Athens: U of Georgia P, 1986.

Latimer, Margery. *This Is My Body*. New York: Cape and Smith, 1930.

Le Sueur, Meridel. *The Girl*. 1978. Rev. ed., Albuquerque, NM: West End P, 1999.

Lumpkin, Grace. *A Sign for Cain*. New York: Lee, Furman, 1935.

———. *To Make My Bread*. 1932. Urbana: U of Illinois P, 1995.

———. *The Wedding*. 1939. Carbondale: Southern Illinois UP, 1976.

McKenney, Ruth. *Industrial Valley*. 1939. Ithaca, NY: ILR P, 1992.

Newhouse, Edward. *You Can't Sleep Here*. New York: Macaulay, 1934.

Olsen, Tillie [Lerner]. *Yonnondio: From the Thirties*. 1974. New York: Delta Books, 1994.

Page, Myra. *Daughter of the Hills*. 1950. New York: Feminist P, 1986.

———. *Gathering Storm: A Story of the Black Belt*. New York: International Publishers, 1932.

———. *Moscow Yankee*. 1935. Urbana: U of Illinois P, 1995.

Rollins, William, Jr. *The Shadow Before*. New York: McBride, 1934.

Roth, Henry. *Call It Sleep*. 1934. New York: Farrar, Straus, & Giroux, 1991.

Sinclair, Upton. *Little Steel*. 1938. New York: AMS P, 1976.

Slesinger, Tess. *The Unpossessed*. 1934. New York: New York Review Books, 2002.

Smedley, Agnes. *Daughter of Earth*. 1929. Old Westbury: Feminist P, 1987.

Steinbeck, John. *The Grapes of Wrath*. 1939. New York: Penguin, 2002.

———. *In Dubious Battle*. 1936. London: Penguin, 2001.

Trumbo, Dalton. *Johnny Got His Gun*. 1939. New York: Citadel, 1991.

Vorse, Mary Heaton. *Strike!* 1930. Urbana: U of Illinois P, 1991.

Weatherwax, Clara. *Marching! Marching!* 1935. Detroit: Omnigraphics, 1990.

West, Nathanael. *The Day of the Locust* and *The Dream Life of Balso Snell*. 1939; 1931. London: Penguin, 2000.

———. *Miss Lonelyhearts* and *A Cool Million*. 1933; 1934. London: Penguin, 2000.

Wright, Richard. *Lawd Today*. 1963. Boston: Northeastern UP, 1993.

———. *Native Son*. 1940. New York: HarperPerennial, 1998.

Zugsmith, Leane. *The Reckoning*. New York: Smith and Haas, 1934.

———. *A Time to Remember*. New York: Random House, 1936.

⤷ Contributors

Lee Bernstein is assistant professor of American studies at San Jose State University and adjunct assistant professor at Vassar College. He is the author of *The Greatest Menace: Organized Crime in Cold War America* (2002).

Donna M. Campbell is associate professor of English at Gonzaga University. She is the author of *Resisting Regionalism: Gender and Naturalism in American Fiction, 1885–1915* (1997) and of the "Fiction: 1900–1930" section in *American Literary Scholarship*. Recent publications include articles on Edith Wharton and David Graham Phillips and on 1920s writers Edna Ferber and Rose Wilder Lane.

Janet Galligani Casey is an independent scholar who has most recently taught at Skidmore College. She is the author of *Dos Passos and the Ideology of the Feminine* (1998) and various essays on gender and class ideologies in American modernist culture. She is the recent recipient of an NEH fellowship for her current book project on women, agrarianism, and the politics of representation, 1900–1940.

Joy Castro is associate professor of English at Wabash College, where she teaches modernist literature and fiction writing. She publishes on modernist and contemporary women writers and on literary pedagogy, and her fiction has appeared in *Quarterly West*, *North American Review*, *Chelsea*, and other journals.

Joseph Entin is assistant professor of English at Brooklyn College, City University of New York, and a former postdoctoral fellow at the American Academy of Arts and Sciences. He is currently at work on a book entitled *Sensational Modernism: Disfigured Bodies and Aesthetic Astonishment in American Literature and Photography*.

Larry Hanley teaches at the City College of New York and the CCNY Center for Worker Education. He writes on proletarian literature, educational technology, and academic labor. He currently edits *Academe*, the magazine of the American Association of University Professors.

Caren Irr is associate professor of English and American literature at Brandeis University. She is the author of *The Suburb of Dissent: Cultural Politics in the United States and Canada During the 1930s* (1998) and co-editor of *Rethinking the Frankfurt School: Alternative Legacies of Cultural Critique* (2002).

David Jenemann is assistant professor of English at the University of Vermont, where he teaches courses on film, television, and critical theory. He has written on Westerns, reality television, and the cinematic theories of Gilles Deleuze and Theodor W. Adorno. He is currently working on a book about Adorno's exile years in the United States.

Andrew Knighton is a graduate student in the program in Comparative Studies in Discourse and Society at the University of Minnesota, and writes about critical theory, literature, and modern and contemporary art. He is currently finishing a dissertation on the development of the concept of idleness in the nineteenth century, especially as it manifests in American literature and painting.

Angela Marie Smith earned her doctorate in English from the University of Minnesota in 2002, with a dissertation on 1930s horror cinema, disability, and American eugenics. She has taught literature and media studies in both the United States and her home country of New Zealand and is currently a visiting lecturer in film at Victoria University of Wellington.

Jon-Christian Suggs is professor of English at John Jay College and the PhD program in English at the Graduate School and University Center of the City University of New York. He is the editor/compiler of *American Proletarian Culture: The Twenties and the Thirties* (Vol. 11 of the Documentary Series, *Dictionary of Literary Biography* [1993]) and the author of *Whispered Consolations: Law and Narrative in African American Life* (2000). His essays on African American literature, proletarian literature, and law and literature have appeared in various journals and collections of essays.

Index